CAPITOL
LETTERS

ALSO BY MITCH GREENLICK:

Greenlick, M., *Managing Research: The Cat-Herd's Toolkit.* Inkwater Press, Portland, OR. 2012.

Hernandez, LM, Liverman CT, Greenlick MR (editors). "National Center for Military Deployment Health Research." Institute of Medicine, National Academy Press, Washington, DC, 1999.

Lamb SJ, Greenlick MR, and McCarty, *Bridging the Gap Between Practice and Research: Forging Partnerships with Community-Based Drug and Alcohol Treatment.* National Academy Press, Washington, DC, 1998.

Hanes PP and Greenlick MR, *Grading Health Care: The Science and Art of Developing Consumer Scorecards.* Jossey-Bass, San Francisco, CA, 1998.

Greenlick MR, Freeborn DK, Pope CR. *Health Care Research in an HMO: Two Decades of Discovery.* The Johns Hopkins University Press, Baltimore, MD,1988.

Arnold C, Greenlick MR, Kuller L, eds., *Advances in Disease Prevention.* Springer Publishing Co., NY, 1981.

Hurtado AV, Greenlick MR, Saward EW, *Home Care and Extended Care in a Comprehensive Prepayment Plan.* Hospital Research and Educational Trust, Chicago, 1972.

Greenlick MR, ed., *Conceptual Issues in the Analysis of Medical Care Utilization Behavior.* US DHEW, Health Services and Mental Health Administration, Washington, DC, Government Printing Office, 1970.

CAPITOL LETTERS

AN INSIDE VIEW OF THE LEGISLATIVE PROCESS

By Oregon State Representative
MITCH GREENLICK, PH.D.

With cartoons by
JACK OHMAN

 Arnica Creative Services
Portland, OR | Los Angeles, CA | Palm Springs, CA

Library of Congress PCN: 2015952469
ISBN: 978-0-9838168-7-4

Publisher: Ross Hawkins
Editor-in-Chief: Gloria Martinez
Book Designer: Aimee Genter-Gilmore

THE OREGON
HISTORICAL
SOCIETY
FOUNDED 1898

NOTE: *The author has directed that all proceeds due him from royalties or other sources will be paid, by the publisher, directly to the Oregon Historical Society. For more information about the Oregon Historical Society, please visit ohs.org*

 PUBLISHING

ideasbyacs.com | Portland, OR | Los Angeles, CA | Palm Springs, CA

Dedicated to my wonderful wife, Harriet, who has been with me every step of the way and to my freshman year Republican mentors, Ben Westlund and Lane Shetterly, who put me on the correct road.

TABLE OF CONTENTS

FOREWORD

BY CONGRESSWOMAN SUZANNE BONAMICI

Mitch Greenlick is an exceptional and brilliant man. He made quite an impression on me the first time I met him at a neighbor's house party back in 2000 when he was a candidate for the Oregon Legislature. I heard about his background and was curious — why would a well-respected, health-care researcher and professor who had a long list of notable publications want to run for a low-paid, part-time job in a legislature where he was virtually certain to serve in the minority? When you read *Capitol Letters*, you will learn why; because Mitch Greenlick is passionate about public service and public policy.

Mitch inspired me so much that I volunteered for his first campaign and, several years later, with Mitch's encouragement, ran for and won a seat in the Oregon House of Representatives. It was an honor to serve as a member of the House Health Care Committee under his leadership and guidance. Mitch led many stimulating and productive discussions about access and affordability, but one topic that really stood out was a philosophical discussion about why health care is a right not a privilege.

During my time in the Oregon House and later the Oregon Senate, I held many interesting town hall meetings with Mitch. He has big ideas, is a forward-thinker, and has no fear of discussing new, provocative concepts or pushing back against proposals he sees as detrimental to his constituents or bad for Oregon. He always maintained a sense of optimism, even through tough decisions and personal health-care challenges that deeply worried his friends and family. I'm convinced that his optimism fueled his recovery.

As an elected official, I can say that one rarely (if ever) finds a book — or even an article — that is as full of unfettered candor as *Capitol Letters*. This compilation of *MitchMessages* from his years in office provides a unique perspective of the joys, disappointments, challenges, and rewards of making public policy from someone who truly loves the job — and is very good at it. And, like me back in 2000, you might find your life changed by this remarkable man with extraordinary intellect, bold ideas, and a gigantic heart. ☐

INTRODUCTION

OREGON HOUSE OF REPRESENTATIVES — HOW I GOT HERE

That busy storefront fascinated me. I am not certain that at nine years old I understood what was happening in that storefront, but there was a great deal of excitement inside. And they had no problem allowing me to hang around. The source of this excitement was the office of President Roosevelt's 1944 reelection campaign, located in the heart of the Jewish ghetto of Detroit. Soon I became a junior volunteer, passing out campaign literature in a neighborhood certain to vote to reelect the incumbent at about the 90 percent level.

I begin this tale with my first political encounter because that seminal experience imprinted me with an excitement for politics that is at the center of my motivation for this book. That political seed went dormant during my adolescence until it was reawakened by John F. Kennedy's "ask not" plea in his 1961 inaugural address. Now, as I find myself a long-term veteran of the Oregon House of Representatives, it feels like an inevitable stop on the political road woven into the fabric of my scientific and academic career. Political action was a part of my life throughout the thirty years I spent as a health researcher at Kaiser Permanente and the decade I spent as a professor and chair of public health and preventive medicine at the Oregon Health & Science University. My experience in politics guided me as I crafted the material for this book.

In the mid-1960s I led a group of "young Turks" seeking to revive a somnolent Democratic Party in Washington County, then a mostly suburban county in the Portland, Oregon metropolitan area. That work led me, in 1968, to run for the Beaverton school board and at the same time, Les AuCoin ran for the Oregon House of Representatives. I lost, but Les won, leading to his successful career in the U.S. House of Representatives. That fired up my enthusiasm for politics and I became involved, in one volunteer capacity or another, in campaigns for Neil Goldschmidt's first run for city council, Ron

Wyden's first race for U.S. Congress, John Kitzhaber's first campaign for governor, Jeff Merkley's U.S. Senate campaign and many others.

I was not motivated to actually run for office myself until 1999. I had retired from Kaiser Permanente in 1995 and was ready to step down as a department chair at OHSU. And I was watching the local political scene. Events during the 1998 election led me to begin contemplating a run for the House of Representatives. Chuck Carpenter, a liberal Republican, had represented my House district. Chuck was openly gay and had been the first openly gay candidate in the country to be elected to a state legislature in 1994. Bill Witt stepped into the primary and defeated Carpenter by fifty-four votes after waging an aggressively homophobic campaign. Witt ran unopposed in the general election, because the district was considered a safe Republican district and no Democratic candidate filed for the race.

After stewing about the situation awhile, I announced I was going to run against Rep. Witt eighteen months hence in the 2000 election. I began working to create a credible campaign, despite the huge Republican registration edge in the district. I got great support once people took my campaign seriously, and because Rep. Witt was so conservative on all social issues. I ran a strong campaign, raising $300,000 and knocked on several thousand doors. However, I lost by nearly 500 votes. I put my lawn signs away and kept running for the 2002 election, which would be in a redrawn district after the 2000 census. The new district (HD 33) as drawn contained a strong Democratic registration edge. I won the seat after winning a hotly contested primary election and a moderately contested general. And that brings us to this phase of the story.

THE MITCHMESSAGE

When I was first elected to the Oregon House of Representatives I decided I would record my reactions to the legislature in a biweekly series of messages to my friends and constituents. Thus the *MitchMessage* was born. I have sent the message to a list of about 3000: to people in my district and across the state, and to a group of health services researchers around the country. Most legislators send out some kind of a newsletter to their constituents, but three things differentiate mine: First, the *MitchMessage* is very personal. I share this journey from my perspective — my view through the windshield. Obviously, I value my perspective, but I try to use as few filters as possible in the telling of the tale. Consequently, it is not only my journey, but also it is told in my voice. And, as the tone reflects, proximate emotional vibrations color it. I used the regular emails as a way to record my experience as a member of the Oregon House of Representatives; I have included not only a reporting of events but also, whenever possible, my reaction to those events.

Secondly, from the beginning I have hoped to use the messages, while intensely personal, as the basis of a book that would be useful to scholars and students of politics and public policy. The six sets of MitchMessages that follow comprise emails that I sent out to my constituents on a regular basis during each of my first six regular and three short legislative sessions. While they represent my effort to communicate with constituents, they amount to an accessible case study, explicating life in the legislature during a critical decade at the turn of the 21st century.

Lastly, I am an experienced behavioral science researcher and therefore observe the process from a different perspective than do many. While I began as a rookie in the legislature, I came to it with a lifetime of experience observing the policy formulation process. As my experience in the legislature grew, I developed a maturing conceptual framework upon which to organize and interpret the events as I reported them. The legislature is unique in many ways, but it also shares elements of its culture with other complex organizations I have studied over my career.

I now have a series of some seventy-five of these documents, spanning six sessions of the Oregon Legislature. Consequently my perspective has emerged over a career. But the messages were written in the moment, not recreated from memory or from notes maintained over that timespan. While the messages represent an aide-mémoir of my experience as a state legislator, I hope they will also help students of the legislative process to get a feeling for the rich fabric of the legislature and to gain an understanding of the complexity of the policy development process.

A TRAVEL GUIDE

Each of the following chapters includes a brief introduction followed by the messages sent out during a single legislative session. The introductions focus on some of the highlights that are discussed in the messages of the chapter. There will be some common themes running through many of the chapters; there will be some absolutely unique elements that show up in some of the chapters. In each chapter, I point out some of the structural elements that define how any legislature does its work. The stories, however, relate specifically to the Oregon Legislature.

For example, the Oregon Legislature is part-time, meeting for five months in the odd years and one month in even years. While there are four full-time legislatures in the United States and another half-dozen nearly full-time, many legislatures are considerably more part-time than Oregon's. Within the time period of my service, we added annual short sessions to our biennial calendar. The importance of limited time frames for legislative activity becomes explicit through the MitchMessages.

INTRODUCTION

A very important element that differentiates the Oregon Legislature from other legislatures is that Oregon does not have term limits for legislators. In 1992 an initiative implemented the strictest legislative term limits in the country in Oregon. In 2002 the Oregon Supreme Court struck down term limits, and subsequently, the voters have resisted efforts to reinstate them. If I had begun in the House in 2003 under term limits, I likely would have moved to the Senate after three terms and would now be in my final term in the legislature. Without term limits I have rejected the opportunity to move to the Senate three times and am very happy with a career in the House.

Oregon has some other unique characteristics. For example, the legislative rules do not allow bills to be amended on the floor. That leads to a strong committee structure. Two other characteristics are important in the legislative process and will be noted in the Introduction to the chapters as they apply. First, the only significant constitutional requirement for the legislature is that it produces a balanced budget, including sufficient revenue to support the services it decides Oregon needs. How the legislature determines what services the state needs to supply flows through much of the controversy reported in the messages, beginning on first day of the first session.

To underscore the second point it is necessary to note that the Oregon House of Representatives consists of sixty members and the Senate thirty members. A majority of the body is required to pass legislation. What defines the legislative process is: "31, 16, and one" or in the case of revenue-raising bills "36, 18, and one." Debating is fine but passing a bill is finer. And it takes agreement between the House, the Senate, and the Governor to change the law. Many important lessons flow from this. And the reader will find a great deal of comment on the difficulty of relations between the Chambers. (Tip O'Neill, a former Speaker of the U.S. House of Representatives, was said to have commented, "the Republicans are our opponents, but the Senate is our enemy.")

Many of the messages feature material on policy development. I note those trends in the chapter introductions. Also because of my special interest in health policy and my growing role as chair of the House Health Care Committee that policy area receives special attention. Inevitably, some of the chapters highlight the strongly held opinions of my constituents and other citizens with regard to policy issues, including my experiences with some of the wackier ones on the right and on the left.

Finally, chapter seven will explore what a reader should be able to make of the whole thing. So hang on fellow travelers and enjoy the journey. ☐

IDEA TO LAW

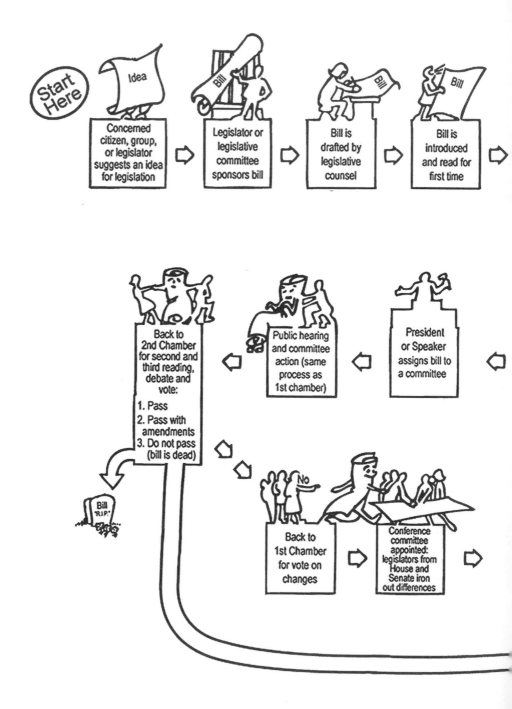

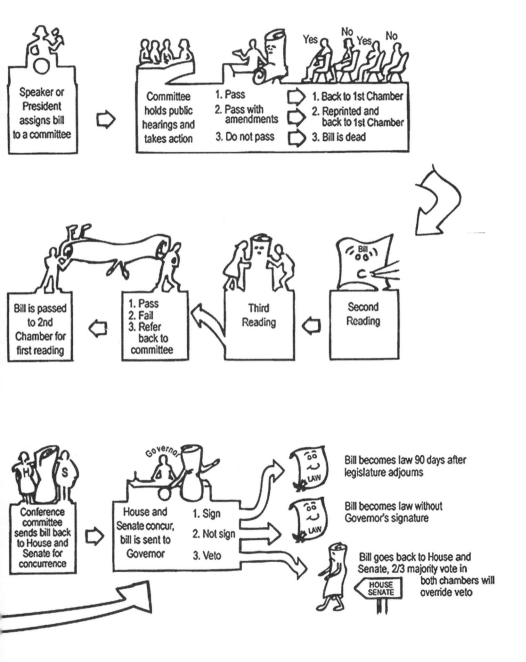

Speaker or President assigns bill to a committee

Committee holds public hearings and takes action
1. Pass
2. Pass with amendments
3. Do not pass

1. Back to 1st Chamber
2. Reprinted and back to 1st Chamber
3. Bill is dead

Yes No Yes No

Bill is passed to 2nd Chamber for first reading

1. Pass
2. Fail
3. Refer back to committee

Third Reading

Second Reading

Conference committee sends bill back to House and Senate for concurrence

House and Senate concur, bill is sent to Governor
1. Sign
2. Not sign
3. Veto

Bill becomes law 90 days after legislature adjourns

Bill becomes law without Governor's signature

Bill goes back to House and Senate, 2/3 majority vote in both chambers will override veto

HOUSE SENATE

Credit: www.oregonlegislature.gov

<table>
<tr><td>CHAPTER
1</td><td>

LEARNING TO BECOME A LEGISLATOR

OREGON HOUSE OF REPRESENTATIVES, 2003
</td></tr>
</table>

THE CONTEXT

As you read the messages from my first legislative session you will note the nature of the communications that emerge as I begin to familiarize myself with the legislative process. Throughout, the messages are characterized by a naïve sense of wonder at the enterprise in which I found myself engaged. My feelings were characterized by an episode that happened the very first day of the session. We were all invited to a reception following the opening day's activities. The reception was held a couple of blocks away from the Capitol. After walking back from the reception, we came to the door of the Capitol. I got out my key to open the door and it struck me with wonder that "I have a key to the Capitol." It was an extraordinary feeling and a residual of it stayed with me for most of the session.

Several things provide background for the events of the 2003 Legislative Session. First, I was in the minority in a legislature where being in the minority had significant consequences. The last time the Democrats had controlled the Oregon House was 1989, having been in the majority for nine terms. The Republicans seemed quite comfortable with the 35–25 majority they had won in the 2002 election, in which they had picked up a net of two seats. (In that same election the Democrats won enough seats to move the Senate to a 15–15 tie, taking control from the Republicans.) You will see how being in the majority mattered in various ways, including the fact that the Speaker did not name me to the Health Care Committee, although I had both a special interest and special knowledge in the health-care field.

The second thing you will notice is how the session was dominated by budget, budget, and budget. At the end of the 1990s, Oregon was hammered by a devastating recession, and the forecasts of state revenue kept diving.

1

1 | LEARNING TO BECOME A LEGISLATOR

During the 2001 session it was extraordinarily difficult to build a rational balanced budget. When the regular session ended on July 7, 2001 the budget situation was very precarious. Then came each new quarterly forecast of the revenue to be expected during the 2001–2003 biennium year. Each forecast predicted lower revenues than the last one had, thereby throwing the budget out of balance. Since our budget must be in balance, each forecast required the Governor to call a special session to bring the budget back in balance; five special sessions were called during the 2001–2002 interim.

In the fifth of the special sessions the legislature passed a measure to provide a temporary one percent income tax surcharge and referred the measure to a special election in January 2003. Measure 28 would have affected both personal and business income tax rates. It was defeated just after the start of the session by a 54 percent to 46 percent margin. That brought us to the beginning of the 2003 regular session, which served as the sixth special session, because it was still necessary to bring its current fiscal year budget into balance, as the work began on creating the 2003–2005 budget. This was an era of thirteen consecutive quarterly revenue forecasts that predicted lower expected revenue than had the one prior.

For students of the legislative process these messages are rich with details about how a legislature works, or at least how it works in Oregon. Notice such things as the roles of the Speaker and committee chairs, with the Speaker controlling committee assignments, including their chairs, and the committee chairs controlling the flow of bills through committees. Bills do not come to hearings without approval of the committee chair and, even after a hearing do not get to a vote without the approval of the chair. There are a few techniques to short-circuit that, but they rarely succeed. This is particularly important because bills may not be amended on the floor.

There are some interesting policy threads to follow in this session's messages, but it was surprising for me to notice, as I reviewed the messages, that health policy issues were hardly mentioned. This is partly because the main health-care issue emerged late in the session, with the deliberations of the Audit Sub-Committee of the Joint Committee on Ways and Means seeking a way to save the Oregon Health Plan. While I was not on the Health Care Committee I decided to sit in on the committee meetings and soon became accepted there. I was invited to join the Audit group when it began working on the development of the hospital tax, which did save the Health Plan. Health policy development will emerge in full bloom in later sessions.

The policy focus for these messages, except in budget matters, largely followed developments in the two committees of which I was a member — transportation and land use. These were definitely areas of interest to me because of my longstanding love for, and interest in, passenger rail and because unwanted annexation was a huge concern for constituents living in unincorporated Washington County.

Finally, the 2003 Legislative Session was the longest session in Oregon's history. It went almost to Labor Day. Consequently there are more messages in this chapter than in any other.

The MitchMessage
December 28, 2002

To my friends: this is to update you on what's happening as I get ready for the 2003 Legislative Session beginning on January 13. This is a very exciting time for me, even as I know I'll be facing some very difficult choices. And one thing I've learned so far is that it is quite humbling to be a freshman representative in a 25–35 minority. That status was quantified by getting the 57th choice of 60 offices, and 58th choice of desks on the floor and parking spots. But it is exciting nonetheless.

Committee assignments came out yesterday. We had been asked to rank our preferences of committees and I ranked health, transportation, education, and environment. And while I didn't get health or education, areas of my strongest expertise, I did get transportation and environment/land use. So I'm pretty pleased overall. I'm sure I'll still be able to affect health and education legislation, at least over several terms in the House.

I've already been working with the Office of the Legislative Counsel having five bills drafted in health care, higher education, and land use. I'll keep you informed on my proposals in future email updates. And I'm very busy meeting with the many groups of people who want to share their opinions on how Oregon should be run.

Of course, the major concern of almost everybody is how we will deal with the budget shortfall. Because most of the general revenue-supported programs are in education, human services, and criminal justice, I'm hearing mostly from these groups. The disastrous cuts to education, senior and disabled services, alcohol and drug treatment, mental health, and the criminal justice system seem almost too difficult to bear. Our first concern must be for the remainder of this biennium, especially if Measure 28 fails — which seems highly likely. But we are also faced with some terrible choices for the next biennium whether or not Measure 28 passes.

Which, of course, leads me to urge you to vote for Measure 28 and to ask all of your friends to do so. Perhaps reason could prevail if we all work hard to make it happen.

Finally, I want you to feel free to contact me at any time. My wife Harriet is coming to Salem with me to manage my office there, as she has managed my campaign office. And Desari Caldwell has signed on to be my legislative staffer. All of us will be there to serve you. We will try to have a community forum each month during the session in Multnomah County and one in Washington County. We'll announce them in the local papers and via email updates.

The MitchMessage
January 18, 2003

It's been an exciting week for new legislators and it seems a good time to share some of my impressions of the first week of the session. From outside the legislature it isn't possible to get a sense of the strength of the culture of the institution. I did, however, get this very strong impression as a part of my training during the week before the swearing-in ceremony. The significance of the fact that this is the 72nd Legislative Assembly came home to me thinking about the 71 groups of legislators who have gathered to the same task since Oregon Statehood. I really felt that the first time I went into the House Chamber and sat at my desk. It was pretty overwhelming.

The emotion came to a peak during the swearing-in ceremony where it became impossible for me to hold back the tears. In talking to freshmen of both parties afterward, we seemed to share the same overwhelming emotion and most reported being in tears during the ceremony. The swearing-in ceremony and the organizing session of the House lasted an hour. Then the House was cleared to get it ready for the inauguration of Governor Kulongoski.

The House members sat at their own desks for the Joint Session of the House and Senate, with two guests joining each of us on the floor. Also in the chamber were the members of the Senate and their guests, the statewide elected officials, the ex-governors, Justices of the State Appeals Court and the Supreme Court, Governors Kitzhaber and Kulongoski and about 100 guests of Governor Kulongoski. It was pretty impressive.

That afternoon the House got down to business with the introduction of about 250 bills, the first of about 700 bills that were prepared in the interim for introduction during the first week of the session of the House and the Senate. We got to work very quickly. Since I'm determined to read (at least quickly) each bill that's introduced, I also got behind very quickly.

I was named to the House Transportation Committee and to the Committee on Environment and Land Use. Both of those committees went quickly to work. I believe I'm going to enjoy the committee work very much and I'm very pleased with the chairs of the two committees, Rep. Bill Garrard (R) of Environment/Land Use and Rep. Alan Brown (R) of Transportation. We also have terrific committee administrators. Reps. Dingfelder and Beyers join me on the D side of Transportation and Ackerman and Rosenbaum on the D team for Environment/Land Use. There will be a great deal to learn in both of these areas but they are very important areas to the health and growth of House District 33.

The House District 33 staff also hit the ground running and they are doing a terrific job. Harriet Greenlick is managing the office and doing my scheduling. Desari Caldwell is our fantastic legislative aide (L.A.). They managed to have the office set up and functioning by last Sunday night and we were ready to get to work exactly on schedule last Monday. I don't think any of us really had a sense of the tremendous pace and the tremendous workload. But they are managing wonderfully. We are on the fourth floor with other freshman legislators, including our neighbors Jeff (Landslide Jeff) Barker and Brad Avakian from Washington County. The staff on the fourth floor has a great time supporting each other and Harriet serves as their den mother. Everybody seems to work very hard and seems very productive. My two committee chairs are also just down the hall, so they can keep an eye on me.

Another strong impression I've had is just how competent my Democratic colleagues really are. In addition to their strong political skills, they are a very skilled group in several other ways. For example, 21 of the 25 members of the Democratic House Caucus have advanced degrees. Many have a great deal of legal or business experience or other professional experience. They also seem like wonderful people. And each Republican with whom I've met so far, including Speaker Minnis, have been universally friendly and helpful. I hope that good fellowship continues as we get to work on difficult and contentious issues.

Now just a comment on what has been a disappointment. As you all know we're faced with a significant budget shortfall. And obviously that disturbs us all. But what troubles me is that I'm not certain that the Governor and the Legislature are willing to face up to the terrible impact the scheduled cuts are going to have on the most vulnerable among us. We must face up to the plight of the senior citizens, the physically and developmentally disabled, and our citizens with mental health and substance abuse problems. The situation is going to be particularly disastrous if Measure 28 fails. I'm working to help that situation, but it's looking quite bleak.

The MitchMessage
February 1, 2003

The failure of Measure 28 dominated the week and left a miasma of concern hanging over the capitol building. The demonstrations and the flood of calls, visits, letters, and email brought home to the legislators the human consequences of the budget cuts that were triggered by Measure 28's failing. I was intrigued to see the supportive reaction of the Capitol State Police troopers to the seniors and disabled demonstration against cuts. The State Police are also being hit hard by the cuts, including the layoff of a number of troopers guarding the Capitol Building.

In spite of the promises of secret plans for saving services by Rep. Dan Doyle and others, I don't see that the Republican majority in the House plans to do much to mitigate the impact of the terrible cuts in human services, education, and public safety during this biennium. The impact will be stunning and terrible if there isn't any relief. There does seem to be a commitment to solve some of the problems for the next biennium, but I sense a clear danger in some of the proposed solutions. I'll continue to comment as plans emerge.

Many of you messaged me that you enjoyed hearing about life as a legislator, so I'll continue to share my experiences as I learn to be a good member of the House. There is a tradition in the house surrounding the first bills brought to the floor by freshman legislators. The Transportation Committee assigned me to carry (present and defend) the first bill out of the Committee onto the House floor. The bill was a housekeeping measure correcting an oversight in the authorization for ODOT. The House was scheduled to hear the bill on Wednesday, January 29, along with bills being carried by freshmen Brad Avakian and George Gilman. The tradition calls for the members of the House to grill the carrier, for as long as an hour, with semi-serious and totally nonsensical questions and comments and to vote in a block against the bill. None of us knew who was going to be the target, so we were all completely over-prepared for the grilling.

However, the defeat of Measure 28 (the day before) and the fact that a serious PERS reform bill was on the agenda created an atmosphere that made the tradition seem too silly to undertake. So Brad and I were spared the hazing and our bills sailed through, as they should have. More importantly during that session the House passed HB 2100, which capped returns in variable PERS accounts at the average expected return, currently 8 percent. The bill saves about $200 million in the next biennium and perhaps $1 billion of the projected $17 billion PERS shortfall overall. It's a good first step and it felt very good for my first critical vote to help PERS with a vote that was supported by all of the stakeholders in the process. I expect the next votes will be more difficult.

My schedule continues to be dizzying, with committee meetings running from 8:30 to 10:30 each morning and the floor session beginning at 11am. There is a caucus meeting 2–3 days a week at lunch, with other lunch meetings on the free days. Then, a steady stream of meetings follows all afternoon — meetings with constituents, lobbyists, concerned citizens, and other legislators. I can have as many as 10–12 meetings during an afternoon. All that followed by one or two dinners, receptions, or meetings held for the legislators and staffs with groups such as the Oregon Bar, Beaverton school supporters, the train lobby, and many other groups who hope their legislators will come and meet their members and supporters.

The Environment and Land Use Committee spent the last two weeks with hearings on HB 2137, the first of several proposals known as the "progeny of Measure 7." These are bills hoping to bring to life a "takings" measure, or to create serious changes in the Oregon land-use system. HB 2137 requires that government pay landowners when a governmental action reduces the value of land by 10 percent. It also provides for other serious weakening of land-use restrictions. After listening to testimony for nearly two weeks, Committee Chair Bill Garrard formed two work groups made up of parties on all sides of the issue (there are more than two sides) to try to achieve some compromise on the issues. If some compromise can be reached it may prevent a new initiative designed to weaken Oregon's land-use regulation system.

I've been working hard to develop four proposals I expect to introduce in the next few weeks. My proposals include:

- A proposal to keep Forest Park, the land surrounding it, and its wildlife corridors out of the urban growth boundary
- A proposal for the eventual merger of PSU and OHSU.
- A proposal for a constitutional amendment creating the right of all Oregon residents to affordable and effective health care, and a plan for a pragmatic approach to achieving it.
- A proposal to create a cabinet-level, state department of public health.

The Forest Park proposal is the closest to being ready to introduce and I've been meeting with many interested parties on it this week. Perhaps I'll have that proposal ready to roll by the end of the coming week. Getting a proposal ready for introduction has many elements, as I've begun to learn. There are questions of the exact wording of the proposal, getting co-sponsors, thinking about trying to affect the committee to which it will be assigned, and generally thinking about strategy and tactics that will enhance its probability of eventually being enacted. As a freshman minority legislator I have a very long view. If I can get three of those four ideas adopted before I leave the legislature my legislative career will have been successful. So much of what's happening now builds the bridges for future success.

In addition to those proposals, I've signed on as a supporter of bills being sponsored by Senator Charlie Ringo and Representative Mark Hass. Those bills include a proposal to bring the lottery commission under better control, and one that will provide an increase in the property tax limitation from 1.5 percent to 1.7 percent if local citizens vote to use the additional .2 percent for a dedicated school fund.

Last Saturday we had a very successful town hall meeting, with Rep. Brad Avakian, at the Cedar Mill Community Library. About 50 people attended and there was lively discussion, with lots of questions asked and even some questions being answered. Brad and I both enjoyed the opportunity to talk to our constituents.

The MitchMessage
February 15, 2003

The fifth and sixth week of the 72nd Legislative Assembly contained some wonderful highs and some disturbing lows. Clearly the low was a meeting this week with the experts from Legislative Revenue and Legislative Fiscal staffs pointing out the likelihood of a significant revenue shortfall for the 2001–03 biennium ending in June. Even as the House Revenue Committee searches through the state's sofa cushions for whatever loose change has dropped and plans raids on whatever savings account balances are left, there is a near certainty of more service cuts looming.

This made even more unsettling the House debate on HB 5075, the bill proposing $15 million to restore cuts in human services and state police services, put forward by House Speaker Karen Minnis as a rescue package. I certainly voted for the bill, and will vote for anything else that seems to help those most hurt by human services cuts. But it really seemed like a charade to me. Representatives who have voted for the terrible cuts in HB 5100 during the fifth special session and who campaigned against Measure 28 stood up, dripping with the milk of human kindness, talking about how special the Republicans were for proposing this miniscule "care package." Their words felt very cynical, even to this freshman legislator.

I believe it is clearly time to look forward to the next biennium. We must begin to bring forth some serious new ideas on how to provide secure future funding for K–16 education and for critical social services. That will be the priority for many of us during the next few weeks.

There were some wonderful high points during the last two weeks. Last Monday I offered the "Opening Ceremony." The opening ceremony is often a prayer, but frequently is something else, such as a song or a moment of silence. I offered a reading from the Torah, with commentary.

On the next day I had the opportunity to carry an important bill onto the floor on behalf of the Transportation Committee. The bill was HB 2176, which creates guidelines for how motorists should behave when they see an emergency vehicle with flashing lights on the side of a road. It was amazing to me to learn that this wasn't covered in the statutes and therefore not covered in the manual new drivers are required to study to get their learner's permit. There have been a large number of emergency personnel killed and injured as they serve the public during emergency situations.

And on that same day I introduced my very first bill, HB 2628. This bill, if passed, would lead to the ultimate integration of Portland State University and Oregon Health & Science University. My purpose in introducing this legislation is to provide the Portland Metro area an integrated, first class university. The lack of this kind of a university in the Metropolitan area has been identified as a major barrier to continued economic development. Further, the ultimate integration of the two universities provides a significant opportunity for increasing the efficiency of each institution.

My press release quote was "These are two totally complementary institutions and this bill provides an inventive solution to an ongoing problem facing both Portland and the state. Our city cannot expect to be the economic engine of the Northwest if we do not take drastic steps to improve our local colleges and universities. Further, neither of these two universities can expect to achieve its full potential without this inevitable move." The bill would simply move operation of PSU under the auspices of the board that currently operates OHSU. The board would be expanded to fifteen members and renamed the Portland Metropolitan Universities Board. The board would be given ten years to integrate the two universities. As of my last conversation with them, the presidents of the two universities could not seem to decide whether they were amused or threatened by the proposal. But certainly neither has embraced it.

My Environment and Land Use Committee has been hearing bills that attack the strict protections on agricultural land under land-use planning and has begun to hear bills attacking Endangered Species Act (ESA) protections in Oregon. More about the ESA later. To help me deal with the land-use issues I've scheduled my next town hall to talk specifically about land-use protection in rural areas. State Senator Charlie Ringo will join me at that session. It has been interesting to me that many rural residents have turned out to testify strongly in favor of restricting non-farm uses on land designated as Exclusive Farm Use (EFU). But many have also testified in favor of allowing landowners to have much more freedom in deciding such things as whether non-farm dwellings should be allowed on prime farmland. Senator Ringo and I are very interested in hearing the opinions of people in our district on this issue. Please attend and share your views with us.

And finally, if you are planning on being in Salem please let my office know. If you can be there during a House session (usually 11am) I'd be proud to introduce you from the floor.

The MitchMessage
March 2, 2003

It's been another exciting and busy fortnight in the legislature. Of course, the budget situation has dominated the bad news side of the ledger. The March 1 revenue forecast came in worse than expected, for about the seventh time in a row. This triggered the budget deal you may have read about over the weekend. The forecast put us about $245 million in the red for the period ending this next June 30. We need to be in balance and the fear is that the news will continue to get worse for the final forecast on May 15. The deal announced Friday would restore many social service cuts, take no more money from schools, and restore forty state troopers and the forensic labs. It will also clean out every account available, including the school "rainy day" fund and will authorize borrowing against the next eight years' proceeds from the tobacco settlement. That will produce total borrowing of about $500 million, leaving some excess in case the final forecast continues to be dismal. And that does not begin to address how bad the situation is for the next biennium, since we've now maxed out all of our credit cards. More about that whole situation in the next *MitchMessage*.

But other than that Mrs. Lincoln, how was the play? The session is getting increasingly intense as the legislative process continues. To highlight that situation, the speaker announced she is aiming for a June 6 end to the session. (To which some wags asked "which year?") With *sine die* targeted for June 6 the rest of the calendar falls into place. March 3 is now the deadline for introducing bills into the house, except that each member can keep two priority bills that could be introduced somewhat later. That deadline caused a great deal of pressure, with me and Desari Caldwell (my high-powered legislative aide) scrambling to make sure all of our bills come out of the legislative counsel's office and are ready for introduction. (Truth be told, Desari is doing most of the scrambling.)

This is an interesting process from the perspective of a freshman legislator. I keep reminding myself that the primary purpose of introducing legislation is to get ideas passed into law. That is, of course, a complex process that can fail at any point along the way. After drafting, the bill gets assigned to committee. Sometimes you can influence which committee to which it is assigned, sometimes not. It is the sole decision of the Speaker. (It pays to stay on her good side.) I've tried to influence only one bill and I don't know yet whether I've succeeded.

Next you try to get a hearing in the committee. Most ideas die in committee without a hearing. That decision is entirely in the hands of the committee chair. Even if a bill gets a hearing there is no guarantee it will go to a committee vote. And sometimes the hearing produces many ideas for amending the bill. Bills can only be amended in committee, not on the House floor. If it gets out of committee, sometimes it needs to go to another committee. And even if it gets through the committee process, it could fail on the floor. If a bill gets out of the House, the process starts over in the Senate.

Consequently, there is a great deal of thought about the strategy and tactics needed to get an idea through the process. A part of that calculation is who should be the sponsor of a bill, who should be primary co-sponsors, and who should sign on as additional co-sponsors. Much of the scrambling this last week was people scurrying around getting other House members and senators to sign on to their legislation.

And sometime strategy dictates finding ways to get bills moved that gives somebody else credit for the idea. This week I arranged to have two of my favorite bills introduced as committee-sponsored bills, rather than introduce them as my bills. My Forest Park protection bill was introduced as a bill of the Environment and Land Use Committee and my bill to create a State Department of Public Health was introduced by the General Government Committee. I believe that will increase the probability that they will get a hearing and that, if passed out of the committee, they will have an increased probability of passing the House.

In the next message I'll include a final list of all the bills I'm sponsoring as primary or co-primary sponsor. Desari tells me she is currently tracking about 30–35 bills that we've signed on to, but I think there are about ten that I'm a primary sponsor on and a few more I'm a primary co-sponsor.

My Portland State/OHSU integration bill is getting lots of comment. It is flatly opposed by PSU and OHSU, and the University System Chancellor has expressed doubts about the bill. But I am still working on the bill. My two universal access bills have been introduced, one of them with twenty-seven co-sponsors. My hope for these bills is that they get a hearing and then I intend to move them to become an initiative for the fall, 2004 election.

I'm working, with Associated Oregon Industries, on a bill to increase the availability of venture capital for Oregon startups, and on a bill to allow local jurisdictions to charge systems development charges for police, fire, emergency services, libraries, and schools as a part of the process of creating new housing developments. And I'll introduce a bill to reduce persistent bio-accumulative toxins in our water system. And several other bills are moving along.

The thing that is frustrating me most as this process moves along is the lack of courageous new ideas about how to produce more revenue for the 2003–2005 biennium. It is clear to me that we need more revenue. We have now wiped out the education endowment and the prospects for social services for the most vulnerable part of our population are exceedingly bleak. And nobody is standing up and championing new ideas for short- or long-term solutions. Something must be done and done soon or Oregon's future will be totally ruined. We've failed to hear any secret Republican plan emerge, but I hope some of us will have the courage to suggest unpopular ideas about how to move forward. We've taken enough ridicule in the national press to damage us for decades. It's time for some ideas.

Finally, if there is something you'd like to see addressed in the *MitchMessage*, please send me an email and I'll put your idea in the mix. I want to be available to all of you.

The MitchMessage
March 15, 2003

March 3 was the deadline for filing bills for the House of Representatives. The frantic sponsor-gathering activity I reported in the last message kept up until 5pm on the 3rd. It turns out it is possible to add your name as a co-sponsor to a bill even after it is introduced. As of this moment I'm the chief sponsor or a chief co-sponsor (three are allowed) of twenty-two bills, of which nine are my bills. I've also sponsored two bills that were ultimately introduced as committee bills. And I've signed on as an additional co-sponsor of another 50 bills. I'll keep you informed about the progress of these bills, if and when they move.

In the last message I raised the issue of Oregon's financial difficulties. Since then the situation has gotten somewhat clearer and somewhat worse. We have had "Special Session Six", right in the middle of the 72nd Legislative Assembly. We have finally done the terrible work of balancing the 2001–2003 budget that should have been completed by the last legislature. The penultimate financial forecast (the final will be May 15) projected a $250 million shortfall in the budget. That was the seventh quarterly forecast in a row that indicated the revenue had been overestimated. In order to deal with the situation a four-bill financial package was crafted by the Senate and House Leadership. The four bills added back a small set of very critical services, while cancelling others; completely drained the school rainy day fund; authorized borrowing up to $500 million from a variety of sources (mainly with bonds guaranteed by the next eight years of tobacco settlement funds); and took about $5 million in transportation funds away from cities, counties, and transportation districts needed to fund aged and disabled transportation services.

These were very hard votes for me and I'm sure for many other legislators. I voted for the bill draining education funds, but delivered a floor speech against the approach and called for others to join me in strong action to do something unusual as we consider the next biennium.

I voted for the bill to add back services, even though I was not happy with the approach taken to cut other services. We certainly needed the buy-back, especially in health care. And I voted for the borrowing because I didn't see we had any choice after the irresponsible action of prior legislatures and the defeat of Measure 28 by the voters. (Incidentally, I was very proud to see that the voters of House District 33 voted for Measure 28, with 58 percent for and 42 percent against.)

Finally, I voted against the bill eliminating $5 million in aged and disabled transportation funds. After authorizing $500 million in borrowing it didn't seem necessary to take this important source of services from seniors and disabled people. However, 36 representatives voted for the bill and their party leadership allowed several Republicans to vote no because they knew there were sufficient votes to pass the bill.

Now we face the terrible reality of the 2003–2005 budget. The Governor presented a "balanced budget", which apparently is out of balance by as much as $1 billion. And that budget doesn't provide sufficient funds to keep our school systems functioning properly, nor does it include sufficient funds to save the Oregon Health Plan, Oregon's Medicaid program. I've been sitting with the Ways and Means Audit Committee, which is looking specifically at the Medicaid program. The Governor's budget doesn't even provide enough money for needed medical care services to the people who are mandated to be covered by Medicaid. And it provides no money for the nearly 200,000 people who have been added to the Oregon Health Plan because they are below the poverty line or are medically needy, but are not a part of one of those mandated populations.

We've heard nothing about a secret Republican plan to save Oregon. In fact, we have heard nothing from any Republicans about what to do now that we have cut services to/through the bone, have maxed out all of the state's credit cards, and emptied all of Oregon's savings accounts. *In my mind there is only one choice and that is to raise revenue and to raise a great deal of revenue for the next biennium.* That is what Republican Governor Atiyeh had the courage to do in the 1980s.

The House Democratic Caucus Leadership announced a plan to provide about $700 million more revenue for the next biennium, while cutting low and middle income tax rates and creating tax credits for true job creation activities in the state. This plan would add an 11 percent income tax bracket for the highest 1.5 percent of Oregon taxpayers, reduce tax breaks by $300 million to support education, and do a variety of other things.

There are others, and I'm among them, who believe the Caucus plan has some great elements, but doesn't produce enough revenue to solve the problem and doesn't do enough to restore education to where it needs to be. Several of us are working with people around Oregon to suggest even greater temporary reductions to tax breaks in Oregon. Currently, income and property tax breaks total more than $25 billion per biennium. We collect less than $10 billion in income tax per biennium. Expect some startling announcements during the next week or so.

I am proposing using $1 billion of reduced tax breaks during this biennium to fund an educational endowment fund. I propose that the proceeds of that fund, more than $45 million per year, be distributed to school districts in amounts proportional to each district's contribution to the total income tax of the state. And that the funds be used to support specific enrichment programs, which could include such things as art, music and drama education, physical education, vocational education, talented and gifted programs, early childhood education, or for reducing class size in K–3. An additional $5 million would be available to be used to enhance financial aid for Oregon's community college and university students.

We can put forward any number of ideas on how to deal with the financial difficulties. But the bottom line is that the Republicans have thirty-five of the sixty votes in the House and it is their obligation to put forward a plan to deal with the situation. There isn't any more room for pretending there are secret plans. There are no more credit cards against which to borrow. It is now up to the majority party to take responsibility for the mess they have created. We can only hope there are enough of them with the courage to face this reality.

The MitchMessage
March 30, 2003

I received an email message from a constituent that asked why the legislature was fooling around with trivial bills rather than solving the real problems of the state. While I had some sympathy with the sentiments expressed in that message, it really got me thinking about what I've been do-ing on a day-to-day basis here in Salem. What has become very clear to me is how complicated it is to run a state. There have been 2800 bills introduced in the Senate and the House, somewhat fewer than last session. Most of these bills do not address huge matters, such as restructuring Oregon's tax system or saving our schools.

The metaphor that came to mind was the complexity of running a house-hold with a couple of active teenagers. Most of the attention in that household is not about life-shaping matters. Most of the discussion in a household is about getting the garbage taken out, figuring out how to get somebody picked up after a soccer game, and determining the rules about television watching.

Most of the bills we consider are analogous to setting TV rules, but unlike the TV decision they are passed unanimously, after having received a great deal of work in the committee setting. We'll vote to give ODOT author-ity to issue the next generation of bonds needed to build highway projects. We passed a bill this week to allow ODOT to accept learning permits from another state when a teenager can pass a test on all of Oregon's laws and wants to take the driver test. We pass bills to extend sunset dates on various taxes and other similar bills.

There are fifteen volumes of Oregon Revised Statutes, each with several hundred pages that define all elements of how the state interacts with citizens and does its business. And these statutes need periodic updating and chang-ing. This alone is an important job. So be patient while we do this job, as well as struggling with the huge issues and debating wonderful new ideas for changing the world, or at least the state.

Incidentally, changing one of the laws I mentioned above gave me a great deal of pleasure. A teenager from Salem came before the Transportation Committee, testifying on the bill to allow the state to accept his learner's permit issued in Arkansas. His father is a Willamette University professor who moved his family to Arkansas for a year. While in Arkansas this young man got his learner's permit and learned to drive. When he returned to Oregon and passed his sixteenth birthday he applied to take the driver test, but was told he needed to get an Oregon learner's permit and wait six months before he became eligible.

He decided that didn't make sense and went to Rep. Vic Backlund for help in changing the law. He worked to get a bill drafted, which Vic intro-duced. He came to the committee, with his father and his grandfather to testify. He sent all the committee members a letter after that session and then visited with each, lobbying for his bill. It passed out of committee and was moved to the floor. He and his grandfather then went office to office lobbying for his bill. This week it passed the House 56–2. I was delighted to make a floor speech in favor of the bill.

It made me think about all of the citizens of Oregon who complain about "stupid" laws and use that excuse labeling the legislature as useless and then vote against taxes needed to provide basic services. This young man was an inspiration to me. An individual can make a difference, even in things harder than the learner's permit issue.

A word about the 2003–2005 budget. Things are beginning to look worse and worse. In the middle of April the Joint Ways and Means chairs will release (perhaps with the agreement of the Governor) an "all-cuts" budget. This is a budget that will be the plan for the state if *NO* new revenues are to be raised. This budget will leave blood all over the floor. The number I hear this budget will have for K–12 education is about $4.6 billion. We know when we considered last biennium's budget, $5.1 billion wasn't enough. The numbers for social services, higher education, the Oregon Health Plan, and the State Police are going to be equally bad, and I believe the whole thing is totally unacceptable. Perhaps this will shock the Republicans into thinking about whether the state can survive these kinds of budget cuts.

Finally, I'm getting a great deal of email from constituents, expressing an opinion on one bill or another pending before the Legislature. I try to respond to each quickly. If you care about a bill coming before the Legislature, please let me know how you feel about it.

The MitchMessage
April 13, 2003

It has been pretty lively around the capitol building since the last *MitchMessage*. The Speaker has set some hard deadlines because she seems determined to get us out of the building in a timely manner. She set a schedule aimed at adjournment mid-June; although she privately acknowledges it could be early July, depending on the budget/revenue talks. That schedule requires most House committees to complete work on House bills by next Friday and to finish all work and close those committees by May 13. I believe that the Rules, Revenue, and Ways and Means Committees will continue to work after that date.

Because of this tight timeline my committees have begun to double their scheduled meetings. As bills begin to move at a faster pace the hearings process has become much less relaxed. If you plan to testify on a bill in the House during the next week, expect severe time limitations. In addition to the committee press, the lobbyist pressure has become more intense as bills have begun to rush toward House votes. Lobbyists, wanting to argue their side of a bill, are increasingly confronting each of us. Generally speaking, I have found the professional lobbyists to be courteous and generally informative. They know that even if you are on the wrong side of their current bill, they will be back in a day or two with a bill that you might find more favorable. They are pretty careful about burning bridges. I've been struck that there is a lot to learn from their behavior pattern. It's clear they don't view this process as a battle between good (those who support their current bill) and evil (those who don't).

On a personal note, I had my first bill passed out of the House. That bill, HB 3014, is a bill I introduced for the Port of Portland, which is headquartered in the district. HB 3014, which is co-sponsored by Rep. Dave Hunt, conformed Oregon law to federal law and allows sales of airport property to be governed by federal law. It passed the House unanimously.

Three more of my bills are being heard this coming week. The most important is my Forest Park Protection bill, HB 2905. My committee on Environment and Land Use will hear this bill tomorrow (Monday) night and I'm hoping it will be passed out of committee and will pass in the House. Since Senator Ringo and I have a similar bill in the Senate, he will take the lead on getting this out of the Senate if it successfully passes the House.

Two other bills are of more recent origin. I have introduced HB 3613, working with Associated Oregon Industries. It is a bill that would encourage the Oregon Investment Council to invest as much as one percent of its investment (part of the alternative investment category of assets) as venture capital for Oregon start-up companies. This bill modifies the definition of a prudent investment for this asset category. It proposes that the council use the classic definition of risk in its risk/benefit assessment, but include benefits that accrue to Oregon's economy as a piece of the benefit assessment.

And finally, there is HB 2661. A couple of weeks ago I did a drive-along with the ODOT Comet. That is a group of specially equipped trucks that patrol the freeway system to aid stranded motorists and to keep traffic flowing. I noticed there were several abandoned cars along I-5. When I asked about them I was told that ODOT used to have the authority to tag and tow these cars, but that the Oregon State Police had withdrawn their authority to do so. When I got back to Salem I asked ODOT and OSP to find out what was happening and found that an Attorney General's opinion stated that OSP could not delegate their authority to ODOT to do this. After a bit of discussion, an amendment to the controlling statute was drafted that would give ODOT that authority. And I was able to find a bill with a relating clause "relating to highways" that could be used as a vehicle. Rep. Garrard had filed that bill, but had decided it wasn't needed. He was able to take his name off the bill and I was able to add mine as sponsor. Now the Committee will do what is known as a "gut and stuff" job, substituting my amendment for the current language of HB 2661. It is likely that it will pass the committee, because there is no opposition and should sail through the House. It was a very interesting process for me to learn.

On the down side I have learned that none of my health bills will get a hearing in the House health committee, including the bill that has become known in the public-health community as "the Public Health Emancipation Bill of 2003." I am working on a bill in the Senate that I co-sponsor with Senator Bill Morrisette, chair of the Senate Health Policy Committee. This is an omnibus prescription drug reform bill. It will be heard in the Senate this week, but has an uncertain future.

Finally, the real elephant in the room — the state budget. It is getting increasingly clear that the budget that will come from Ways and Means this week will be totally inadequate. I mentioned in my last message that this $11 billion budget will include about $4.6 billion for K–12 education. The quality education model just released says $6.9 billion is required for a really quality education. That obviously isn't going to happen, but it shows the total inadequacy of $4.6 billion (or even the $5 billion plus in the Governor's budget). While everybody wants to live within our means, the situation with education shows that isn't possible. The amount left for social services and the criminal justice system is equally catastrophically inadequate.

After the last *MitchMessage* I was asked by one of my constituents to be taken off my mailing list because I wasn't willing to just "live within our means" and kept talking about new revenue. I answered, in the removal message that I recognized that I was giving an unpopular message. But that as long as I was the District 33 representative I owed it to my constituents to tell them the truth as I saw it. And I frankly don't see how Oregon can survive this economic downfall without doing what Governor Atiyeh did in the 1980s. We must raise more revenue. Governor Kulongoski acknowledged that in today's *Oregonian* and some of the very conservative Republicans in the legislature have recognized the reality. I hope that recognition leads to action.

In the meantime, I want to urge all of you to work for the local tax increases if you live in Multnomah County or in the Beaverton School District area. The May 20 elections give us a chance to provide some respite next year for the eight school districts in Multnomah County and for the Beaverton School District. I'll be working very hard supporting both of the May 20 measures. I hope all of you see fit to do the same. Our endangered schools are vital to the economic and social viability of Oregon. We can't let them starve.

The MitchMessage
April 27, 2003

A busy fortnight has passed since the last *MitchMessage*. The big news around the capitol has been budget, since both the co-chairs' "no-new revenue" budget and the Governor's redo of his budget were released. They are quite similar, both inadequate in a variety of key ways, and neither suggesting major new sources of revenue. For example, in education the Quality Education Model suggests we need $6.9 billion to properly educate Oregon's children. The so-called current service level budget would be $6.0 billion. The equivalent current service level (CSL) minus the 2002 cuts to education would require $5.6 billion. The Governor's budget included $5.05 for education. The co-chairs budget is $4.95 billion. They also make some wild assumptions about PERS savings to get to that number.

The total budget adopted on July 1, 2001 was $12.344 billion. The legislature eventually cut that budget to $11.2 billion after several special sessions. The co-chairs budget was $10.83 billion. This really does represent belt-tightening, to an extreme degree. As you go through the budget as we've been doing there are cuts proposed to make everybody angry and I expect to get angry emails from school supporters, people worried about public safety, and supporters of the poor and the elderly. I've already gotten angry messages about the Governor's proposal to move hunting and fishing fee income into the general fund. Higher education is badly mauled by this budget, as are many other things. Please keep the emails coming, whatever your perspective.

We are going to be getting a couple of key PERS bills during the next week or two. First we will have two options for the "successor" plan — that is to say the plan that will be available for new hires under PERS. One of the competing models was designed by Rep. Greg Macpherson and is a combination of a defined benefit and a defined contribution plan. The alternative is a plan by the majority of the PERS committee and is a pure defined contribution plan — sort of like a 401K plan. I expect to vote for the Macpherson plan. But the big PERS change will come when HB 2003 is sent to the floor, perhaps on Friday. That is the bill that overhauls the PERS system for existing PERS members. That is likely to be very controversial and will most certainly end up being decided in the Supreme Court. More on that in my next message.

This has been a particularly busy period for my legislation. Those of you who are interested in the workings of the legislature would have been most interested being a fly on the wall during some of the meetings relating to three of the bills I'm working the most. The first, HB 2661, passed out of the Transportation Committee by a 7–0 vote and was put on the Consent Calendar (voted on without debate) of the House. That is the bill I talked about in the last *MitchMessage* that will allow ODOT to arrange to tow abandoned cars off the freeways. That should pass the House this week without controversy and with any luck will breeze through the Senate. But you can never tell.

I found that out with the roller coaster ride I've had during the last two weeks on HB 2905, the Forest Park Protection bill. I thought I had that bill completely arranged for a unanimous vote in the Environment and Land Use Committee and a great chance on the floor. At the last minute (9pm on the night of the hearing), the City of Portland announced opposition to the bill because of a couple of key issues. While I got the bill out of committee on a 5–2 vote it was clear I couldn't win on the floor if the city continued to oppose the bill. While I was negotiating with the city to clear their objections, Oregonians in Action (OIA) stole the bill, added an amendment they were interested in and tried to stuff it into a terrible bill attacking land-use protection generally. I succeeded in keeping it out of that bill, but OIA guaranteed me I could pass the Forest Park bill if I accepted their amendment. I rejected that offer and arranged to bring the bill back to committee to die. But it now looks like we have the city's objections taken care of with some amendments and there is the possibility we can get approval to bring it back out of committee in an amended form. But maybe we won't get approval. There really is a great deal to learn as a freshman legislator. As we left that terrible committee hearing, with my plans for the bill in tatters, Harriet said, "This sure is a tough business." It certainly can be.

This week will be the "do or die" week for HB 3613, my "Invest in Oregon" bill. This bill, which I'm working in conjunction with Associated Oregon Industries (AOI), proposes that the Oregon Investment Council invest up to 1 percent of its investments in Oregon start-up companies. (There are several Republican and Democratic co-sponsors on the bill.) As I said two weeks ago, the Oregon Investment Council currently invests up to 13 percent of its funds in alternative equity investments, mostly with venture capital partnerships and most outside of Oregon. This bill suggests they look to Oregon investments first. Treasurer Randall Edwards is fighting it furiously, saying that the legislature should not be introducing policy considerations into investment decisions.

There was a great hearing on the bill, with many Oregon business leaders testifying on behalf of the bill and the Treasurer and his team against. Several unions raised concerns and we have developed a set of amendments that take care of their concerns (I think). The bill will be debated on the House floor sometime this week. It's been instructive to watch AOI bring their pressure to the legislature. The bill passed the committee 4–3, with two Republicans and two Democrats voting for the bill and two Republicans and one Democrat, Rep. Mark Hass, one of the bill's co-sponsors, voting against. How is that for bi-partisan? The floor count looks good at the moment, but a major glitch is that we want to pass the bill in the House and amend it in the Senate. That is a pretty common approach when the time pressure begins. The Speaker wants it to move to the Senate for amendment, rather than back to committee. This makes some people nervous. Once again, we'll see how it plays out.

The other key issue we have been working on these last two weeks is bulk purchasing of prescription drugs. We had a hearing before the Senate Health Policy Committee on a bill by Senator Morrisette and me on bulk purchasing. Senator Morrisette put together a workgroup, led by Senator John Minnis to work out a compromise on this bill. The workgroup includes representatives of the pharmacy industry, the state's pharmacists, the AFL-CIO, the Governor's office, others and me. There is the possibility that we can actually work out an agreement for a bill to begin putting together a bulk-purchasing program, at least for government groups and school districts. But that still has a long way to go.

I've been getting a great deal of email from you all and I really appreciate it. While school funding always remains a favorite for emails, other issues take the forefront each week. During the last two weeks I've gotten a number of messages about an open-source software bill, which may or may not still be alive in a house committee and on major league baseball. Insurance reform wakes up the insurance industry and apparently Verizon put an insert into its bills suggesting its customers use a specially designed website to get email messages to their very own representative suggesting I not add to my constituents' phone bills. I can't find a specific bill that is the target of that approach. But as I said, I really do appreciate email and I really do listen to my constituents. However, since I get messages on both sides of most issues (not counting Verizon), I am going to have to say I agree with some and disagree with others. And sometimes I haven't had a chance to review the bill carefully, so I punt.

As I've said in this message before, life as a freshman in the minority can be very fascinating. My super-extraordinary legislative aide, Desari Caldwell, says sometimes it gets too "fascinating" for her tastes. We really have a great team in Salem, with Harriet keeping the office moving and in order and Desari doing the heavy lifting on policy issues and on counting votes. I occasionally remember the Chinese curse "May you live in interesting times." These are certainly interesting times.

The MitchMessage
May 11, 2003

House Bill 3613 passed the House on April 30 after a lively debate. This bill, which has the wonderful support of Associated Oregon Industries, has stirred up a great deal of controversy. State Treasurer Randall Edwards led the controversy. HB 3613 "encourages" the Oregon Investment Council (OIC) to direct a small proportion of the funds it invests as venture capital for start-up companies in Oregon, when it is prudent to do so. The Treasurer argues that the Legislature has no business telling the Oregon Investment Council anything. Labor was nervous about the bill until amendments were drafted that ensured the OIC would not be required to make inappropriate investments. The bill, which has the support of many leading finance figures in the state, passed the House on a 32–26 vote, with ten Democrats and twenty-two Republicans supporting the bill. It moved to the Senate Rules Committee, where co-chairs Senators Kate Brown and Bev Clarno have committed to include the agreed upon amendments as they consider the bill. A hearing is scheduled Tuesday afternoon in the Rules Committee.

The last two weeks did see the passage of key PERS reform bills by the House and the Senate and the bills were signed by the Governor. The final action on HB 2003, which restructured PERS for Tier 1 employees (those who have been covered by PERS for several years) and current retirees, passed the House 39–20, with eighteen Democrats and two Republicans voting against final passage. While this bill could reduce a large chunk of the unfunded PERS liability, I voted against HB 2003 because I firmly believe that the Supreme Court will overturn some of the provisions and we will be back into crisis mode. I also did not believe it was fair to take away the retirees' 2 percent annual cost-of-living adjustment. We have heard a great deal about people who retired with more than their salaries, but most PERS retirees are receiving a pension that is far less than their final salary. And for many their final salary was not inappropriately high, compared to other similar careers in Oregon.

The baseball bill, HB 3606 was also a highly controversial bill. I started out determined to vote no on this bill, but I changed my mind as the bill changed and as I considered the issues. I wanted to be certain that no state money would be spent on the stadium and that none of the bonding capacity of the state would be used to secure financing for it. As I studied the final bill I became convinced that the current version of the bill met those criteria, since the only state money to be used would be taxes collected on the ball players' salaries. And the final consideration for me was the potential for restarting our economy with the many construction jobs that would be available if the stadium were actually to be built. Building the stadium would be the construction equivalent of building six Fox Towers. Our construction trades currently have an unemployment rate in the neighborhood of 40 percent.

I received a great deal of constituent email on HB 3606, almost as much as on PERS. The messages ran about 10–1 favorable, although I knew that many of the messages were from friends and family members of people with an economic stake in building the stadium. The bill passed the house on a 33–25 vote, with twelve Democrats and thirteen Republicans voting no. As Desari Caldwell, my legislative aide, reviewed the voting pattern, she noted there was an obvious gender bias in the vote, with a large majority of women in both parties voting against the bill. The bill moved on to the Senate.

There is still no apparent movement from the Republican caucus in the House on finding additional sources of funding for education, in spite of the pressure. It is clear that some of the leaders are waiting for the outcome of the May 20 election. If the votes in Multnomah County and Beaverton fail, the clear message will be that the voters do not want to invest new revenue in education. Please work very hard to get these measures passed.

On a personal note: when I campaigned for office I argued that because of my experience in the business world and in academia I would be able to build bridges across the party lines and across interest groups to help get good legislation. And I have worked very hard to do just that. But lately, it's apparent to me that everybody does not necessarily appreciate this kind of effort. It seems particularly strange to some that a Democrat would be leading the way on a bill strongly supported by Associated Oregon Industries and opposed by the Democratic State Treasurer. To others, my working toward a compromise on bulk purchasing in order to get some action on a bill seems strange because we might actually get a bill that is supported by the pharmaceutical industry. The fact that Oregonians in Action captured my Forest Park Bill has caused some consternation (including by me).

I've taken some real heat when I don't behave according to some stereotype of me, whether that stereotype is based on my party affiliation or based on some previously accepted notion of who I am. I've pledged to try to represent all of my constituents. I can't take a poll of my constituents to tell me how to vote on issues, nor would I want to do that. But I try very hard to be sensitive to the needs of this whole very diverse district and to the needs of the people of the state of Oregon. There are very few issues upon which I will find no possibility of compromise. Certainly a woman's right to choose is one of those issues.

But I believe two things. First, I believe we need to consider many more alternative solutions to a problem than are usually brought to the table. (In fact, I usually try to redefine the problem to stimulate consideration of new alternatives.) And secondly, I believe the solution to most of the problems we face can be greatly improved by working with folks on all sides of the issue to get a consensus solution. Consequently, look to these two beliefs if you are looking for a clue to my future behavior.

Finally, please keep the email coming. I really want to hear from you. Since I try hard to answer all email from my constituents promptly, it helps if you keep the messages somewhat brief. And please feel free to pass on the *MitchMessage*. There are more than 1000 people on the list now, but it's pretty easy to handle new additions.

The MitchMessage
May 25, 2003

We're getting down to nitty-gritty time in Salem as the session rolls toward *sine die* with little progress on crafting a budget that will fund schools, critical social services, and other important functions of the state. The House policy committees have announced they are through with their work and are closing down. Of my committees, only Transportation is still functioning, although there was an announcement of an informal work group to look at the state of the mental-health system that I've been invited to join.

There was a fascinating battle in the House Friday when the Democrats tried to force HB 3636 to the floor for debate and a vote. HB 3636 was sponsored by Reps. Mark Hass and Ginny Burdick and co-sponsored by thirty other House members, including me. This bill would require that $6 billion be included in the 2003–2005 budget for K–12 education, rather than the less than $5 billion in the co-chairs' budget. Since it had thirty-one House members as sponsors it seemed possible that it could get a hearing on the floor. Further, it seemed an appropriate day to consider the bill since Friday was the last day of school this year for the Hillsboro schools.

But that was not to be. The Republican caucus treated the effort to discuss the bill as a threat to the Republic and completely stifled debate. First, they invoked a very strict rule for debate, limiting any comments in support of the motion to the question of withdrawal, not allowing comments on the merits of the bill itself. Consequently, they ruled out of order most of the comments on the floor. They moved to close debate, with many of the bill's sponsors (including me) in the queue to speak to the motion. The vote to stifle debate was along straight party lines, with six Republican sponsors of the bill voting against bringing the bill to the floor. That was a very informative debate for me, as were several of the things discussed below.

There was also a very partisan debate this week on the question of requiring health insurance companies to cover oral contraceptives when they cover drugs for other purposes. The debate came on a minority report to a bill that made minor changes in the regulations covering health insurance companies. As in other sessions the Women's Health Caucus couldn't get a contraceptive parity bill out of the Health Committee so a minority report was used as the mechanism to bring it to the floor. Despite brilliant speeches by Rep. Diane

Rosenbaum, Rep. Mike Schaufler, and others, the bill failed, largely along party lines. It's clear that being in the minority is not as nice as being in the majority. But nobody switched party over this debate, as Rep. Jan Lee did in the last session. That switch led to her defeat in the 2002 election.

I was very proud of the role I played as the carrier in the House of SB 795, which requires children (under 16) to wear helmets when engaging in "roller sports." That includes skateboards, roller skates, in-line skates, and scooters. Sen. Bill Morrisette sponsored the bill with Sen. Bev Clarno. She had introduced it on behalf of her grandson Tyler Henley, whose close friend had been seriously injured skateboarding. In my floor speech I quoted testimony by the mother of a boy, Tyler Amundson, who had been killed in a skateboard accident. She also testified that her son's friends put their helmets on to ride to where they were going to skateboard and then took them off to skateboard. Her testimony was very moving and the bill has become known as Tyler's Bill. After somewhat lively debate the bill passed 48–7. The very next class that visited me in Salem quizzed me on my sponsorship of this bill. It amazed me how fast the word had spread. There is going to be a signing ceremony on this bill next week.

Life was much more exciting in another bill I carried in the House last week, SB 289. This bill, sponsored by Senators Atkinson and Courtney, would allow some people with macular degeneration to test for a driver's license if they meet some very strict criteria, take exhaustive rehabilitative training, and use a bioptic lens for spotting signs in the distance. A young man named Aaron Mathews, who graduated from high school as an honor student and was a varsity basketball player who made all-conference despite having a childhood form of macular degeneration, stimulated this bill. The bill was heard on a day when the House passed 73 bills, most of them unopposed and without debate. I opened the debate with preliminary material. There was no debate at all on the bill, so I didn't provide much other information since I assumed the bill was unopposed. I received the shock of my brief legislative career when I looked up at the scoreboard and saw that the bill had been defeated 23–30.

Senator Courtney came down to the House floor and was not very happy with the situation. Rep. Terry Beyer, who had voted no and therefore was on the winning side, provided notice she was going to move for reconsideration. Then Senator Courtney, Senator Atkinson, and I got to work explaining the bill person-to-person in the House. It seems most people just looked at the bill and decided it was giving blind people the right to drive and voted no, even though it had passed 25–4 in the Senate. After a great deal of lobbying to ensure I had the 31 votes necessary to reconsider the bill on the floor, Rep. Beyer moved for reconsideration and that motion passed.

Then I rose to give the closing I hadn't given the day before, explaining that the bill would only apply to about 150 people who have been taught to use their peripheral vision to drive, that they would need to be certified by a vision specialist, and pass both written and driving tests, and they could only drive in the daytime and on roads with speed limits of 45 mph or less. Further, they would have to be retested every two years to prove they could drive safely. I discussed a study estimating additional risk for allowing these drivers an opportunity to prove they could drive safely. Finally, I read a statement by Marla Runyon, the Olympic runner who has this same condition and drove ten years in California (one of several states that allows this option) under this restricted license. The bill passed 51–6. Senator Atkinson said the 28-vote turnaround was the biggest he had ever seen in the House. It was a one-trial learning experience for me, ensuring I will take nothing for granted when I'm carrying a bill.

Desari, Harvey Mathews from Associated Oregon Industries, and I continue to work very hard to get HB 3613, the bill to increase venture capital investment in Oregon start-up companies, through the Senate. The bill had an excellent hearing in the Senate Rules Committee May 13. Many well-known high-tech executives testified on how important the bill would be to economic development in Oregon. We have all of the amendments ready to go that satisfied the unions that this bill wouldn't put pension money at risk. All of the unions appear to be at least neutral on the bill with these amendments. The Treasurer remains opposed, but I am pretty confident that it will pass out of the Rules Committee, perhaps this week. Then we will continue working to get the needed votes in the Senate.

I've become concerned about the proposal in the co-chairs' budget to delete funds that support the two trains from Eugene to Portland. While it is clear to me that education and social services are the number one budget priority it does not seem to me that deleting $9 million in support for these trains is really good public policy. That is the only support for trains in Oregon's budget. It doesn't make sense to me from either an environmental or a transportation policy perspective. The transportation package is finally coming to my Transportation Committee this week, but it's about repairing and replacing bridges, not about trains. Consequently, I've announced the formation of a bipartisan Choo-Choo Caucus to see if we can find a way to keep those trains alive. My concern was heightened when I rode the inaugural run of the Lewis and Clark Explorer train from Portland to Astoria that will highlight the Lewis and Clark Bicentennial celebration. It was a great ride and promises to provide a wonderful economic stimulus to Astoria. I just sat and contemplated the economic potential of high-speed rail between Eugene and Seattle. We can't go backwards now.

Finally, I want to congratulate the voters of Multnomah County and of the Beaverton School District on the vote on school support on Tuesday. That vote makes it so much easier to consider increased revenue for schools in the state budget. The Governor also got into the act this week declaring that $5.5 billion is the minimum required for schools. And Tuesday's school board election in Portland put Bobbie Regan, from House District 33, onto the Portland School Board. Congratulations to Bobbie and thank you so much for taking on that difficult challenge.

Finally, keep your emails coming. I really pay attention to them and I try to answer each one the same day it's received. I also appreciate your editorial suggestions. You'll find I use "despite" in this edition after a complaint about my use of "in spite of". I checked with my editorial consultant Gary Miranda, who said either was acceptable, although he reminded me that it was usually better to use one word instead of three. (He also pointed out that I had spelled helmet incorrectly in a prior edition.) So, at least this week, I opted for parsimony.

The MitchMessage
June 8, 2003

We finally saw the transportation package emerge from behind the curtains of high-level negotiation to a public hearing before a joint session of the Transportation and the Revenue Committees. The package is more properly a roads-and-bridges package. It will provide the revenue to allow the sale of $1.6 billion in bonds to fund about $1.3 billion of work on some severely cracked bridges and $300 million on roads. The revenue will come from an increase in the registration and title fees for cars and an appropriate share from an increase in weight-mile taxes on trucks. The bill passed the Transportation Committee, but is currently being held up in the Revenue Committee. The holdup is caused by a flap over an amendment Speaker Minnis added to force a new negotiation between the cities in Multnomah County and the county on an agreement for fund-sharing for the maintenance of roads in the county.

Since the last message I spoke on the floor against several measures, even though I'm trying very hard to speak only when necessary. I spoke (and voted) against two education bills, mostly because I remain concerned that we have not yet passed an appropriate education budget. The first measure was HJR 18 that called for a referral to the voters to allow the state to issue bonds to help build schools. That is basically a good idea, and one that we voted for in a prior referral. But there is no money that goes with the bill, nor is there an identified source for future funds. Consequently, it felt to me like an empty promise at best and, at worst, a phony attempt to fool the citizens into believing we were actually doing something to fund education. Enough people felt the same way I did that the bill did not receive the 40 votes needed to pass and was sent back to committee to remain alive. I hope we get it back as a part of a real package to fund schools.

The second bill that particularly concerned me was HB 2894, which was passed originally but was sent back to the House for a vote to concur with Senate amendments. This time it ran into a buzz saw. The current law allows a school district to be out of compliance with state regulations for one school year before it is necessary to take action against the district. The major compliance issue is, of course, having a sufficiently long school year. This bill would allow school districts to have a second year to get into compliance if there was a shortage of funds that caused them to close early. I believe that it is a terrible message to admit that we are not going to provide sufficient funds to keep schools open. *The Oregonian* quoted from my floor speech in which I argued that passing this bill at this time would be "hoisting the white flag of surrender" in our battle to adequately fund schools. After a heated debate the bill passed and was sent on to the Governor. He'll probably sign it.

Another bill that caught my attention was a bill to expand the definition of the crime of bestiality. We passed a bestiality bill in the last session and somebody thought it was necessary to expand its definition. I'll try to keep this discussion G-rated, but I decided the legislature had gone over the falls when it proposed adding the new crime of sexual abuse of an animal carcass to our law books. I get email from constituents all the time telling me they are growing impatient with us wasting time with foolish things when we should be seriously addressing issues like school funding. I said on the floor that this had to be a prime example of that kind of time wasting. As it turned out I was one of two no votes on the measure, and the other member changed his vote from no to yes. I kept mine no in protest.

I get quite a bit of email each week and I thought you might be interested in what's stirring up my constituents. *The Oregonian* article reporting that PGE paid only the $10 minimum corporation income tax and reporting on how many corporations were in that same category caused a flood of email. It looks like the Democratic revenue plan, that is beginning to emerge from both the House and the Senate caucus, will certainly include a proposal to increase that minimum in some significant way. My guess is that a proposal to do so will get some support from the moderate Republicans.

I've also received a great deal of mail supporting funding for the Oregon Poison Control Center that is included in HB 2709. That bill would use some of the money collected in the modest 911 charge included on phone bills to fund the center. I've been surprised by the broad nature of the support I've been hearing. I don't have an indication yet about whether that bill will emerge from the Revenue Committee. Stay tuned.

I continue to get questions about bulk purchasing of prescriptions. There remains a real possibility that SB 875, a bill sponsored by Senator Bill Morrisette and me will get to consensus and will get passed out of the Senate Health Policy Committee. We are close to getting a bill that would create a mechanism for bulk purchasing of prescription drugs that would have the support of the pharmaceutical industry, the unions, and the Governor. The bill would only provide a starting mechanism in the area and still has a long way to go. But there remains the possibility.

Finally, one of my constituents chided me for picking on the Republicans in my last messages. I'll close with a comment on that issue. I ran for the legislature on the promise that I would work hard to build bridges across the aisle. And I've worked very hard to do that. I have reached this point in the session with a close working relationship with both of my Republican committee chairs. I have built close relationships with several other moderate Republicans. Just the other day the Speaker told me how much she believes I had added to the legislative process. And in truth, most of the bills that come to the floor have no partisan element to them. A very large proportion of the bills we vote on pass 58–0 or 55–3 or something like that.

But sometimes things move very specifically to a battle between the Republican caucus and the Democratic caucus. That is usually the choice of the Republican caucus since they are in charge of the House. The model that has emerged over the last several years is to exert close control over the debate in the House according to the dictates of the majority party. Sometimes that turns things into R *vs.* D.

One such time was the discussion I reported in the last *MitchMessage* about the Democratic attempt to get HB 3636 to the floor so we could debate explicitly whether to provide $6 billion for K–12 education. As I pointed out in that message there were 31 co-sponsors of the bill, seemingly enough to pass it on the floor. But the Republican caucus decided we would not be allowed to have a debate on the substance of the issue. Consequently, many Republicans were forced to vote against having the debate even though they favored the substance of the bill. I hope that when the Democrats next control the House we will adopt rules that broaden the rights of the minority party. That should remind us that when the chips are down it's not about party politics, it's about representing the citizens of Oregon.

The MitchMessage
June 22, 2003

On June 11 I took the opportunity to deliver the opening ceremony (sometimes a prayer) and used the occasion to comment on the Torah portion from Genesis concerning Joseph's interpreting Pharaoh's dream. Joseph told Pharaoh that there would be seven years of abundant harvest, followed by seven years of famine in the land. That interpretation led Pharaoh to put Joseph in charge of gathering surplus food supplies and storing them to feed the land during the difficult times. The lesson I drew from this message was about economic cycles. Oregon failed to save for difficult times during the wondrous decade of the 1990s and we are suffering now. But it feels important to me, during these difficult times, to remember that good times inevitably follow bad times. Consequently, we must be careful not to destroy the institutions that are critical for maintaining the kind of Oregon in which we all want to live. I remain concerned that our crisis mentality will allow us to destroy elements of Oregon we need to sustain the society we desire. The education system, the social safety net, the environment, the multimodal transportation system are all at stake as we work to balance the budget.

Elements of the budget have begun to work their way through the legislature, without any of us having a clear picture of where we will end up. Many of the budget bills cause me no problem because they don't require any general funds or lottery funds. For example, we passed the budget Friday for the Board of Nursing, which is funded by fees and other miscellaneous funds. But we have also begun to pass budgets with general fund or lottery expenditures and several of us are worried that the passage of these bills will reduce the degrees of freedom in the budget negotiations when the difficult budgets come into play. I voted against SB 5542, the budget for the Department of Administrative Services for just such a reason and the bill passed the House with a thin margin. The problem will become much more serious when such budgets as the one for the criminal justice system come to the House. That bill will add $100 million to the co-chairs budget, most for services that I support, but not if that $100 million comes out of the education budget or the social safety net budget.

The promise many of us made to fund education first cannot be kept when the negotiation process leaves the education budget to the very last. I believe that the education budget should be the first thing tackled, and all else should follow from that.

In addition to the leadership's negotiations on the key elements of the budget there is a group beginning serious conversations on a basic restructuring of the tax system. The group was begun by moderate Republicans and has now expanded to include some moderate Democrats. Many Republicans have begun to realize that any budget they are willing to live with will require an additional $1 billion in revenues. (Most Democrats believe that number is more like $1.5–2 billion.) But even the lower number requires new thinking about revenue. It is not going to be possible to find that much money searching the sofa cushions for loose change. While talk about taking money from year-end reserves continues, talk about a change in the tax structure has begun, including use of the S word. (That is, sales tax, as proposed in *The Oregonian* by Rep. Max Williams, Republican from Tigard.) Stay tuned.

There were some interesting floor debates during the last two weeks. I got embroiled in the debate on SB 880, a bill that gives the tobacco industry special court treatment. Currently, when a jury awards a very large settlement in a civil trial the defendant must post a bond in the amount of the award. When an Illinois jury awarded a settlement of several billion to a plaintiff against a tobacco company there was fear in all of the states that have become addicted to money from the Master Tobacco Settlement that Phillip Morris would go bankrupt, leaving the states high and dry. Consequently SB 880 was quickly rushed through the Senate to protect the tobacco industry if something like that happened in Oregon. This bill creates a maximum of $100 million for an appeal bond for any tobacco company in court in Oregon. This troubled me, particularly because it only applied to a tobacco company and I helped fight it in the House. We defeated it one day, but the proponents unleashed a counter-attack and it passed on the second try the next day. My comments about Oregon "being in bed with the tobacco industry" were quoted in *The Oregonian* story about the bill.

On the good news side, the prescription drug bulk-purchasing bill (SB 875) passed out of the Senate Health Policy Committee on a 6–0 vote. The bill had the support of the pharmaceutical industry, the Administration, and the Oregon State Pharmacy Association. The unions (AFL-CIO and SEIU) provided some reluctant support for the bill. Their reluctance wasn't about the basic approach, but rather because they believe (as do I) that the scope of the bill was too narrow and that not enough people would be included in the purchasing pool. But this bill, which was the product of intense negotiation over the last two months, has now moved further than any similar bill in Oregon's history. Senator John Minnis is carrying the bill in the Senate and the pharmaceutical industry representatives are actively supporting the effort. It should be voted on in the Senate in the next two weeks.

On Thursday, the Senate Rules Committee will consider House Bill 3613, a bill I've been working with Associated Oregon Industries (can you imagine that?). This is a bill that would require the Oregon Investment Council to increase their participation in Oregon venture capital opportunities. I believe this is critical to mitigating the impact of the next economic downturn on Oregon's well being. This bill is getting wonderful support from the new-industry leaders in the state. We believe we have a set of amendments that make the bill acceptable to most interested parties. This movement is the result of very intense negotiations, guided by Desari Caldwell (from my staff) and Harvey Mathews of AOI. They have both worked very hard on this bill and we are feeling quite optimistic about its ultimate passage.

The Choo-Choo Caucus is chugging along. We are planning a press conference supporting the Cascade trains that run between Eugene and Portland (and on to Seattle). This will be held at the Capitol on June 30 and will feature the mayors of the cities along the line between Eugene and Portland. (Portland Mayor Katz has not yet confirmed, but we will at least have one of her representatives there.) As some of you may have heard me comment on OPB this week, I believe that interest in the caucus is high, because it is clear that no transportation system in Oregon can be successful without a significant rail component. The system needs to include short-line freight, class 1 railroads (the Burlington Northern and the Union Pacific), Amtrak passenger rail, and commuter rail. Saving the Cascade trains is the immediate priority of the caucus, but we will also be working to help support the total rail system in Oregon.

Finally, my grandson Jim Taber and my granddaughter Hannah Snyder served as honorary pages last week and another granddaughter, Megan Taber, will be serving this week. The kids get a great introduction to the Capitol and work as a page during the floor session. It seems both interesting and a great deal of fun. If any of you have friends and relatives in the 12- to 16-year age range who would like to serve as pages please send Harriet an email at *rep.mitchgreenlick@state.or.us* and she'll help arrange it. And keep the emails coming.

The MitchMessage
July 6, 2003

The development of the budget continues to dominate the news from the legislature. It seems as if there is some movement for the first time — for better or worse. The key negotiations have moved into a smaller room, with just six people present: the Governor, House Speaker Karen Minnis, Senate President Peter Courtney, and one staff person each. Prior to this there were as many as 30 people in the room at the negotiations. Reports out of that room are that they began by focusing on the education budget. While they moved closer together, they did not agree on a number for the K–12 education budget. *The Oregonian* reports that they have moved to talking about an overall budget number. It seems to me that isn't possible to do without having fixed on an education budget number first, as the K-16 budget represents half of the general fund budget.

In the meantime, Speaker Minnis is going to change the House rules tomorrow to allow budget bills to move through any House Committee, rather than processing them through the Joint Ways and Means Committee, as the current rules require. I believe this will be only the second time in the state's history this has been done. Speaker Larry Campbell also did this several years ago and it produced the longest session ever in the legislature, ending on August 7. I'm hoping we'll be done by then this time, but nobody is betting on *sine die* by August 7. The problem with processing budget bills without buy-in of the Senate side of Ways and Means is that most of the budget votes will become party line votes. The budgets that have come through so far have received bipartisan support. If important parts of the budget move to the Senate on a 35–25 party-line vote, they will certainly get bogged down there. Consequently, I'm rooting for the budget negotiations to be successful. Otherwise it's going to be a mess in Salem.

The next most important news is that hearings began last week on tax reform in the Revenue Committee of the House. Since it is now clear that any of the budget numbers being discussed will need more revenue, it's hard to believe it took six months of a session for the Speaker to allow these hearings to take place. Three moderate Republicans, Max Williams, Lane Shetterly, and Ben Westlund, are using these hearings to push for the addition of a sales tax to Oregon's tax structure. Democratic House Leader Deborah Kafoury will be testifying tomorrow, providing the caucus's perspective on the nature of a tax reform that could be accepted by the Democrats. She is going to argue that we can support a tax reform proposal if it meets a set of criteria, providing that it is adequate to meet the needs of Oregon, is fair and equitable, is stable, is business friendly, leverages federal and other revenues, is developed with the input of a broad range of stakeholders, and is efficient (minimizes the administrative costs of collecting revenue). No tax proposal can pass out of the House without Democrats supporting it, partly because none will have majority Republican support and also because any revenue bill requires a 3/5 majority (that is 36 votes).

As you can imagine I've been getting a flood of email on both sides of the issue of adding a sales tax in Oregon. I think they are running about 50–50, which is about how the polls look. I'm about 50–50 myself. I've never voted for a sales tax, but our tax structure is really in trouble. On the other hand, at the heart of Oregon's financial problems is the state of the national economy and the problematic decisions coming from Washington D.C. There are about 42 other states in trouble, including California with a $38 billion shortfall. (Compare that with our total budget of $11 billion.) And most of those states have sales, property, and income taxes. So the question of how to vote on a tax change depends on the details of the tax itself. However, given the late start of tax restructure deliberations, I'd be astounded if an actual long-term restructuring proposal emerges from this session. I don't think there are enough Republican votes to move a bill out of the House at this late date.

I continue to be troubled by the potential for the education budget. The Speaker's number for K–12 education is just under $5 billion. The Governor's number appears to be about $5.3 billion. The House Democrats are holding out for $5.6 billion. The problem is that even $5.6 billion will only fund programs at the level of the 2001 beginning budget. While $5.6 would assure full school years and even adequate class sizes, it still leaves schools short of critical programs such as music, art, social studies, full library services and many other important things. And strangely, at this critical time in budget negotiations, the huge numbers of parents, teachers, and students roaming the Capitol lobbying for schools seems to have disappeared. It appears that as summer started the folks are doing other things. Please don't stop fighting for schools at this critical time.

I mentioned in my last message that I had fought against SB 880, a bill that gave the tobacco industry special advantage in posting appeal bonds in court cases. I was pleased to hear that the Governor is going to veto that bill. It really is bad social policy. Bills I'm working on are moving along, although some more slowly than others. HB 3613, which Desari Caldwell and I have been working with Harvey Mathews of Associated Oregon Industries, is scheduled for a vote in the Senate tomorrow. Senator Kate Brown will carry it and we expect near total support for the bill. We were able to craft amendments that gained the support of all of the parties involved, including the State Treasurer. The bill passed out of the Rules Committee by a 5–0 vote. This measure, which should move swiftly now, will free up venture capital for emerging Oregon industries and should provide a substantial boost to Oregon's economy over the next decade.

I'm still working to provide support for the Cascade passenger trains between Eugene, Portland and Seattle. The Choo-Choo Caucus had a wonderful press conference last Monday urging support for the Governor's version of the transportation budget (which includes support for the trains). The mayors of Eugene, Albany, Salem, and Oregon City spoke at the press conference, as did Republican and Democratic legislators from all of the cities along the route. We continue to have hope for the Cascade trains and are urging support for the whole of Oregon's rail system.

The biggest partisan political flap of the year was a battle, on June 25, over HB 2652, which extends pollution tax credits to corporations. The battle started with Rep. Mark Hass moving to re-refer the bill back to the Revenue Committee. He argued that since it has been announced that PGE has received a huge tax credit for decommissioning the Trojan Plant the committee should reconsider the bill. There was a narrow debate, only on the question of re-referring the bill and the motion failed on a straight party vote. Then the Majority Leader moved to close debate on the measure itself, before any Democrats had a chance to argue against the bill. Since there had been a call of the house (all members had been called to the House floor and were required to stay there) caucus meetings were called at two corners of the House floor. Tempers were really high and the motion to end debate carried on a straight party vote. The bill then passed, with several Democrats voting for the bill, but most Democrats felt really abused by the process. It seemed very unfortunate to me, especially after the Minority Leader suggested a compromise, with three speakers allowed on each side of the measure. I personally felt I was denied a chance to speak on behalf of many of my constituents who had contacted me opposing the bill.

The big social happening of the last week was the events surrounding the departure of my star Legislative Aide, Desari Caldwell. Desari left on July 1 to join the staff of Congresswoman Darlene Hooley. While Harriet and I are delighted to see Desari get that great job, we are very sad about her departure. Desari has been a critical person in the legislative life and the social life of our part of the fourth floor. Our section is known as Democrat Freshman Row, since five of the six Democratic freshman have offices there. We have a great group of LAs on the floor, but Desari has been a special person for us all. She promises to hang out once in a while, watching the movement of HB 3613, which has been her very special baby. So we'll still get to see her on occasion.

The MitchMessage
July 20, 2003

"The development of the budget continues to dominate the news from the legislature." That was the lead sentence in the *MitchMessage* on July 6 and it is every bit as true on July 20. Rumors are floating all over the building as Speaker Minnis has been meeting one-on-one with every member of the Republican caucus. These meetings feature her effort to strong-arm her members into supporting her totally inadequate budget and her weird plan for raising an additional $100 million to support the inadequate budget. Apparently her budget calls for $5.05 billion for schools with an additional amount to go to schools only if state revenue is very much above forecast. This will allow her to claim that there really is more money for schools than there is in her budget. And social services would be decimated by her proposal. Those meetings should be interesting because some of the Republicans believe her budget is too generous and some realize they will have trouble winning their districts if they vote for an inadequate school budget.

Since she doesn't seem to be able to engage in serious negotiations with the Senate President and the Governor it probably would be a good move to get her version of the budget over to the Senate where rational people can get to work on a real budget.

The big news for me this past two weeks was the passage of HB 3613, my bill to encourage the Oregon Investment Council to look to Oregon companies first when investing their venture capital funds in emerging companies. The bill, which had Treasurer Randall Edwards opposing strenuously at first, passed the Senate on a 26–1 vote and passed unanimously out of the House. The Governor is going to sign the bill in a major press conference/signing ceremony Wednesday afternoon. HB 3613, which I worked with Harvey Mathews of Associated Oregon Industries, is getting a great deal of attention (and not simply because it represents a combined effort of AOI and a liberal freshman Democrat). The lead article in the business section of today's *Oregonian* was an excellent discussion of the bill from several perspectives. The *Valley Times* had an editorial on the bill this week as well, and it was covered on TV by KATU. I really believe this may be the most important economic development bill passed this year, because it has the potential to produce thousands of jobs and billions of dollars of revenue for Oregon.

I have been getting a great deal of email about the sales tax (still running 50–50), as the House Revenue Committee hearings have come to an end. It is clear that no major tax-restructuring bill will emerge from this session, although there is some movement toward a formal interim process. This approach could produce an integrated proposal to be acted upon by a special session — perhaps the first of several special sessions this year. On the other hand, there isn't any indication that we will get to *sine die* anytime soon. Before the beginning of the session Harriet and I bought tickets for an Alaskan cruise with my daughter and her family leaving on August 16. The longest session in history up to now ended on August 7. I now have an excused absence for that week, but I don't know what I'll do if the session is still dragging on August 15. Harriet has lots of offers from people willing to take my place, but she continues to hold out for me.

The transportation package should clear the Senate this week and should re-pass the House easily. While I'm disappointed that it only covers roads and bridges (not trains), it will have funds in it that have special importance to HD 33. Replacement of the Sauvie Island Bridge is important to this district. In addition to Oregon funds for the bridge, most of the money will come from the federal government. Multnomah County Commissioner Maria Rojo de Steffey announced this week that she received word that $500,000 has been appropriated by Congress to cover the next stage of design for the bridge. That is great news.

We are still working hard to move SB 875, the prescription drug bulk-purchasing bill. As I reported the bill has broad bipartisan support, including from the public employee unions, the Governor, the pharmaceutical industry, the Oregon Pharmacists, and advocacy groups such as AARP. The bill, which is sponsored by Senator Morrisette and me, passed out of the Senate Health Policy Committee on a 6–0 vote. It is currently stuck in the Joint Ways and Means Committee because the Department of Administrative Services has increased its estimate of the fiscal impact of the program. The program would include in the purchasing pool many state agencies, local governments, school districts and individual people 55 years of age and older whose income is under 185 percent of the Federal Poverty Line. We are working closely with the Governor's staff and the program's supporters to find the $950,000 it would take to kick-start the program.

There was an excellent article in Saturday's *Oregonian* about my colleague Jeff Barker's fight to save the inclusion of funding for emergency contraception in the Rape Victims Relief Fund passed last week by the House. Senator John Minnis had stripped funding for emergency contraception out of the bill as the bill passed the Senate and Jeff was not allowed to introduce an amendment to the bill during hearings by the House Judiciary Committee. Consequently Jeff drafted a minority report including E.C. funding in the program and personally gathered sufficient Republican support to pass the minority report. That convinced the Republican Caucus to move the bill back to committee to allow a bipartisan show of support for the addition of funding for emergency contraception. Jeff, a retired Portland police officer, said he had seen too many rape victims not to do everything possible for them. He played "good cop" to Senator Minnis's "bad cop" on this issue and won — at least in the House. Congratulations Jeff!!

The MitchMessage
August 3, 2003

This is the third message in a row where the development of the budget is dominating the news from Salem. I'll talk about that topic below. But first I'll share my experiences on several other things that transpired in the House during the last two weeks.

One of the loyal HD33 constituents asked me to explain the situation of the Forest Park bills and asked particularly if the rumor was true that 1000

Friends of Oregon was opposing me on Forest Park. First, the rumor is not true. 1000 Friends and others are now all on the same side, but it is a really interesting story that isn't quite over yet. I proposed the original Forest Park protection bill, HB 2905. That bill would have named Forest Park and the surrounding areas an "area of special state concern" and would have required LCDC to create a special plan for the protection of Forest Park, the Balch Creek Watershed, the wildlife corridors into the park and some surrounding areas. 1000 Friends was neutral on this bill, but at the last moment the City of Portland came in and opposed it. Before that happened I had the votes to pass the bill in the House, and the bill did pass out of committee to the House floor. Marge Kafoury (City of Portland lobbyist) told Deborah Kafoury, the House Minority Leader, that the city would oppose the bill. So I moved the bill off the floor and back to committee.

At that point, Oregonians in Action took a special interest in the bill and proposed to add an amendment that would require Multnomah County to partition 22 acres of forestland owned by Dorothy English into eight parcels. I objected to the amendment and OIA created another bill, HB 3631, comprising my Forest Park language and the Dorothy English amendment. I opposed HB 3631, even though Marge Kafoury came to me to tell me the city was now neutral on the bill. HB 3631 passed the House, although I voted against it. It went to the Senate. In the Senate, Senator Ringo amended the bill to substitute some City of Portland Forest Park language and to reduce the number of lots for Dorothy English from eight to six. The Senate passed the bill and sent it back to the House. Now 1000 Friends and Multnomah County were dead set against the bill. Just then the Governor announced he was going to veto the bill because of the Dorothy English provision, which he views (as I do) as a special interest bill bypassing the planning process. Currently, I am trying to get the bill into a conference committee so we can keep the Forest Park language, but strip out the Dorothy English provision. But Oregonians in Action are trying to negotiate with the Governor, so the bill is back in the House awaiting action. I hear the current plan is to concur with the Senate vote and send it to the Governor for a veto.

Now about more pleasant topics. The highlight of my last two weeks was the ceremony at which the Governor signed HB 3613, my bill to increase the amount of venture capital available to Oregon's emerging industries. The ceremony was at the Teseda Corporation headquarters in downtown Portland and was attended by many local business people, by Senator Kate Brown who carried the bill in the Senate, and by Rep. Dave Hunt, representing the Bipartisan Economic Growth Caucus. The Caucus picked up HB 3613 as a prime priority bill and supported it strongly in both the House and the Senate committee hearings. It was a great feeling to have sponsored the bill, which has been referred to by some as the most important economic development bill of the session. It was great to work with Harvey Mathews, of Associated Oregon Industries, and Desari Caldwell moving the bill through the process.

An important health-care bill, the Oregon Patient Safety bill (HB 2349), quietly passed the House last week. The bill was sponsored by Reps. Alan Bates, Jeff Kruse and me and creates the Oregon Patient Safety Commission that will begin working with hospitals to create a patient safety database and to help health-care institutions develop plans to improve patient safety when evidence of adverse patient outcomes becomes apparent. Deaths from medical misadventures have reached epidemic proportions in the United States and folks in the health-care community can be commended for working together to move this program.

SB 875, the prescription bulk-purchasing bill, has reached a critical point. All parties, including the public employee unions, AARP, the pharmaceutical industry, the Oregon pharmacists, and the Governor's office, are now in full agreement supporting the bill. The problem we're now facing is reducing the fiscal impact sufficiently to allow the bill to escape from the Ways and Means Committee and get to the Senate floor — where it will certainly pass. Hard work by Dr. Bruce Goldberg and the Department of Administrative Services reduced the price tag from $950,000 to $200,000 after SEIU, AARP and the pharmaceutical industry all agreed to take on part of the task. But the bill is still in trouble because of the tight fiscal situation.

I found myself in an awkward position a week ago that resulted in me missing my very first floor vote. I had agreed to join Reps. Brad Avakian and Greg Macpherson speaking at the City Club of Portland on July 25. We were to present "City Club members as Freshman Legislators." We had accepted the invitation months ago, since we assumed the session would be over by then, or if not we'd have no problem because Friday floor sessions usually went from 8:30am to 10:30am. That day the House was to vote on the Republican education package and the debate was scheduled for 8:30am. When the House convened at 8:30 the Republican caucus was in total disarray, because many of their members were not interested in voting for the terrible education budget the leadership presented. (In truth, several were also opposed because they thought it was too generous to schools.) They went into a stormy caucus and were still hard at it when we needed to leave for Portland. We decided, since I hadn't missed even a single vote at that point, that I would go to Portland and Brad and Greg would try to join by phone. The City Club was not able to arrange the phone link, so while I had to miss an important vote, I got the stage all to myself and I was able to use the time well. While I enjoyed the opportunity to share my perspectives, I felt really terrible about not being able to record my no vote on the budget, which passed 32–26 with Rep. Zauner and me missing.

1 | LEARNING TO BECOME A LEGISLATOR

Tomorrow the House will pass a totally inadequate Health and Human Services Budget. The budget will be a minimum of $50 million short of what is needed for the barest adequate service package. All of the Democrats will likely vote against the budget and it will move on to the Senate for further action. Many of us will make a floor statement on the inadequacy of the budget. We likely will also pass the natural resources budget to the Senate without the money needed to implement pesticide reporting. But it too will pass the House. The report we are getting is that the Speaker wants to pass out all of her unacceptable budgets and adjourn *sine die*, leaving the Senate to figure out what to do. Apparently we can leave for three days at a time, before getting called back into session. That should be interesting.

You have been hearing the Speaker and the Governor are only about $300 million apart on the total budget. The House passed an education budget that might be considered as much as $5.05 billion. (It's really more like $4.9 billion.) Schools need $5.3 billion at the minimum to stay open for a full year. It is ironic that House members from Multnomah County and Beaverton, where the schools will be least harmed by the Speaker's budget are fighting hardest to save the schools in the district represented by people who are arguing for the least adequate budget.

And the Health and Human Services budget is about $50 million short. We don't like the other budgets very much either, but we can probably live with them. That adds up to only $300 million difference between the Rs and the Ds in a budget in excess of $11 billion. It doesn't seem like much. But it does present a huge problem to the Republicans. Just to meet the budgets the majority has already passed, the ones coming down the pike, and to make up existing revenue shortfalls they need a plan to raise an additional $1.2 billion. They hate to face that idea and are struggling to find any possible way to avoid raising revenue. If you add $300 million to that amount they know they can't raise an additional $1.5 billion without being honest about short-term revenue increases. That idea has them paralyzed.

Finally, there is still talk about tax reform. But the only plan that could possibly pass is one to name an interim committee to deal with the issue, with the requirement to bring back an actual plan in about January or February. Then the legislature would return in a special session, just to consider a tax reform plan. We'll see.

Most of the old hands around the building are betting the legislature won't finish the session before Labor Day. I'm telling people October 12 seems more likely. Stay tuned.

The MitchMessage
September 1, 2003

The 72nd Legislative Assembly was pretty exciting right up to the moment when the House concurred with the Senate resolution to adjourn *sine die* (without a day) last Wednesday evening. In this *MitchMessage* I'll focus on events of the last couple of weeks. In a later message I'll share my perceptions of the entire session — but I need a bit of distance from the session to do that adequately.

As I mentioned in my prior message I had been planning to join my family on a cruise to Alaska since January, assuming the session would be long over by August. But it wasn't. However, on Saturday, August 16 with no indication there was a final deal in sight, I reluctantly joined my family and drove to Seattle to board the ship. The ship left Saturday evening. On Sunday night I received a message from the caucus office saying that a deal had been struck and that I needed to return to Salem immediately. Twelve legislators, three from each of the four caucuses, had been working all weekend long to get agreement on the budget deal. The twelve included three moderate members of the House Republican caucus, not including any of the caucus leadership. I was told that between 11 and 14 moderate House Republicans would join with most of the House Democrats in voting for the final package. They were ultimately named "the Rat Bastard Caucus" (RBC), by other House Republicans. It seemed critical to me that this plan needed to fly, because if it didn't I could see us still working on a balanced budget at Christmas time.

On Monday I flew out of Juneau, Alaska and returned to Salem early Tuesday morning to begin work on putting the budget to bed for the session. Harriet reluctantly remained on the cruise as I assured her she would be back in plenty of time for session-ending activities. Other members of my caucus welcomed my return, as the finishing touches had not been settled yet, and it was clear that all hands were required on deck (see how nautical I became after 36 hours on a ship) to work out the final details. The heart of the matter was HB 2152, which would carry most of the revenue components of the final settlement. All of the elements of the final plan would come to the House from the Senate stuffed into bills that had already been passed by the House. That meant that the Speaker could not bury the bill in a committee to thwart the plan. When a bill comes back to the House from the Senate it is brought directly to the floor for concurrence. Only a majority action of the House can re-refer the measure to a committee. This was critical because there was no assurance that the Speaker would move the bills of the package, even though she ultimately declared she would not interfere with the deal.

The agreement reached by the negotiating team was that all elements of the package would be supported and that votes would be delivered in the House for all agreed upon elements by a combination of RBC and Democrat members. Revenue raising matters required 36 votes in the House, while other elements of the deal only required a simple majority of 31 votes. The package included agreement on the education expenditure bills, both K–12 and Higher Ed, and on the social services package. All other major expenditure bills had already passed the legislature. The deal included agreement that the K–12 budget would be $5.2 billion, plus the possibility of an additional $100 million if the revenue picture improved late in the biennium. There was also an additional $50 million added to the budget for Human Services above what had already been approved by the House majority.

The revenue needed to pay for these services would be in two bills, HB 2152 for revenue raising measures and HB 2148 which included a set of revenue transfers that only required a majority vote. Several substantive matters were also included in the final deal, including two that were of great interest to me - SB 875 my prescription drug bulk-purchasing bill and final funding for operation of the Willamette Valley train service.

I expect you have all read about the revenue deal. HB 2152 included a modest three-year income tax surcharge generating $544 million over the biennium. There is also an increase in corporate income taxes raising $74 million, a three-year reduction in corporate tax credits worth $16 million and other changes in corporate taxes, such as an increase in the corporate minimum tax raising an additional $56 million — and several miscellaneous revenue changes raising about $100 million. Nobody with income under $30,000 pays any additional income tax under the plan. Taxpayers with income between $50,000 and $70,000 per year pay an additional $98 per year. All this is happening in a year when we are all receiving the benefit of a federal income tax reduction.

The political activity was furious on Tuesday and Wednesday preceding the House vote on HB 2152. The Senate easily passed the amended bill over to the House on Tuesday. I have a suspicion that if I had not been back in town on Tuesday the bill would have come to a vote Tuesday afternoon. As the pressure mounted on the RBC by the other Republican caucus members the suspense mounted. There were rumors all day Tuesday and on Wednesday morning about which members had changed their mind and were going to vote yes or no on HB 2152. I counted possible Republican yes votes (out of the 34 Republican caucus members) as high as 20 and as low as 9 during the day. There were as many as 5 Democrats (out of the 25 in the Democratic

Caucus) who expressed an interest in voting no at one time or another. But through that whole time the leaders of the RBC and the Democratic Caucus expressed confidence that things would work out fine. It was nail-biting time for those of us watching the proceedings. (Being a House member gives one an excellent view of the game.)

When the actual vote began the suspense mounted. The decision had been made to have a voice roll call on the measure, instead of using the electronic system where all members vote at the same time. The RBC leadership wanted a roll-call vote beginning from Z and going to A (with the speaker voting last), so they called for a roll call on the vote just before HB 2152. That roll call started at A so the next one would begin at Z according to House rules. The yes vote was at 35 at the end of the roll call, with Brad Avakian, the third from the last, voting no. I can feel the adrenalin raising even as I write about the vote. Brad, who was the only Democrat voting no, stood up and changed his no vote to yes before the gavel could drop, assuring the passage of the bill. In the end all 25 Democrats joined 11 Republicans voting in favor of the revenue package that needed to pass to support the rest of the agreement. It was stunning, and certainly the most dramatic moment of the session for me.

The rest of the package rolled out over the next week, with plenty of intrigue and plenty of suspense. HB 5077, the K–12 budget, passed the House 40-18. HB 5030, the human services budget, passed 38–17. Those bills only needed 31 yes votes. HB 2020, the PERS successor plan, passed 43–15. The only glitch came on the vote on HB 2148, a necessary part of the package to transfer money from other budgets, including the Education Stability fund and the lottery. It also carried some of the money for operating the trains. Several Democrats unexpectedly voted no on the bill when it came up the day before the final day of the session and the bill failed. A member switched his vote from yes to no and announced he would seek reconsideration the next day. After much negotiation and a little pressure on some of the no votes, the bill passed on the final day of the session to seal the deal.

As I said above, the money to operate the trains was in the final package and the operating funds were passed as expected in HB 2152 and 2148. However, some capital funds for upgrading the tracks upon which the trains run were also required. This money was expected to come from lottery-backed bonds, but that authorization wasn't put into the lottery bond bill. It was placed in another bill, from which it was removed at the last moment. Attempts were made to put the authorization into several other bills over the frantic weekend, but each effort was blocked. It's not clear at this moment what will happen to the trains as a result of this problem, but the picture should become clearer during the next week. It would be terrible if we have money for Amtrak to operate the trains, but no track upon which to run them.

Things were happening on my bills, right up to the last moment. The House had passed HB 2661, my bill to give ODOT authority to tow abandoned cars off the freeways. However it was stuffed with 17 pages of amendments to clean up the speed limits laws. This offended Rep. Randy Miller and the bill went to a conference committee, to which I was appointed as a minority member. During the conference committee proceedings the bill was further stuffed with some good and some bad things, including a measure that had previously passed the House to give ODOT authority to raise speed limits on the Interstate highways. I had voted no on this bill in its original form, but ultimately decided that the good things in the bill outweighed the bad and voted for it in the committee and in the House. The Governor will sign the bill, I think, but I hope ODOT is very careful about raising the speed limit.

On the totally good side, my bill to create an Oregon bulk-purchasing plan finally moved right through the legislative process. I had been working this bill from before the session began. After hours of negotiation and a dozen various amendments I reached consensus with all the key actors. SB 875 was backed, in its final form, by the pharmaceutical industry (PhRMA), the Oregon Pharmacists, SEIU, Oregonians for Health Security, AARP, OS-PIRG, Metropolitan Alliance for the Common Good, Oregon Health Action, and many other organizations. SB 875 creates the Oregon Prescription Drug Program for the bulk purchasing of drugs for state agencies, local governments, special districts, and all people over 54 years of age earning less than 185 percent of the federal poverty line. The bill passed, without a single no vote, out of the Senate Health Policy Committee, the full Ways and Means Committee, the Senate, the House Rules Committee, and at 8:30pm, just before *sine die*, out of the House of Representatives. It was a very emotional moment for me as I carried the bill on the House floor, since I had promised this bill in each of my election campaigns and had been working on it since just after my election to the House. It was the fifth of my bills to pass. That made it feel like a successful session and I was able to move to the *sine die* ceremonies with an easy mind and a smiley face.

The MitchMessage
September 28, 2003

I've been stalling a bit before writing my review of the 72nd Legislative Assembly to give myself sufficient distance from *sine die* for a calmer analysis of the session. Here it is. As in the previous *MitchMessages* I'm presenting a very personal perspective on things. I'll leave the objective reporting to *The Oregonian* and the *Willamette Week*. It feels to me as if the session was extremely productive, both for me personally and for the State of Oregon generally. I continue to hear people say that this was a terrible session, especially since it took 227 days to get its work done. It did take that long to get revenue and budget deals. But while the assembly struggled with that most critical part of its work, it also did a lot of great work for the citizens of Oregon. There were 2922 bills introduced this session and 869 of them passed out of the legislature.

IMPORTANT THINGS THAT HAPPENED DURING THE SESSION

There were many important measures passed, but of course the budget/revenue package was on everybody's mind. And we finally got that job done. The budget passed by the 2001 session was for about $12.3 billion in general fund and lottery expenditures. As the revenue forecasts got worse and worse the budget was recast several times and the final approved budget was reduced to $11.2 billion. That was a very minimal budget. I commented previously on the final budget and revenue deal reached by a group of moderate Republicans and all of the Democrats. That package still is a modest package, with $11.7 billion in spending, nearly $600 million less than was passed by the 2001 Legislature. The extra revenue for that package comes from a series of temporary income tax surcharges, an increase in corporate minimum tax, and several other temporary tax and fee increases. If that revenue package is rejected by the voters expenditure authorizations will be reduced by at least $800 million, including a $400 million reduction in school funding and $400 million more across the general fund budgets.

Reform of the Public Employee Retirement System (PERS) was high on our agenda and several bills passed that will make a great difference in the way PERS is managed. I voted for some of these bills and against others, based on my reading of the constitutionality of the bills and their fairness to retirees and workers. However, all in all they will make a major difference. Changes in the laws will save Oregon approximately $300 million in this biennium and will reduce the PERS shortfall by billions of dollars over the next several cycles, depending on the outcome of court challenges to the measures. One very important bill creates a successor plan for future employees that is both fair to the employees and saves billions for the future.

Maintaining adequate support for our schools was a very important matter for most of the legislators — at least they campaigned as if it was an important issue. We struggled with the K–12 budget. The budget debate raged across a range of numbers from a low of about $4.6 billion proposed by the House Republicans to a high of about $6 billion proposed by the House Democrats. The final budget compromise includes about $5.3 billion for K–12 schools, which will be reduced to $4.9 billion if the revenue package fails.

Passage of the transportation package was critical to Oregon and its passage was clearly a bipartisan triumph. The chairs and co-chairs of the House and Senate Transportation Committees guided this package, which provides funds for roads and for rebuilding a large group of critical bridges. Not only will the projects funded by that package keep people and freight moving, but it will also create a very large number of construction jobs to stimulate the Oregon economy. It is clear to me that this bill is the most important economic stimulus bill we passed during the session.

I sat with the Ways and Means Audit Sub-committee, which was charged with redesigning the Oregon Health Plan, and it was fascinating to be a part of that struggle. The committee made several major changes in the Health Plan, but generally retained both the coverage scope and the number of people served by the plan, although they certainly made priorities. The final salvation for the Health Plan was that both the nursing home industry and the hospitals came forward with a plan to tax their services to get money for a federal match that would fund paying for their services. Every $.40 in tax paid by the industries brings back $1.00 to them in reimbursements. That certainly seems like a good deal for everybody. And the plan was saved!

We spent some time and effort addressing the question of support for a major league baseball stadium. This issue was among the top three email generators for me, along with K–12 funding and the sales tax. I was against the baseball-funding package as the session began. But I eventually changed my mind as the plan emerged with more safeguards, including the certainty that the only state funds committed to the project would be taxes collected on players' salaries if a team actually came to Oregon. And I was moved, once again, by the possibility of 1500 construction jobs required by the stadium construction.

As I reported in earlier messages I became the leader of the Choo-Choo Caucus. That came about because I saw in the Transportation Committee that all of the effort was focusing on funding roads and bridges. While I think roads and bridges are clearly important, I believe that Oregon's future depends on a well-rounded, multi-modal transportation system. And that passenger rail, commuter rail, short-haul railroads, mass transit systems, and class I freight lines all need to be encouraged and protected as a part of Oregon's transportation infrastructure. We did important things for West Side Commuter rail, for mass transit, and for the short-haul railroads, but I'm very proud that we were also able to save the two Cascade trains from Eugene to Seattle.

The legislature provided the funds to support the operations of the trains and last week the Governor announced that he had worked out a deal with the Union Pacific for the track upgrades that are needed to keep the trains running. It was great to work with ODOT, with the Governor's staff, with train advocates, and with legislators from all over the state on this issue. All of us believe that the $10 million supporting the trains probably should have been a part of the $1.6 billion overall transportation package. One dollar for supporting passenger rail out of $160 supporting roads doesn't seem like too much for trains.

BILLS PASSED THAT I SPONSORED

I was personally gratified to have five bills pass in which I was the sponsor or chief co-sponsor. The Governor signed all five. That is certainly a better record than I expected to achieve. The first bill that passed was HB 3014, a technical bill that I introduced on behalf of the Port of Portland. (The headquarters building of the Port is in HD 33.) This was a simple bill that brought state law into compliance with federal law concerning the sale of airport property. While it wasn't high on my legislative agenda, the first bill passed had a special meaning for me, and is framed and on the wall of my office. The other four bills are much more important to me.

I introduced HB 3613 in cooperation with Associated Oregon Industries (AOI) and it is designed to increase the amount of venture capital available for emerging Oregon industries. HB 3613 encourages the Oregon Investment Council to look to Oregon first when investing their venture capital funds in emerging companies. It provides a target of $100 million in this type of investment over the next eight years. Harvey Mathews (AOI) and Desari Caldwell, of my staff, worked very hard on this bill and did a terrific job with a complicated measure. Treasurer Randall Edwards originally opposed the bill, but he ultimately supported the final version, which also included some changes his office wanted in the Oregon Growth Account program. The public employee unions were strong supporters of the bill as soon as it included a set of safeguards to ensure that the investments would be made using all the standards for prudent investments. At the bill signing ceremony the Governor said that HB 3613 was one of the most important stimulus bills of the session for the future growth of the Oregon economy.

The only bill I passed that was on my original legislative agenda was SB 875, the Oregon Prescription Drug Purchasing bill. In my 2000 and 2002 campaigns I promised to introduce this bill as my most important health bill. In early strategy sessions we decided to move this bill through the Senate, rather than through the House. Senator Bill Morrisette and I became the chief co-sponsors of the Senate bill. After working with all interested parties I was able to bring together a broad coalition to support the final version of the bill, including the pharmaceutical industry (PhRMA), the Oregon Pharmacists, SEIU, Oregonians for Health Security, AARP, OSPIRG, Oregon Health

Action, Metropolitan Alliance for the Common Good, and many others. It creates the program for the bulk purchasing of drugs for state agencies, local governments, special districts, and all people over 54 years of age earning less than 185 percent of the federal poverty line. It could ultimately have a significant impact on prescription costs for those populations. The bill passed without a single no vote in three committees, the Senate and the House. The Governor's staff is organizing a signing ceremony for it.

HB 2661, my bill to give ODOT authority to tow abandoned cars off the freeways, had a strange trip through the legislature. The bill, which was one paragraph long, easily passed the House. Unfortunately, in the Senate it was stuffed with 17 pages of amendments to clean up the speed limits laws. This offended Rep. Randy Miller and the bill went to a conference committee, to which I was appointed as a minority member. During the conference committee the bill was further stuffed with some good and some bad things, including a measure that had previously passed the House to give ODOT authority to raise speed limits on the Interstate highways. I had voted no on that bill in its original form, but ultimately decided that the good things in the bill outweighed the bad and voted for it in the committee and in the House. The Governor recently signed the bill. I'm ambivalent about the final product, but I'm pleased ODOT can now tow abandoned cars off of our freeways. And I hope ODOT is very careful about raising speed limits.

Another important health-care bill, the Oregon Patient Safety bill (HB 2349), quietly passed the legislature. The bill was sponsored by Reps. Alan Bates, Jeff Kruse and me and creates the Oregon Patient Safety Commission that will begin working with hospitals to create a patient safety database and to help health-care institutions develop plans to improve patient safety when evidence of adverse patient outcomes becomes apparent. Deaths from medical misadventures have reached epidemic proportions in the United States and folks in the health-care community can be commended for working together to move this program. It's possible it will really make a difference. A bill-signing ceremony is also in the works for this bill.

BAD THINGS THAT DIDN'T HAPPEN

There were several bad things that could have happened but actually didn't happen. Most of those things didn't happen because the Senate was evenly divided and because the Governor was there to backstop bad things. Among the measures that fit this category were a slew of bills designed to overturn land-use planning and endangered species protection. I was particularly interested in the large number of bills that were designed to let any number of bad things happen on productive farmland. I was strengthened in my resolve to protect farmland by a town meeting in the Helvetia area of my district. About 100 people came out to remind me that agriculture is very important to HD 33 and that they felt there was already more than enough intrusion of development interfering with the farmers' ability to bring their crops to market. I believe we will have an interim committee looking, once again, at the land-use planning system.

I was quite disappointed because we weren't able to get a serious look at tax reform. Nor did we do anything to reduce tax expenditures (tax breaks and tax credits) under the Oregon tax code. We only collect about $.45 of each $1 we could collect because of a forest of tax expenditures that have been introduced over many years. We passed a bill to create a tax reform commission to bring proposals back to a special session of the Legislature in early June and I hope that work addresses tax expenditures as well as looking at an overall tax restructure. I'm sure most folks think sales tax when they think about tax restructure. But there are many other approaches possible for reforming our tax structure, most of which will have a better chance of passing a state-wide vote.

And finally, we didn't kill the Oregon Poison Control Center. The center was clearly in danger of being phased out of existence. That brought me a great deal of email, as you can be sure. A last minute deal between OHSU and the Governor allowed us to include some funding for the center in the final funding package, while OHSU agreed to keep the center in operation with some internal funds. I was fascinated to see how much support emerged for the center.

GOOD THINGS THAT DIDN'T HAPPEN

I had four bills that I would include in the "good things that didn't happen" category. One of my intentions as a freshman legislator was to introduce some "big" ideas that I understood would take several years to actually happen. The bills would have referred a constitutional amendment designed to ensure universal access to health care for all Oregonians, provided land-use protection for Forest Park and the Balch Creek Watershed, created a cabinet-level Oregon Department of Public Health, and one that would have moved toward consolidation of Portland State University and Oregon Health & Science University. Each of the bills started debate and discussion, as I had hoped. I'll continue to work with each of the ideas, moving them forward for more serious discussion during the 2005 session.

The Forest Park Protection bill really took a strange turn, just as I had it wired to pass out of committee. First it turned out that the City of Portland wasn't happy sharing responsibility for the Park with anybody. They rejected the idea that Forest Park was a treasure that needed state-wide attention. Next the bill was hijacked by Oregonians in Action and stuffed with a section that would have given special sub-division rights to one resident, Dorothy English, who owns 22 acres out on Skyline Blvd. Their version of the bill passed the Senate and the House (I voted no) and was quickly vetoed by the Governor. I intend to work with all parties during the interim to get a version of the bill that is acceptable to all, except perhaps Oregonians in Action.

I had intended to move an initiative on a practical plan for universal health-care access during this interim, but I now think I'll step back and see how an AFL-CIO proposal for an initiative on universal access for children flies. We've waited this long for solving the health-care problem that I think we can wait another two years.

But I am going to work very hard on the PSU/OHSU idea during the next few months. This is an idea that seems so completely obvious to me I'm having trouble understanding why the presidents of the two institutions can't see it as well. It almost makes me wonder if ego ever gets in the way of organizational objectives. Surely not!! However, as long as having a tier-four university hampers economic development in the Metro area I'll keep pushing for the immediate creation of a tier-two university, which is what happens if PSU and OHSU are integrated as a single institution.

I have reason to believe that an interim committee will be taking a close look at the way the Department of Human Services is organized to deliver services in Oregon. That will give me ample opportunity to advance my State Health Department idea as a part of that review. A majority of states do have an independent State Health Department and it puts us at a competitive disadvantage not to have one.

THE FUTURE

I'm back working at OHSU, at least part time, and I'm looking forward to the interim. The interim committee assignments will be announced early in October and I have turned in my preferences for interim service to the Speaker. I'm finding my responsibilities as the Representative for House District 33 are also keeping me busy. In addition to my official assignments I will be working with interested folks in the Choo-Choo Caucus to craft plans for the continued development of Oregon's transportation infrastructure and on other issues of importance to the district. I'll be sending out *MitchMessages* periodically as things come up during the interim that I think would interest you. And you, please keep those emails coming about things that concern you. □

LIFE IN THE MINORITY

OREGON HOUSE OF REPRESENTATIVES, 2005

THE CONTEXT

This chapter chronicles my sophomore term as an Oregon legislator. My education clearly was continuing, with specific emphasis on being a successful member of the minority. My focus as a minority member was in working to improve bills of importance to members of the majority and finding allies from the majority to help move bills that were important to me. Many of the messages from this session deal with the nuts and bolts of legislative process, mostly emerging as a topic of discussion as I learned the process or, in some instances, when I was smacked in the head by it. I learned that matters such as how the leadership manages the legislative calendar to complete the work in a timely manner becomes critical to an individual member's ability to move his or her legislative agenda.

The *MitchMessages* cover the meaning of first, second, and third readings, the consent calendar, minority reports, attempts to force bills out of committee, and other parliamentary procedures. And as in the previous chapter, this chapter includes a great deal of discussion about the budget process. One cannot be reminded too often that the one constitutional obligation of the legislature is the creation of a balanced budget. This is a theme that suffuses each legislative session, whether the budget situation is bleak or rosy.

In the 2005 session getting to the final budget deal was somewhat more complicated because Republicans controlled the House and the Senate was in Democratic hands. The final deal crafted in any session comprises a complicated set of bargains that settles contentious budget disagreements as well as a few policy arguments. The primary actors in the final negotiation are the Speaker of the House, the President of the Senate, and the Governor. Sometimes the Minority Leaders of the House and the Senate are included, especially if the final deal requires a super-majority vote in order to raise taxes to balance the budget. The most contentious budget fight during the 2005 session involved the final budget number for the support of K–12 schools, a fight that arose early in the session and was not resolved. As usual, the final agreement was achieved with a compromise that everybody hated.

Getting to a compromise this session was also complicated because the Speaker took the unusual step of dissolving the Joint Committee on Ways and Means. Budgets crafted in Ways and Means require a majority of the members of both chambers. With separate budget committees each chamber's committee is required to develop each budget and differences need to be mediated as a separate negotiation. This is a central theme in the messages in this chapter, as I followed the developments as they occurred.

A few themes dominated my focus in the messages of this session. Land-use issues continued to be central, both because the question of forced annexation was central to the Washington County half of my constituents and because of my role as vice-chair of the House Committee on Land Use. Fortuitously, Rep. Bill Garrard, the chair of the committee had a similar situation with his constituents in Klamath Falls and we became close allies in working the legislation to deal with the situation. I say fortuitously, because if the land-use committees in the House and the Senate had been chaired by members with a different view of annexation, it would have been very difficult to achieve the legislative successes in the area we were able to achieve.

We were less successful in dealing with Measure 37. This statute was put into law as an initiative by the voters and was intended to protect landowners from gratuitous government action reducing the value of their land. However, the measure was so badly written that it could not be implemented. The backers of the measure (Oregonians in Action) presented another "will-of-the-voters" argument, demanding that the legislature amend the statute so it could be implemented. That created a very high-octane battle, which was reported in the land-use discussions of this chapter's *MitchMessages*. But we were not able to develop a compromise, and the problem remained at *sine die*.

The reader will find some focus in these messages on my work on child welfare in the Committee on Health and Human Services and on the Sub-Committee on Child Welfare. I found that work to be one of the most stressful activities I have undertaken as a House member. In the interim following the session I asked the Speaker to release me from that sub-committee; as I was dealing with treatment for lymphoma and felt I did not need the extra stress created by worrying about protecting the children for whom the Department of Human Services was responsible.

The session was also highlighted by a scandal sufficiently significant to cause the resignation of a House member. It is my impression that the Oregon

Legislature is relatively corruption-free, with problems at the edge of ethics rather than of a frankly illegal nature. In the messages from future sessions there is more discussion about changes in and clarification of rules regulating member behavior, especially around the use of campaign funds and the relationship between lobbyists and members.

The messages will also point out several things that did not happen, including passage of SB 1000, the bill to create civil unions for gay and lesbian couples. As you will find, the bill created a great deal of communication — support from my district and opposition from other parts of Oregon. The Republican leadership made sure that measure did not get to the floor. I also failed, once again, to pass my PSU/OHSU bill and my Forest Park bill.

Many of the *MitchMessages* from later in the session were suffused by a growing sense of disappointment, and even anger, at some of what seemed to be outrageously partisan behavior on the part of Speaker Karen Minnis and, to a lesser extent, majority leader Wayne Scott. Some of the anger was perhaps a result of naiveté. It is possible the tone would have changed had I served future sessions in the minority. I am happy to say I have not experienced any more sessions in the minority. It is clear that some of the expression of righteous indignation at the partisan nature of the session reported in this set of messages was well deserved.

The MitchMessage
January 8, 2005

Here we are getting ready for Oregon's 73rd Legislative Assembly to begin on Monday at 8:30 and *The Oregonian* is already reporting a potential fight over the rules. Today's *Oregonian* article reports that the rules to be presented by the Speaker on Monday will change the office of Clerk of the House from an elected position to that of one that serves at the whim of the Speaker. While the Republicans have not made the proposed rules available to the Minority, this one could cause quite a stir, since it departs from 145 years of tradition.

I'm quite pleased with my committee assignments for this session, having been named vice-chair of the Committee on Land Use, and a member of the Committee on Health and Human Services and the Committee on Election and Rules. Work on all three of those committees should be quite interesting. The Land Use Committee will certainly be charged with trying to make Measure 37 work. That will be a challenge. And as you know, I'm very interested in issues of health and human services, starting with trying to ensure the survival of the Oregon Health Plan.

I've been meeting with constituents since the end of the last session in late August 2003 and I'm developing a very large legislative agenda. I have between 15 and 20 bills already at, or soon to be at, the Legislative Counsel's office for drafting. I'll focus on various of my proposed bills in subsequent *MitchMessages*, but many will sound familiar, because I discussed them during the last session. Among my highest priority bills this session will be the integration of PSU and OHSU, the protection of Forest Park, and the development of a referral or an initiative to increase access to health insurance availability for all Oregonians.

Among the new high priority bills this session is a proposal to allow the citizens of unincorporated Washington County (half of House District 33) to consider the formation of a new city, several proposals on the health of children, and consideration of the creation of a drug czar position in Oregon government to help integrate substance abuse prevention and treatment activities. But more about all of these and others in future *MitchMessages*.

The dynamics of this session should be quite different from the last session for several reasons. First of all, the defeats of Measure 28 and Measure 30 over the last years have taken away any interest in raising revenue, except for a couple of minor things such as reinstating the ten cent cigarette tax. The thing that extended the 2003 session was the search for 36 votes in the House for a proposal to raise revenue. Eleven Republicans eventually came over and voted for the revenue increases that were finally referred and defeated in Measure 30. No such thing will happen this session. We are definitely going to be facing budgets for K–12 education, higher education, health care and human services that will be painfully inadequate. It is not going to be possible to fund essential services with the money available. There are going to be some very painful votes.

The dynamics will also be different because of major shifts in the political distribution of the body. The Senate, which had been Republican dominated for many years, went to 15–15 for the 2003 session. That made for an unusual dynamic. This session the Democrats have taken control of the Senate, 18–12. The Republicans have dominated the House for 14 years. But things have also changed in the House this year. In 2003 the Republicans held a 35–25 majority, but about 12 of the Republican members were somewhat moderate. (My two chosen informal mentors were Republicans, Ben Westlund and Lane Shetterly). The House now has a 33–27 Republican majority, but almost all of the moderates are no longer in the House. They have either been defeated for reelection, been elected to the Senate, or have left political office for other pursuits.

So the real question will be the extent to which the Republican majority in the House and the Democratic majority in the Senate can find ways to work together for the good of the citizens of Oregon. I am somewhat hopeful and I look forward to a shorter (over by early July) but perhaps productive session. I certainly intend to do my part to make that happen.

The MitchMessage
January 23, 2005

The first two weeks of the 2005 Legislature have been pretty busy and quite interesting. The first day of session is always special (I even wear a tie). Particularly moved were the 20 or so freshman in the House whose friends and family filled the House Chamber. Following the swearing-in ceremony a joint session began with the entry of the Senators, several past governors, the Supreme Court, Appeals Court, and Tax Court justices and the Governor. The Governor presented his State of the State address, half of which excited the Republicans in the chamber (no new taxes, live within the budget, stimulate business) and half of which excited the Democrats (stimulate business, save the salmon, addition of sexual orientation to anti-discrimination laws.) The most controversial part of the speech was his passionate statement about the lack of an exit strategy for the Iraq war. He has been attending the funerals of Oregon soldiers and he has obviously been moved by the experience.

We went to work immediately after the morning session, beginning our committee work. The Health and Human Services Committee has been focusing on the work of the DHS division of Children, Adults, and Families, with particular concern for their Child Protective Services group and their work on foster care and adoptive services. The committee is worried about the extent to which the division is protecting children in the State's custody, after two tragic incidents where children were killed or injured by their parents or other family members. But some members of the committee seem very concerned about whether the rights of parents or other family members are being protected by the agency. I was impressed with the competence of the director of the group, Ramona Foley, but it is clear they have a terrible job to do and perhaps with insufficient resources to do the job.

The Committee on Land Use also went quickly to work looking at the land-use system. We had a joint meeting with Senator Ringo's Senate Committee on Land Use and Environment, looking at the impact of Measure 37. There does seem some determination on the part of the chairs to try to make Measure 37 work while reviewing the whole land-use system. We hope to make land-use work even better, in the face of Measure 37 implementation. There certainly are strong opinions on Measure 37, but we heard testimony that until some of the uncertainty about the measure is cleared up, title companies may stop issuing title insurance and banks may stop offering mortgages. Not too good.

Several of my bills were introduced this week or will be introduced next week. These include one aimed at reducing light pollution in the Oregon sky, one to increase the reach of SB 875 that I passed in the last session to begin a pool for the bulk-purchasing of prescription drugs, and a bill to require a double-majority vote for annexations. Senator Bill Morrisette, the co-sponsor of the earlier bill, is jointly sponsoring the SB 875 expansion bill. The annexation bill is co-sponsored by Rep. Bill Garrard (R. Klamath Falls), the chair of the House Land Use Committee and Rep. Brad Avakian who, like me, represents a large portion of unincorporated Washington County. I'll have the actual bill numbers for you in the next edition of the *MitchMessage*, along with other bills introduced in the period.

There are about 20 other bills on my work list currently, including the one to remove the ability of Beaverton, Portland, and Hillsboro to veto the formation of a city within three miles of their borders. That one is at the Legislative Counsel's office. I'm continuing to work on a referral to the voters of a constitutional amendment that would facilitate increasing health insurance coverage in Oregon. A Republican senator has agreed to co-sponsor that referral, which would declare that access to affordable, effective health care is a right of all Oregonians.

I met this week with the Treasurer's office to discuss their efforts to implement HB 3613, which I passed last year (working closely with Associated Oregon Industries) as my primary jobs bill. That bill would ensure that at least $100 million would be invested in emerging Oregon industries by 2008. I have been concerned that the Treasurer needs to take stronger steps to make sure the Oregon investments are actually considered and made, if it is prudent to do so.

Senator Ringo and I are working on the development of a bill to create open primary elections in Oregon. You may have read ex-Secretary of State Phil Keisling's op-ed piece on the topic. It is an intriguing possibility that could improve the quality of candidates we see in the general election, especially in districts that are heavily Democrat or heavily Republican. Both parties will probably object to it, but if it doesn't come out of the legislature it is likely we will see the proposal as an initiative in November 2006.

There has been a heavy load of email during these two weeks. Please keep the communications coming. The highest number of emails this period has been messages concerning annexation and a mass mailing of emails concerning the Public Utility Commission's upcoming decision of the sale of PGE to the Texas Pacific Group. I remain strongly opposed to the sale (I've said I oppose anything that starts with Texas). There doesn't seem to me to be a great deal that the legislature can do about it pending a PUC decision. On the other hand, Senator Rick Metsger is holding hearings on the topic, apparently groping for some way to influence the decision. Since the House Water Committee heard a fluoridation bill last week, mail on fluoridation (which I support) has been picking up.

Keep in touch.

The MitchMessage
February 5, 2005

It's hard to believe that four weeks of the session have already gone by. The last couple of weeks have been pretty traumatic for members of the House because of the scandal surrounding the financial activities of Rep. Dan Doyle. While Doyle was not among the most popular of our colleagues, we are all extremely embarrassed by his activities, which include the apparent conversion of as much as $80,000 from campaign funds to his personal use. Doyle's resignation from the House left many of us still waiting for his "secret" financial plan to save Oregon, which he floated during the battle on Measure 28. A good thing coming out of the Doyle fiasco was the announcement this week by Speaker Minnis and Democratic Leader Jeff Merkley of a bipartisan proposal to reform the manner in which campaign funds are handled.

It is likely that the House Committee on Election and Rules, of which I am a member, will address this issue. This committee has already announced that we will be holding eight hearings, all over the state, to take testimony on how the election process in Oregon can be improved. While I'm not excited about winter travel to Pendleton, Bend, Prineville, Grants Pass, Medford and Newport, I think it is a useful activity. I'm particularly interested in examining how well prepared we are for recounts, after the experience following the recent election in Washington State. It's amazing to elect a governor by 125 votes out of several million and after three recounts.

Most of us are frantically working to get bills ordered for drafting and gathering co-sponsors for the proposals when they are ready for introduction. The deadline for requesting bills to be drafted from the Legislative Counsel office is 5pm Monday so the stakes are getting high. After Monday we will only be allowed to request two priority bills before the end of session. I have requested more than 20 different measures to be drafted and have already introduced eight or nine, including a couple for which I am the chief co-sponsor. I'll list the individual bills I've introduced already at the bottom of this message. The 50th day of the session is the deadline for introducing bills.

Beaverton announcing plans to eventually annex about 50 percent of my House district has brought annexation to the forefront, at least for the Washington County delegation. I'm in a unique position because my district is 50/50 Multnomah County and Washington County. I serve as a member of both the Washington County delegation and the Portland delegation. So annexation without representation has become the focus of the "Washington County Tea Party." It turns out my constituents don't want to help Beaverton become the second largest city in Oregon, at least not without a chance to vote on their annexation. Consequently I've introduced a bill (HB 2484), with the chair of the House Land Use Committee Bill Garrard, Brad Avakian, and Jerry Krummel to ensure that no annexation takes place without the consent of the voters (and land owners) of an area to be annexed. There are folks in the Senate doing the same thing, so we will have several opportunities to ensure the voices of the citizens are heard.

Because I decided early in my legislative service that it was necessary to create bipartisan alliances to accomplish anything in the legislature, most of the bills I'm proposing have at least one Republican chief co-sponsor. I've worked hard to develop the kind of relationships with my Republican colleagues that make this possible. As I reported in the last *MitchMessage* my most critical legislative priority is the bill to ultimately create an integrated comprehensive university by merging PSU and OHSU. That bill has begun to gather momentum, with the announcement that Rep. Linda Flores, a Republican who is chair of the House Education Committee has joined me as an enthusiastic chief co-sponsor. Yesterday the story broke on the front page of the *Portland Business Journal.* I'll be introducing this bill in the next week or so, after I gather a few more co-sponsors.

Senator Ben Westlund, a Republican from Bend, and Senator (Dr.) Al Bates, a Democrat from Ashland, joined as the chief co-sponsors of my proposal to refer an amendment to the constitution to the voters. The referral (HJR 6) would put into the constitution the right of all Oregonians to affordable and effective health care and would give the legislature, working with all stakeholders, four years to create a pragmatic, incremental way to do that. In the likely event I can't pass HJR 6 out of the legislature, I'm beginning the work to gather signatures for an initiative to be voted on in November, 2006.

I've been getting a great deal of email and I try hard to keep up with it. The mass mailings of the last couple of weeks concern protecting individual privacy, funding for K–12 education, hospital infections, and annexation. But I've also gotten email from you on a great many other topics. Please keep the email flowing. And I'll try to keep answering it.

Here are some of the bills I've introduced during the past two weeks. You can find the language of the bills on the legislative website at *www.leg.state.or.us*

- HJR 6 — the constitutional referral for improved access to health care
- HB 2311 — to reduce light pollution
- HB 2426 — to expand the scope of practice for dental hygienists in poverty clinics
- HB 2483 — to allow state agencies to name units of higher education as state agencies when applying for grants

- HB 2484 — annexation reform
- HB 2507 — to reduce the danger in the handling of sodium azide, the explosive in airbags
- HB 2523 — to allow local areas to impose system development charges for education, police, fire, and parks
- SB 329 — to expand the bulk-purchasing pool for prescription drugs created by my bill SB 875 last session

The MitchMessage
February 20, 2005

The legislative session is marching along, although there have been significantly fewer bills introduced so far this session than last session. The lobbyists are joking that it isn't difficult to find a parking place near the Capitol this session. That will change on Monday when hundreds of school children and their parents will be in the Capitol lobbying for adequate school funding.

During the last two weeks I received many emails supporting two women's health bills (HB 2497 and HB 2498). The first bill continues the insurance mandate for several important women's screening services, including mammography and pap smears, as these mandates are scheduled to sunset. HB 2498 adds a mandate that clinical breast exams be included in health insurance coverage. These bills were heard in the House Health and Human Services Committee (of which I'm a member) this week. There was terrific testimony on these bills, including that by four legislators. Dr. Elizabeth Steiner, a resident of HD 33, did a wonderful job testifying on HB 2498. Both bills were passed out of committee by a 7–0 vote, with the sunset clause removed. They should move easily through the legislature.

Annexation was a very hot topic in the legislature this week. The week started with Nike holding a dinner at their headquarters for a very large number of legislators, arguing that they must be protected from Beaverton's annexation designs. Several of us maintained that Nike must make sure that their desires echo those of their 190,000 neighbors in unincorporated urban Washington County. The highlight in the annexation debate came at a hearing on HB 2484 before the House Land Use Committee (of which I'm vice-chair). This bill, sponsored by Chair Bill Garrard, Brad Avakian, Jerry Krummel, and me would require a majority vote of the voters (or land owners in industrial or unoccupied land) in an area as a condition of annexation. With the amendments we propose, it would also outlaw most island annexations.

It was a very lively hearing (which can be heard on computer via the legislative website archives). The most vigorous opposition to the bill was by the cities, with Portland leading off with testimony that they only annex with permission; but saying that they didn't want to give up any of their current authority, even though they don't plan on using the authority to annex without approval of the residents. But there was also very strong support for the proposal. Rep. Garrard has agreed to the creation of a workgroup to try to achieve consensus on the issue, but strongly believes that we need to deal with annexation during this session.

The Land Use Committee is also working on Measure 37 legislation. There are so many ambiguities in the measure passed by the voters that it cannot possibly work as written. But there is absolutely no consensus emerging as to what to specify and how to make it work. Opinion goes from leaving it alone and letting the courts clarify the ambiguity, to making sure the legislature clarifies things to match "what the voters thought was in the measure", to nullifying the measure and doing something else that will satisfy the voters. I'm cautiously watching the debate and am not yet taking very much of a position, although I do think we need to make things work, one way or another.

I introduced my PSU/OHSU bill (HB 2560) and it is beginning to get some traction. Last Sunday *The Oregonian* had a long article on its front page about how Washington has improved its economic development potential by supporting the University of Washington as an economic development engine. That article commented on HB 2560 as the only proposal dealing with the problem in Portland. The lead editorial in today's *Oregonian* comments very favorably on HB 2560, which would create a comprehensive, integrated university in the metro area by ultimately integrating PSU and OHSU. The proposal would remove PSU from the Oregon University System, expand the public corporation board that governs OHSU and rename it the Oregon Metropolitan Universities Board, put PSU under the OMU board, and give the board ten years to integrate the institutions. The bill was assigned to the House Education Committee and subsequently to the Joint Committee on Ways and Means. Education Committee Chair, Linda Flores, is the chief co-sponsor of the bill with several other co-sponsors.

I've introduced a bill to create a better way to deal with disposing of sodium azide (the explosive that is used to deploy airbags). The bill, which will have a hearing in the House Committee on Environment, has begun to get some attention. Sodium azide is a deadly biocide (poison), highly explosive, and becomes hydrozoic acid when exposed to water in an acid environment. Consequently its proper disposal is of interest to auto recyclers, auto crushers, and auto manufactures. I first became interested in the issue while reading a mystery book by J.A. Jance. When I contacted her she led me to scientists at the University of Arizona who were working on the issue. There will be a hearing on the bill on March 1 and it is likely there will be speakers from around the country talking about the issue, including a representative of the group that produces ISO standards in the auto industry.

While I introduced a couple of new bills during this period (including one that would limit school vending machines to milk, juice, and water) I still have 18 or 19 concepts for bills that have not emerged from the legislative counsel's office. LC turns ideas into bill drafts and they are quite busy. But since all bills, except my two priority bills, must be introduced no later than February 28, they will be getting me the rest before the next *MitchMessage*. I'll provide a full list of my bills in that message.

Email has remained hot and heavy. The women's health issue led the list during this fortnight, closely followed by mail about school funding (the most recent set suggesting an increase in lottery profits go to schools), fluoridation, and suggestions to eliminate toxic mixing zones in the Willamette River. Please keep the emails coming. I love to hear from my constituents.

The MitchMessage
April 17, 2005

The budget remains on the front burner, as it is now clear that the compromise budget will not provide sufficient resources for K–12 education, higher education, services for the elderly, people without access to health care, and the mentally ill. It's likely that I will be voting against each of those budgets. I've said in this message many times that most things in the legislature are not partisan issues, but the question of whether there is enough money to fund critical services is clearly becoming partisan. We had two very interesting debates in the House since I last wrote that point out the nature of the partisan split. It is clear to me that we do not have sufficient revenue to fund the services that we all agree are necessary. And it's my view that our tax code gives away (through weird tax loopholes) far too much that should be collected. We spend more on tax loopholes than we spend on programs. One of those debates was about reconnecting to the federal tax code.

For many years the Oregon tax system was connected to the federal income tax structure. But during the 2003 session we decided to partially disconnect from some of the tax reductions that had been passed in Washington, D.C., especially the corporate tax breaks. Our House revenue committee debated reconnecting and produced a bill to reconnect fully with the federal tax code. The Democratic minority on the committee produced a minority report that proposed reconnecting except for two huge tax breaks to multinational corporations. The difference between the majority and the minority approach was tens of millions of dollars that could have been collected from these multinationals to support Oregon schools. There are currently only nine states in the Union that have lower corporate taxes than Oregon. The debate went along strict party lines, as did the vote. I'm hoping sanity will take over in the Senate, allowing us to reconnect with most of the federal tax code, but preserving Oregon's ability to determine its own tax policy.

Another debate over tax policy produced my most embarrassing event of the session so far. Following the income tax debate we had a similar debate over connecting to federal inheritance tax changes. The question was whether to raise the limits for when an estate would be taxed. Again there was a majority and a minority report. The minority report proposed raising the limit significantly, but also proposed raising the tax rate on the really large estates so the change could be done in a revenue neutral way. After the minority report was defeated (along strict party lines) I rose to speak against the bill. I favor raising the limit, but I'm opposed to anything that takes revenue out of the current system. I gave a passionate speech against the bill and when it came time to vote I spaced out and pushed the "aye" button without noticing. Later somebody asked me if I intended to speak against the bill and then vote for it. When I realized what I had done I joked about being able to claim both sides of the issue, like a comic politician. But I had to go through the embarrassing process of asking the Majority Leader to ask for a suspension of the rules the next day to allow me to change my vote on the bill. It is only allowable to do that if the vote change won't affect the outcome of the bill and this bill had easily passed without my vote.

I've spent much of the last two weeks traveling around Oregon with various committees. The most interesting of these has been our visits of the House Sub-Committee on Child Welfare where we spent much of two days in the child protective service offices in Clackamas County and in Gresham. I had the privilege of listening on the phone while hotline screeners took calls from people concerned about children's safety. These workers have an extraordinary task, because each call (and there are more than 40,000 per year to the hotline) has the nugget of disaster within it. They do a great job of keeping people on the line and getting the information they need to make an informed choice on whether to take immediate action on the call or to simply file the information away for future reference. The two other committee members observed a variety of tasks for the agency, including riding along on a drug bust with kids in the home and observing in foster homes. There was an excellent piece on our work on the 11pm news on Channel 6 on Tuesday night. We'll continue to work to figure out how to ensure that we are doing everything possible to protect the children generally, but especially those children who are in the custody of the state. I feel the need to protect these children especially because they are "our" children when we take custody of them.

I also travelled with members of the Elections Committee, Health and Human Services Committee and the Land Use Committee to Heppner, Pendleton, Baker City, Grants Pass, and Medford. It was clear that Oregonians around the state really appreciated the opportunity to talk to the legislature without having to travel to Salem. It felt important symbolically and allowed us to gain insight into significant issues. For example, we took testimony Friday night in Medford on Measure 37. There were 29 witnesses who testified between 6:30 and 9:30 on Measure 37. I was surprised to hear so many of the farmers and ranchers from three counties around Medford say that they believe the intent of Measure 37 was to pay for "takings" and not to allow people to do whatever they wanted to disregard land-use regulations. The real estate people who testified had the opposite position. In Salem we are more likely to hear from the real estate lobby than from so many ordinary citizens. We have about 15 Measure 37 bills in the House Committee on Land Use, but we've been waiting for Sen. Ringo to craft a compromise in the Senate before we take a serious look at the situation. He reports success on moving toward a compromise.

I was assured we were going to pass HB 2484, one of the main annexation bills, during our hearing in Medford. But one thing and another intervened again and we didn't move the bill. To complicate matters in this area SB 887, the bill Sen. Ringo and I sponsored continues to move from one committee assignment to another in the Senate and did not get to the floor. We were hoping to have that bill over to the House to work on it. I continue to be assured we will pass HB 2484 and we are planning to take up Rep. Avakian's annexation bill in the House committee soon. I continue to be hopeful that we will move a good bill. But I've begun to bite my nails, recognizing the difficulty on moving anything in this area because of the strong and confounding forces that are muddying the annexation waters.

Several other of my bills have begun to move. We passed HB 2755, a technical land-use bill, out of the House on a 60–0 vote. HB 2428, having moved out of the House, passed to the Senate floor out of the Senate Health Policy Committee on a 7–0 vote. That is a bill to improve access to dental hygiene services in poverty clinics, schools, and other places with limited access to dental care. HB 2507 should move out of the House Committee on Environment this week. I reached a compromise with all parties on this bill, which requires deploying all airbags in wrecked cars to protect against misuse of sodium azide, a very dangerous chemical. I understand the content of HB 2517, my bill to limit the contents of school drink machines, is going to be added to a Senate bill. Two of my health insurance reform bills will also be heard in the House Committee on Health and Human Services. At least one will pass out of committee and out of the House. I also have gotten a compromise on a modest version of my Forest Park bill (HB 2704) and expect to move it out of committee this week. And we had an excellent hearing on HB 2897, a bill to create a commission to study extending the Washington County Commuter Rail line to Salem. I only requested a hearing to highlight the issue, but independent work has begun to study the problems related to extending the line. It has been hard to generate a sense of urgency for the extension since the first segment of the line won't be completed before 2008. But I believe we need to be moving on the project in order to have the first passenger by 2017, just about the time my plan for OHSU/PSU comes to fruition.

It's very difficult for legislators to think 12 years off in the midst of a busy legislative session, with immediate deadlines, committees closing down, and things happening in committee rooms all over the Capitol. But I think raising issues to create a better future is one of my most important functions as a legislator. My experience as a health services researcher feeds my approach to considering legislation. While I work on immediate and pressing things each day, I always try to imagine a better future. And I ask myself what steps need to be taken today to move a little step towards that better future. I told a story in the committee hearing on commuter rail about Napoleon. It is told that he brought his arborists in and told them he wanted them to work on a plan for trees that would completely cover one of his favorite roads. They told him it would take 100 years to get trees to look the way he envisioned. He responded, "Then begin TODAY." Not too many other legislators share my commitment to move towards the future.

Please keep your messages coming. This week I had a great deal of mail on SB 1000, the bill to create civil unions in Oregon as they are in California and against HB 2409 that would change the minimum wage for restaurant workers. And mail continues on my responsibility to make certain the budget includes adequate funding for schools. I also had a rash of "spam" favoring a bill I'm co-sponsoring requiring drug companies to report financial arrangements with doctors. I considered it spam because I got more than 250 email messages, triggered by Consumers Union, from all over Oregon. I was angry because with 250 messages, almost all from people who aren't my constituents, it hampered my ability to answer my constituents' email. I simply deleted them in mass after finding only one in the first fifty that was from a constituent. It's my habit only to answer mass emails from constituents. I think most other legislators do the same, although most have their staff answer the emails, whereas I do it myself.

The MitchMessage
May 1, 2005

I began the last message saying that the budget dominated the legislature and the same thing is true this week. The Speaker of the House announced last week that if a budget number on K–12 education wasn't agreed upon by Friday evening (last) she would break up the Joint Ways and Means process and create a House budget without the Senate. Friday evening came and went and there was no word on a budget agreement and no word about breaking up Ways and Means. It's my belief that the House Leadership does not really want to break up Ways and Means because they don't want to be exposed alone having to back such an inadequate budget. The current negotiations appear to be stuck between the House Republican K–12 budget number of $5.175 billion and the Senate Democrats number of $5.325 billion. While that seems like a minor difference, the stark reality is that neither number is adequate to prevent schools from taking another hit. And we are committed to a total budget of $12.393 billion, neither more nor less. But it also isn't clear where that money will come from.

The House Democrats held a school budget hearing this week with the Senate Democratic caucus leadership. About 80 school administrators and school board members attended. All but three school representatives said that if the final budget number was below $5.4 billion it would necessitate further cuts in school days or increases in class size. And most said that because of the need to complete their budgets they were basing their budget on state money between $5.1 and $5.3 billion. I think a barrier to getting to a reasonable school budget number is that the negotiators don't seem like they share the objective of getting to a solution. It seems like they have political objectives, rather than pragmatic ones. I was talking to one of the key participants in the negotiation yesterday and the process was equated with a negotiation in a divorce. I have announced I will not vote for a school budget below $5.4 billion, when even that number will harm so many school districts.

There were several interesting floor debates the past two weeks, and I managed to press the button I intended to press each time. The much-heralded vote to require schools to provide an opportunity to recite the Pledge of Allegiance started the fortnight. It stimulated a great patriotic fervor and finally passed with only ten negative votes. The objective of this bill seemed to be to get some political fodder for the next election for members brave enough to vote their conscience against the bill. I voted aye, mostly because I grew up saying the pledge in school and having fond feelings for it. If fact, if memory serves, the school day went downhill from there.

There was an interesting political fight between the podiatrists and the physicians over whether podiatrists should have a seat on the Board of Medical Examiners. I had provided a yes vote in committee so the bill could be brought to the floor, but voted no on the floor. The bill passed 50–8. It seemed to me the decision on the bill was a political, rather than a policy decision. The seat was an important symbol to the 200 or so podiatrists and to the several thousand physicians.

There were two interesting land-use bills on the floor last week. The first would allow existing dwellings clustered in rural areas to be served by a sewer system. That could happen either by local government action or because the homeowners could create their own sewer system. Historical arguments against this were based on the assumption that rural homes should not have urban services. The bill came to the Land Use Committee and we were able to work out a compromise that all sides accepted. It passed in the House easily.

The more important bill was HB 2484, which was my first annexation bill. It requires that when a city wants to annex land under ORS 195 a majority of voters in an area to be annexed agree to the annexation, as well as a majority of voters in the city. There was a lively debate on the floor and the bill passed with 45 yes votes. It now moves to the Senate. Because some cities can also annex under ORS 222, which includes the island annexation provisions, we also need to amend ORS 222. Senator Ringo and I sponsored SB 887 aimed at fixing ORS 222. That bill stops Beaverton from doing forced island annexations for the next two years, provides for an interim work group to look for a permanent fix for annexation statutes, and provides some guarantees for Nike and Columbia Sportswear. The bill passed out of the Senate last week and is headed for my House Committee on Land Use. I expect it will be amended and passed back to the Senate for agreement. There is also a bill sponsored by Brad Avakian and me (HB 3084) with similar provisions to SB 887 that will be heard this week in the Land Use Committee. We might pass that on for Senate consideration as well.

There has been a lot of action on my legislative agenda in the last two weeks, and more scheduled for the coming week. So far four of my bills have passed out of the House of Representatives and another one will be passed on Wednesday. In addition SB 887, of which I was a co-sponsor, passed out of the Senate. HB 2426, co-sponsored by Rep. Dalto and me, passed out of the Senate on a 27–0 vote and will go to the Governor for his signature. That bill expands dental hygiene services to areas with limited access to dental care, by allowing certain hygienists to practice without direct supervision of a dentist. SB 329, a bill co-sponsored by me and Sen. Bill Morrisette, passed out of the Senate Committee on Human Services on a narrow 3–2 vote. I'm not sure what that means for passage on the Senate floor, because it will also face a minority report. This bill is one vehicle to expand the drug purchasing pool. I'm hoping it passes out of the Senate over to the House where I'm already working on a compromise measure that has a chance of passing the House. SB 329 in its current form has no chance in the House. However, if it doesn't pass the Senate, there are ways to get a vehicle in the House if we can work out a compromise, as we did for the bill (SB 875) we passed during last session.

I expect committee action during the next two weeks on four other of my bills. HB 2507 will probably be passed out of the Committee on Environment Wednesday. That is the bill dealing with proper disposal of sodium azide (contained in airbags) during the dismantling of automobiles. I have reached agreement with everybody interested in the topic and the Speaker has rescinded a subsequent referral to the Committee on Ways and Means. The House Committee on Health and Human Services is scheduled to act on HB 2706 tomorrow. This bill was introduced at the request of two of OHSU's preventive medicine residents, Michelle Adler and Abbas Hyderi, who have worked very hard on the bill. It is aimed at improving the HIV testing rate as a part of obstetrical care. My Forest Park bill (HB 2704) was moved out of the Committee on Land Use last week. But because of a subsequent referral, it moved to the Committee on Agriculture and Natural Resources. I'm working with the chair of that committee and hope to get action there, because I have reached consensus on that bill with Metro, the City of Portland, Multnomah and Washington Counties, and the State Department of Land Conservation and Development. Finally, it's likely that HB 2560 (PSU/OHSU) will move out of the House Committee on Education to the Joint Committee on Ways and Means. It will be a busy two weeks.

The last two weeks have been busy email weeks. As many of you know I read and answer all email from my constituents myself. So occasionally I fall a day behind. But here are the big issues currently. I've received a great deal of email about SB 1000, which I support. This bill provides for civil unions and supports other areas of equality for gays and lesbians. I've had heavy email on both sides of SB 861, which prohibits force-feeding of birds. I am tending towards opposing SB 861. Fluoridation (HB 2025) also got a fair amount of attention. That bill passed the House and was heard in the Senate Committee on Environment and Land Use. I testified in Committee in favor of it, both as a member of the Oregon Health Policy Commission, which proposed the bill, and in my capacity as a professor of public health and preventive medicine. It's facing rough sledding in Senator Ringo's committee, but I still have hopes for it.

HB 2605, which would require parental notification before performing an abortion on a minor, has stimulated a great deal of mail. I oppose that bill. Under current law (ORS 109.650) a minor 15 years of age or older may give consent to hospital care or medical or surgical diagnosis or treatment by a physician. It doesn't make any sense to me to treat an abortion decision differently than any other procedure. I think that bill will come to the House floor this week and is likely to pass. It will die in the Senate. Finally, I've been hearing a great deal about Measure 37 and annexation. Most of the emails on Measure 37 suggest we pay the claims, rather than granting waivers. Currently that isn't possible, since the claims present a potential liability of about $1 billion. But I'm still hoping we can figure something out to get a compromise. Senator Ringo is working on SB 1037 which could be that vehicle and I think we'll begin working on something in the House Land Use Committee this week.

As you can see from this message, crafting a bill, getting it through a committee in one chamber, through that chamber, and starting the process over in the other chamber is rather complicated. Major issues are just beginning to emerge and things should get much more interesting in the next two to three weeks. If a budget compromise emerges in the next couple of days we should be done by July 1. But if not, we could be in Salem again through the summer. I'm still betting on July 1.

The MitchMessage
May 15, 2005

The release of the latest revenue forecast yesterday stimulated the feeling that we are moving toward the end game. The fact that the forecast increased the revenue estimate by some $218 million won't increase the expenditure number (set at $12.393 billion) but it will eliminate any need to increase revenue. Figuring out how to increase revenue would have been nearly impossible in the current environment and would have kept us in Salem trying well into the summer. Now the fight will begin in earnest to settle the budget. The Senate passed out a $5.325 billion school (K–12) budget. But the House Republican leadership is holding out for $5.2 billion. I think we'll have a debate this week in the House on the House Democrats' budget proposal for $5.4 billion for schools. That will probably be defeated on a straight party-line vote. But it really feels like it should be possible for the House Rs and the Senate Ds to come to some compromise on the K–12 budget. When they do, the rest of the budget falls into place. And I'm going to hate all of the budgets, but you've heard from me before on that one.

I'm right in the middle of two very interesting situations that are featured in two external reports. Last week, the Child Welfare Sub-committee (I'm one of three members) received a report on the state of Child Protective Services in Oregon. The report highlighted the same situation we had observed visiting

CPS offices in Oregon City and Gresham. It is clear that the caseload is unmanageable, the work is organized differently in each office, morale is very low causing very high turnover, and the tasks are extraordinarily difficult ones. The report, done by a national expert brought in by the DHS director, suggested more resources for the agency, completely rewriting their policies, providing much more direction and clearer supervision for the workers, and more standardization among the different offices. The situation seems like a ticking time bomb to our committee members. Incidentally, the report also suggested Oregon's situation isn't all that different from that in most states.

The other ticking time bomb, the Oregon State Hospital, is the subject of a report focusing on the basic question — what will it take to make the hospital viable? The report will be presented to a joint meeting of the House and the Senate committees on human services on Monday. According to news reports we'll hear that the hospital, parts of which were built in the 1880s, cannot be remodeled and must be replaced. I expect we'll also hear about the state of the community mental health system, which is required to support the OSP if it is to be feasible to run. After having visited the hospital, which was the featured location in the movie *One Flew over the Cuckoo's Nest,* it was clear that the building must be demolished and a new hospital built. I don't really see any alternative.

We'll be dealing with critical land-use issues in my House Committee on Land Use during the next two weeks. This week we should move an amended version of SB 887, the annexation bill sponsored by Senator Ringo and me. The bill will stop Beaverton from using island annexations until January, 2008, will require a majority vote of the people living in an area to be annexed under ORS 195, will provide annexation exemptions for NIKE and Columbia Sportswear, and will create an interim workgroup to create a new model for the whole annexation process. We're considering about 14 amendments to the bill, some of which will clearly make it into the final bill including, I hope, a couple of mine. Chair Garrard and I are working with Sen. Ringo to ensure that any bill that passes out of the House will be in a form that will be accepted by the Senate. It's not an easy job, but I think we'll move it on Wednesday and have the votes to get it out of the House and back to the Senate for concurrence on the amendments.

And Senator Ringo is working on a final version of SB 1037, a bill to implement Measure 37. He expects to move it out of his committee on Tuesday. He knows there is still a great deal of work to be done on it and is moving it to the House to allow us an opportunity to improve it. He also is introducing a companion bill in the House (with Rep. Hunt) to create a funding source for compensation for future claims. That will have hard sledding in the House, because it requires a new tax, which isn't too popular in the

House. But there are certainly demands from all over the state to compensate landowners rather than providing waivers to allow uses that aren't currently allowed by law. This battle is a long way from being over.

Some interesting bills passed out of the House since I last wrote, including a minor bill of mine, HB 2518, requested by a constituent. The House passed the bill to change the school speed zone approach, scrapping the 24/7 version to an approach that puts the 20-mph school zone in force from 7am to 5pm during school days. The schools also have the option of putting in flashing lights that control the operation of the school speed zone.

The House cut the capital gains tax, provided a tax break for foreign corporations, cut the inheritance tax, expanded the death penalty by defining an unborn fetus as a "human being", and passed a few other things that will die in the Senate, as will all of the above. Most of these bills were designed to force a cynical debate to provide ammunition for the next election cycle, rather than as an earnest attempt to craft public policy alternatives. But there were also many good bills passed over to the Senate as a part of clearing the decks. One very good bill that passed almost without objection was a bill to increase the earned income tax credit for low-income wage earners. Also we passed HB 2662 that provides protection of unemployment compensation for victims of domestic violence, sexual assault, or stalking who needed to leave a job to protect themselves.

I expect to pass two more bills out of the House during the next two weeks. HB 2706, a bill suggested by two preventive medicine residents to improve OB care by making HIV testing more likely, will be on the floor on Monday. I don't expect a serious problem on the floor. And HB 2507, my bill to ensure proper disposal of airbags containing sodium azide, is scheduled for the third reading on May 18. A bill gets its first reading when it's introduced and is then assigned to a committee. And it gets a second reading when it's passed out of committee. The third reading, no sooner than a day after the second reading, is when the body votes on it. I understand the legislature was set up this way to allow a citizen a chance to ride his horse to the Capitol upon hearing of the likely voting on a bill so he could demonstrate, or shoot the sponsor, or something. If these two pass as scheduled, it will make seven of my bills (where I was the sponsor or the chief co-sponsor) that have passed out of the House, although only one has passed the Senate so far.

Three of my bills moved out of committee since I last wrote and went to the Ways and Means Committee (or the House half of the committee). Those are the PSU/OHSU bill (HB 2560), a bill to create a drug czar (drug policy advisor) (HB 2955), and my bill to increase enrollment in the Children's Health Insurance Program and FHIAP, an insurance program for low-income working people (HB 2712). SB 329, a bill co-sponsored by Senator

Morrisette to increase the drug bulk-purchasing pool, passed out of its Senate committee, but hasn't been heard yet in the whole Senate. I understand it's having problems there because the drug companies are fighting it. I'm still optimistic about working out a compromise on the bill in a House version. In fact, I remain cautiously optimistic about each of these bills, although I recognize they won't all make it through the process. But the longer we stay in session, the more time there is to move the bills.

The two bills that have caused the most email during the past two week period have been a bill to limit the use of fire-retardant chemicals in clothes and SB 1000, the bill to provide civil-unions for gay and lesbian couples. But I've also heard about a number of other important matters, so please keep the messages coming.

The MitchMessage
May 30, 2005

The last week was highlighted for me by two non-legislative events. First I filed for re-election to be your representative for House District 33. I received a call from someone interested in running for this office and asking if I was planning on running in 2006. I decided to save him and others speculation about whether there was going to be an empty seat and filed my re-election papers on Friday. I hope you all continue to support me. But the second event was much more important. On Wednesday I filed a petition for a constitutional amendment initiative and had a great press conference with my co-chief petitioners — Republican Senator Ben Westlund and Democratic Senator Al Bates. The "HOPE for Oregon Families" initiative is aimed at improving health-care access for the 600,000 Oregonians without access to affordable and effective health care.

The House Republican leadership rolled out its school budget last week and we had an interesting debate on it. Everybody (except the House Leadership) seems to recognize that the $5.22 billion they propose for K–12 education is hopelessly inadequate and will continue the sharp decline of Oregon's schools. Just one week earlier the House Leadership did backflips to prevent a debate on the House Democrats' proposal for a $5.4 billion K–12 budget, because they didn't want to be embarrassed voting against an adequate budget. They tricked this budget up a bit by adding an adequate amount for community colleges ($437 million) and spent most of their debate time talking about the community colleges component. We announced we'd all vote for that if it were in its own bill. The vote for the K–12 budget had all but one Republican voting for it and all Democrats, plus the one Republican (Rep.

Debi Farr) voting against it. The Senate has already sent out a bill calling for $5.375 billion (including $55 million from a school support fund). It's not clear where things will go now, but the Governor has gotten into negotiations and a deal should be reached in the next 2–3 weeks.

We had double sessions the last two weeks (11am and 3:30pm) and bills came zooming out of the House, some very good ones, and some goofy ones. On the very good side, two of my bills passed the House with a combination of one "no" vote. On May 16 we passed HB 2706 on a 55–1 vote. That bill improves the process to enable more pregnant women to be tested for HIV. And on May 18 we passed HB 2507 (with zero "no" votes). This is the bill that requires safer handling of air bags containing the very deadly sodium azide when an automobile is dismantled. This makes seven bills I've passed out of the House. These two go to the Senate Rules Committee for consideration.

On the goofier side were two House Memorials. These are bills that are passed only by the House and have no standing anywhere. In my mind that makes them goofy, regardless of the topic. The first memorial requested the Congress to enact legislation to protect firearms businesses from "abusive and ill-conceived" tort actions (HM 3). The second was expressing support by the Oregon House to the Congress and president to permanently abolish the federal estate tax. This one had some more propaganda in the resolution. As you can imagine they were loudly debated and passed along pretty strict party lines, as they were intended to be. I must admit I don't pay much attention to this sort of nonsense, because I consider it simply political theatre and find it pretty boring.

There were many more interesting bills that passed and debates that took place. HB 3363 is an important piece of legislation that passed the House this period. The bill establishes minimum efficiency standards for specific new commercial appliances. This bill takes effect slowly, but would, if passed in the Senate and signed by the Governor, be our first step in reducing power use by requiring more efficient appliances. We also passed HJR 39, a proposal for a constitutional referral that would amend the Oregon Constitution creating a commission to develop the redistricting plan after each census. If you remember the fight over redistricting in 2001 you might find this proposal worth looking at. Both party leaderships dislike the proposal so it can't be all bad.

There was a big fight over HB 2583. This bill requires proof of citizenship to register to vote. Sounds like a good idea on its face. But, in fact, it's not a good idea. My House Committee on Elections and Rules held hearings all over Oregon on this bill and there wasn't a single case where it had been proven that a non-citizen had attempted to vote in Oregon. The testimony was overwhelmingly against the bill. When people sign up to register now they must sign a form that reminds them the penalty for false statements on the registration form is a fine of $100,000 and several years in prison.

This bill would require a person to show their birth certificate or passport to register to vote. Federal law reminds us that voting is a right, not a privilege, and we must do all we can to ensure all citizens vote. This bill, if it goes forward, would make it very hard for both young people and older people to register. Our committee chair assured us that the bill wasn't moving, but the House Leadership decided it would be a good political move to get people on the record. The Democratic minority on the committee offered a minority report on the bill, suggesting substitution of a proposal to eliminate registration gatherers from being paid by the registration card. We did hear evidence that people were being paid by the card of a certain party and were throwing away cards they gathered that were registrations for the other party.

We also passed HB 3458, after a passionate debate about how legislators should be compensated. This bill, among other campaign finance reforms, makes clear that legislators may not use campaign funds to support legislative activities for which they are already compensated by the legislature. This practice, which is currently legal, has gotten a few legislators headline coverage in *The Oregonian* and *Willamette Week*. The bill puts in place the six reforms that Speaker Minnis and Minority Leader Jeff Merkley proposed after Dan Doyle resigned from the legislature under a major cloud of investigation for campaign finance misdeeds. Incidentally, it has just been announced that Doyle's wife is now under investigation for campaign finance irregularities in a local election in Salem.

The Senate has also passed a couple of bills for which I was the chief co-sponsor — SB 887, which I sponsored with Senator Charlie Ringo, and SB 329, which I sponsored with Senator Bill Morrisette. SB 887 is an annexation bill, which passed out of my House Committee on Land Use on Friday. As amended it has many components, including ones that stop Beaverton from annexing without citizen approval for the next two years, that provide for a task force to review the whole annexation question and prevents annexations under ORS 195 without a vote of the affected people. After fierce lobbying in the committee, it also provides annexation protection (against Beaverton) for many years for Nike, Tektronix, Columbia Sportswear, and ESI. I believe it will pass out of the House next week and go back to the Senate for concurrence on the amendments we made in the House.

SB 329, a bill to expand the prescription-drug-purchasing program, will not receive such kind treatment in the House. We did have a great hearing on the bill, which was scheduled from 4:30pm to 6:30pm on the Friday of Memorial Day weekend. Testimony took the hearing until nearly 7:30pm, with only Chair Billy Dalto and me still there at the end. But it was good testimony by a great many people. The Oregon State Pharmacists and the industry representatives from PhRMA were the only people opposing the bill.

Unless I can reach a compromise with those two parties (and they supported my original bill — SB 875), the bill is dead in the House. To make sure it doesn't slip out the Speaker has required a subsequent referral to a committee that hasn't even met this session. She doesn't appear to be taking any chances on it accidently getting out of the committee and on to the House floor.

I'm monitoring action on several of my bills in the Senate this week. HB 2722, which eliminates a city's ability to veto any new city within three miles of its borders, is awaiting action in Senator Ringo's Committee on Environment and Land Use. I'm hoping he'll pass it out this week. And I'll be working to get hearings and work sessions on HB 2706 and HB 2507 in Senator Kate Brown's Committee on Rules. They should both pass easily if I can get them in the process. And I'm working to get a hearing in the House Budget Committee on my PSU/OHSU bill.

I continue to get a great deal of email from my constituents. (I answer all email from constituents and very little from anybody else.) Mental health parity continues to get a great deal of mail. (I support parity.) SB 1000, the civil union bill, which I support, is getting a lot of attention from both sides. I'm hearing about SB 545, a bill to provide very modest regulation of the payday loan industry. I support that bill and stronger ones. That business is unbelievable. I continue to hear about fluoridation, which I support. And I've begun to hear about SB 389, which seems to be a new assault on cougars, under the guise of a bill to regulate hunting using the Internet and remote controlled weapons. (Don't ask me!!) Keep the email coming.

The MitchMessage
June 11, 2005

Friday presented an ironic juxtaposition of the Republican House leadership's response to the "will of the voters" on two different measures. There was significant action on bills reacting to two measures overwhelmingly passed by the voters — Measure 37 (61 percent yes vote) and Measure 3 (67 percent yes vote). You remember Measure 37, but to remind you, Measure 3 was an initiative that required a conviction for a crime before the police could proceed to civil forfeiture of assets seized during an arrest. Measure 3 also required that assets seized be spent on substance abuse treatment programs. There was an appeal of Measure 3 on the grounds that it was a constitutional amendment that covered more than one topic. It is awaiting an Oregon Supreme Court decision.

We are hard at work in the House Land Use Committee to make sense out of the words of Measure 37, using HB 3120 as the vehicle for this work. We have been told that we must implement the "will of the voters" and make

Measure 37 work despite its obvious flaws. On the other hand, the leadership of the House handed us HB 3457 to gut the "will of the voters" on Measure 3 and hand back to the police agencies broad powers to seize property and use it mostly for police purposes. I had to ask a question four times to get the carrier to admit that seized property would not be returned to a person, even if that person had ultimately not been charged with the crime or had been acquitted of the charge. That caused me to vote against the bill, although it easily passed the House. I hope the Senate amends the bill to assure the rights of innocent people.

We had another example of the House leadership's devotion to the "will of the voters" this week with action on SB 389. The first time I visited the legislature in 1999 the House was debating a cougar/bear-hunting bill. When I attended the only time in 2001, the House was debating a cougar/bear-hunting bill. In 2003 the leadership took a shot at overturning the "will of the people" who voted overwhelmingly to ban dogs in hunting cougars. And on June 6 they took another carefully aimed shot at the "will of the people" through an amendment to a Senate bill that would ban hunting over the Internet. The amended version of SB 389, would give counties the right to allow hunting of cougars with dogs and baiting for bear hunts. It easily passed the House. I hope the Senate will refuse to concur with the House amendments and kill the amendments or the bill in conference committee.

The outcome of my first conference committee this year turned out happily Friday. The House had unanimously passed a bill (HB 2498) to require insurance companies to pay for complete clinical breast exams. The bill only required payment for exams in women older than 40 years of age. It was clear that the age limit was a drafting error and it was announced that the age should be lowered in the Senate. The Senate passed the bill and amended the age limit to 18 years of age. The Chair of the House Health and Human Services Committee, Billy Dalto, refused to act on the bill for nearly a month. He finally moved for non-concurrence and a conference committee was named. I was named to serve on the conference committee. We worked with Chair Dalto and reached an acceptable compromise, which actually strengthened the Senate language, ensuring that any clinical breast exam would be covered by insurance. The conference committee unanimously approved the compromise. It will now certainly pass the House and the Senate.

This is the time of year where it is easy for the non-partisan approach to legislation to break down. There were two blatant examples of partisan muscle exhibited recently. They happened, not for any real purpose, but simply because the majority in the House could make them happen. The first was in response to SB 6, a bill sponsored by Senate President Peter Courtney to prohibit school personnel from promoting, suggesting, or supplying performance-enhancing supplements to students. It passed without serious opposition in the Senate and passed out of the House Education Committee on a 6–1 vote. But after a weird debate in the House the bill was defeated. It felt like a shot at Courtney.

An even more blatant example happened on a purely technical bill (SB 134) relating to the Commissioner of the Bureau of Labor and Industries. This bill passed in the Senate and had no opposing testimony in the House committee. The committee voted 7–0 and the bill was put on the Consent Calendar. Bills on the Consent Calendar are viewed as non-controversial and are not debated. But when this bill came up one of the Republican members stood up in the front of the House with his thumb down to remind his caucus members to vote no. There obviously was a caucus decision to defeat the bill. The bill was defeated on a strict party-line vote. Two Republican members forgot to vote no and had to change their vote to make it straight party line. I had never heard of anything like that, and could only guess that somebody was mad at Dan Gardner, the labor commissioner.

Another strange partisan action came out with a happier outcome. Rep. Mark Hass has been working for two sessions to get a bill that would encourage the placement of automated external defibrillators in schools. Rep. Linda Flores had a similar bill for AEDs in health clubs. The Health and Human Services Committee was convinced these were good ideas, but rather than passing a bill with Hass and Flores' name on the bill, introduced an identical committee bill. That bill (HB 3482) passed the committee and to respect Mark's contribution he was assigned to carry the bill in the House. It passed easily and I think Mark felt pretty good about it. But it felt strange to me nonetheless. On the other hand, one of my principles as a legislator is expressed in the phrase *Qui facit per alium, facit per se.* That roughly translates as "He who does through others, does through himself." That was a lesson I was given by one of my mentors in my first session, Rep. Lane Shetterly. He told me you could get a great deal done if you don't care who gets the credit.

But speaking of credit, this has been a pretty good period for the annexation bills. The three key annexation bills of which I am either the sponsor or the chief co-sponsor moved along. HB 2484, ensuring that both voters in the city doing annexation and in the territory to be annexed need to approve an annexation, passed the Senate Friday and is on the way to the Governor's desk. SB 887, sponsored by Senator Ringo and me, passed out of the House Land Use Committee and will be on the House floor this week, with the chair of the committee Rep. Bill Garrard and me carrying it on the floor. It has been amended so it will need to go back to the Senate for concurrence. And HB 2722, my bill to take away cities' ability to veto the formation of another city within three miles of its borders passed out of the Senate committee and will be on the Senate floor this week, with Senator Ringo carrying the bill. A technical land-use bill I sponsored, HB 2755 passed the Senate this week and is coming to the House for concurrence on a "conflict amendment." A conflict amendment is used to make sure two different bills passed in the same session don't conflict with each other.

Three more of my bills will be heard in Senate committees during the next two weeks. HB 2518 is being heard in the Senate Judiciary Committee on Monday. And HB 2706 (an HIV bill) and HB 2507 (the sodium azide airbag bill) are in the process of being scheduled in the Senate Rules Committee. I'm fairly optimistic about the outlook of all three bills. The running total is that seven of my bills are out of the House and two that began in the Senate are out of the Senate and in the House. Two of the seven are either signed by the Governor or will be soon. The only one that is in serious trouble is SB 329, which expands the Oregon Drug Purchasing program. It passed the Senate and passed out of the House Committee on Health and Human Services to the House Budget Committee. PhRMA continues to oppose the bill, and it is seen as a possibility for trading in the end game, when the majority of the House and Senate and the Governor begin to bargain on the final package.

This has also been a good period for my constitutional amendment initiative, HOPE for Oregon Families. If HOPE were passed it would establish that Oregon residents have a right to affordable and effective health care. The Attorney General has issued a draft ballot title, including the ballot summary. They are available on the Secretary of State's website (www.sos.state.or.us) I only have one minor problem with what the AG did and have commented on that issue. The time for comments on the draft ends Friday and then it moves to the next stage. If things continue to move as planned, we will be able to begin to gather signatures about July 15. Contributions have begun to come in and we have established a bank account for HOPE. If you would like to help in any way, please let me know.

The email traffic has been the heaviest this last two weeks on two issues. The most frequent were requests to vote against the DEQ budget proposal coming from the House Budget Committee. I certainly will vote against it for more reasons than are noted in the email — that the bill would prohibit DEQ from enforcing automobile emissions standards. Among other problems it is unconstitutional to put that kind of policy matter into a budget bill. But equally serious is the nature of the budget itself that kills funding for significant environmental programs. The second most frequent emails copy me on a message to the Speaker and committee chairs urging that key bills to reduce the cost of medical care (including SB 329) be brought out of committees and brought to the floor of the House for a vote. Since I'm a key sponsor of several of the bills, I certainly concur. It really does show the difference between being in the majority and in the minority.

The MitchMessage
June 25, 2005

I've been swamped with Walmart related email these last three days, receiving more than 100 emails supporting Sen. Ringo's amendment to HB 3310. One message, from Lake Oswego, opposed the amendment. The other 100-plus, mostly from the Cedar Hills/Cedar Mill area, supported the amendment. HB 3310 is a rather important land-use bill, improving the periodic land-use review process. Sen. Ringo added an amendment that would make it more difficult for Beaverton to approve the application for a Walmart store at the intersection of NW Cedar Hills Blvd and NW Barnes Rd. in my district. I support the amendment and testified in favor of it before the Senate Environment and Land Use Committee. It passed out of the Senate and comes back to the House for a vote on concurrence with the Senate Amendment. I believe the Republican House leadership will not allow concurrence (perhaps on Monday) and the bill will go to a conference committee.

The deliberations on SB 887 had a similar result, although in the opposite direction. SB 887 is one of the key annexation bills sponsored by Senator Ringo and me. It passed out of the Senate with a ban, for two years, on Beaverton doing any non-voluntary annexations. It established an interim task force to look at annexation generally, created a mediation model to smooth the annexation process, and protected NIKE and Columbia Sportswear from non-voluntary annexation by Beaverton until 2020. As I discussed in the last message, the bill got into a cement mixer in the House Committee on Land Use and came out with major changes, including the addition of Tektronix and ESI to the list of protected companies and extending the protection of all the companies to 2040. High-power lobbyists were heavily involved in the process and I thought it was a mess.

However, I carried the bill on the House floor, saying my constituents needed to be protected from Beaverton so I was willing to go along with the other changes. In my floor speech I recollected the old saying that people with weak stomachs should not closely observe either the manufacture of sausage or the creation of legislation. In my closing remarks I recommended that my colleagues hold their noses and vote for the bill. About 35 of them did so, for a variety of reasons including close relationships with powerful lobbyists. It was a bipartisan vote with 15 no votes coming from Democrats and seven from Republicans. When the bill got back to the Senate for concurrence, Senator Ringo moved to "not concur" and the bill is assigned to a conference committee. We shall see what we shall see.

Probably the most important thing in the House this last two weeks (and certainly the most entertaining political theatre) revolved around the Speaker's proposal to stabilize school funding. I think stabilization is a great idea, but not at what I view as an entirely too low a level and not without proper inflators included. When she proposed her model Jeff Merkley, the Minority Leader, went to Speaker Minnis and suggested that we negotiate the approach to come out with a bipartisan bill. We believe that a few changes (for example those suggested in a recent *Oregonian* editorial) could actually make her plan work. She rejected that offer out of hand. About ten days ago word emerged that the Speaker had worked out a deal to include a plan to allow Portland Public Schools to keep funds from a revenue source that apparently had expired. The bill would allow that without a vote of the people in Portland.

The members of the House who represent the Portland Public Schools District had not been informed about the plan. We (I represent Portland, Beaverton and Hillsboro public schools) clearly saw that as a cynical attempt by the Speaker (with the collusion of PPS Board members) to embarrass Portland Democrats. As a part of the deal two PPS board members published an op-ed piece praising the Speaker's plan. When it came time for the Speaker to roll out her bill, she found she didn't have the votes in her own caucus to pass the measure out of the House. Reportedly she has been storming at recalcitrant members of her caucus and has decided to bring it to the floor for a vote, probably on Tuesday. Rumors are that she has been trolling for a Democratic vote or two. The drama will continue next week, wasting time and energy from efforts to really seek a solution to this most critical issue and to get a K–12 budget compromise for this biennium.

This has been a good period for my own legislation. Two more of my bills are on the way to the Governor's desk. HB 2722 passed out of the Senate with a minor amendment and received a vote to concur in the House. This is the bill that takes away a city's right to automatically veto the formation of another city within three miles of its borders. I'm really pleased this moved forward. HB 2755, which is a technical bill about land use, passed the Senate with a couple of amendments and achieved concurrence in the House. And HB 2518, a bill to help public safety workers with claims before the Public Safety Memorial Board passed the Senate without amendment. I think that makes a total of five of my bills on their way to the Governor's desk. Two more of my bills, HB 2507 (Sodium Azide) and HB 2706 (HIV) are awaiting action in the Senate Rules Committee. I have been assured there will be no problem passing these two, but I'm holding my breath on them anyway. I introduced HB 2942 early in the session. This bill would require that only self-extinguishing cigarettes be sold in Oregon. It's an issue I have been working on for about 20 years. I haven't been able to get a hearing in the House, but a similar bill is moving forward in the Senate.

We had a number of interesting floor debates in the House over the past two weeks. HB 3474 came out of my Committee on Land Use on a party-line vote and was debated on the House floor. The bill prohibits any regulation that restricts the use of any land owned by a religious organization, except for some design restraints. This would prohibit, for example, restriction on the development of St. Vincent Hospital, or on a halfway house for sexual offenders built on land owned by a religious organization. In committee we tried to get a compromise that would limit the prohibition to actual church buildings, but that was rejected. We tried the same argument on the floor, but logic was also rejected and the bill passed along party lines. The debate on SB 618 was also interesting. This began as a bill to require employers to allow unpaid rest time for an employee to nurse a baby or express breast milk. It was designed to help new mothers get back to work more quickly. But business fought the bill, even those companies who already had those policies. And it came out with no mention of breasts and in a form that would "allow" an employer to accommodate employees who are nursing. You can imagine the dumb debate on this bill.

We spent a great deal of time during this period dealing with appropriation bills for state agencies. Most agency bills are pretty straightforward and pass with about 50 votes. (There are always a few who have a problem with any agency.) But there was high drama and a great deal of debate on HB 5135, the budget bill for the Department of Environmental Quality. I received a ton of email on this budget. The House Special Committee on Budget, besides cutting budgets for important environmental functions and providing no funding for pesticide reporting, included a budget note forbidding DEQ from imposing Automobile Clean Air Standards. The Legislative Counsel's office told them it was unconstitutional to mix policy in a budget bill, but they did it anyway. The bill passed on a straight party-line vote. It won't get through the Senate in this form.

Wednesday we had a press conference on HB 3500, sponsored by Rep. Billy Dalto, Sen. Alan Bates, Sen. Ben Westlund and me. We introduced this bipartisan measure, which would refer to the voters a proposal to raise the cigarette tax by $.60 per pack. The money would go to fund health care for all children without health care, double the number of people covered under the Oregon Health Plan Standard plan, fund smoking reduction activities, and provide some funds for the State Police to do more cigarette tax enforcement. (It's interesting to note that every pack of cigarettes sold costs Oregon $3.00 in health-care costs.) The bill has caused some excitement in Salem and we had an extensive interview with the editorial board of *The Oregonian* on Friday. It's probably too late to actually pass this bill this session, but it is a beginning of the discussion on how to get more Oregonians covered with health insurance.

Our HOPE for Oregon Families initiative continues to move through the process, and it seemed to Senators Bates and Westlund that HB 3500 would be a good companion piece to the HOPE initiative on the ballot in November 2006. HOPE for Oregon Families is a constitutional amendment that would make access to affordable and effective health care a protected right for all Oregonians. We have received the ballot title for the Hope initiative, but it was challenged at the last hour by a law firm on behalf of a client. The next step is the Secretary of State's and the Attorney General's response to that challenge. I think we'll hear on that in the next week or two. I'm still planning on being able to gather signatures by the end of July.

There will be a press conference on Monday on House Memorial 38. While I hate these memorials, I've agreed to be a co-sponsor on this one, called "Homeward Bound: Calling for a Plan for Withdrawal from Iraq." This memorial recognizes that 40 Oregonians have died in the war, out of the 1700 Americans who have died. We are carrying twice the casualty burden as would be expected by our population. This memorial is designed to support our troops in Iraq, but also responds to the growing number of Americans who think we should be figuring out how to extricate ourselves from the Iraq War. The memorial is sponsored by Rep. Chip Shields.

The only non-Walmart issue that stimulated mass email during this period was civil union. There are two different versions of a civil union bill working in the Senate and it looks as if SB 1000 will pass out to the House. The mail from constituents is running about 90 percent favorable, although I'm getting heavy phone calling from outside the district to oppose civil unions. I've also been getting some health-care email about bills stalled in the House — SB 329, my bill to increase the Oregon Prescription Purchasing Pool, and the several bills that would provide mental health parity. Remember folks, SB 329 is my bill and I support mental health parity. Generally speaking I ask you to send emails and continue to do so. But you really don't have to send me a message to support one of my own bills. It's likely I will support it even without your email.

The MitchMessage
July 9, 2005

The last two-week period ended in a most unusual fashion. At the end of each floor session the Speaker asks the senior member of the House, Rep. Bob Jensen, to move to adjourn and fills in the time and date to reconvene. It is usually some time the next day. At the end of Wednesday's session Speaker Minnis, without any warning to the Democrats, asked him for a motion to adjourn until 5pm on Sunday. That caused quite a bit of turmoil, with the Democratic Whip breaking in and asking for a recess for a caucus. We held that meeting and put up a substitute motion to adjourn until 11am the next day. It caused an interesting bit of political theatre, with the Democrats being quite outraged that we would take a three-day vacation (with pay) when there was so much work yet to be done. Of course, we were voted down on a straight party-line vote and the House closed down with dozens of bills buried in one committee or another.

We'll be back at it on Sunday night, but the Speaker might do it again after that session. There is all sorts of speculation about why she did it, the best being that too many of her caucus members would be sitting around and getting into trouble by talking to Democrats and lobbyists. There is a hope that the break provides a better opportunity for the leadership of both Houses to spend time together crafting the bargain that will allow us to get out of Dodge. Of course, the fact that the Senate was fully engaged in their business still makes me wonder why it was necessary to shut down our work to allow the leaders to meet.

A great deal of the work during the past two weeks was voting on budget bills brought out of the House Special Committee on Budget, the committee charged with producing budget bills after the Speaker broke up the Joint Ways and Means process. The breakup of Ways and Means is quite unusual and ensured two things — the process would take longer to get to a balanced budget since parallel process needed to be set up in the House and the Senate and that the process would be politicized. Both of these things have happened. While we hear there is agreement on about 60 of the 105 or so budget bills required to be passed to get to the final budget, many of the others include ridiculous partisan elements that would never be placed in a bill that had to be agreed upon in the Joint Committee. Several of those came to the floor during the last two weeks and provided the opportunity for me to vote against bad budget bills. For example, I voted against the Department of Agriculture budget because, for the second session in a row, it did not have funds for pesticide use reporting. I was a no on the Department of Land Conservation and Development budget because it had no funds for paying Measure 37 claims against the state and because the Committee had withheld $600,000 that was needed to conduct a new and complete review of the land-use planning system in Oregon following the passage of Measure 37.

I voted against the Department of State Lands budget. I had no trouble voting against the Department of Higher Education budget because it was totally inadequate and provided no vision about how we were going to return to supporting the higher education system in Oregon. And I voted against the Department of Corrections budget for a variety of reasons, not the least of which was that the budget eliminated a large proportion of the substance abuse treatment resources of the department. It has been proven that a dollar spent on treatment in the prison system saves several dollars in future prison costs.

And I voted against the transportation budget because the Republican leadership decided to withhold funding for one of the two Cascade passenger trains running between Eugene and Seattle. It appears they decided they wanted to keep the train funds as a bargaining chip for the final negotiations with the Senate in the end game. This one seems most foolish, since much of the cost of those trains is covered by the Washington Department of Transportation and the service has been increasing ridership at a high rate. This is not the time to cut back on passenger rail service. This got me into action and I have convened the bipartisan Choo-Choo caucus to try to reverse the situation. There are 60 members of the legislature whose districts come within 25 miles of one of the stations between Eugene/Springfield and Portland. There is great local support for the trains and Eugene, Albany, Salem, and Oregon City have all spent a considerable amount of money refurbishing their stations. We hope we can turn this around.

There were several other interesting debates, including one on HB 2450, which the Speaker ran out last week. That is her plan for permanent inadequacy in K–12 funding. Her original plan was to include taxing authority for Portland Public Schools to get back some of the taxes that are running out during the next biennium. That plan caused the Portland School Board to jump on a bandwagon for the Speaker's scheme. However, it turned out that the Speaker couldn't get the votes to pass her bill from within her own caucus with the Portland tax piece in the bill, so she stripped out the Portland component, leaving PPS high and dry after board members had supported her. Politics can get brutal in the Capitol, and the Portland School Board members came out looking pretty naive.

Another interesting brouhaha emerged when a plan came out of the Budget Committee to move the State Fair from independent status to place it under the State Parks and Recreation Department. The Fair has been a consistent money loser and is currently about $24 million in debt. The plan was to make it the functional equivalent of a park and fund the deficit using lottery money that had been dedicated by the voters in Measure 66 to funding parks and salmon reclamation. The Democrats erupted about the plan and refused to give the bill a rule suspension. The next day the Speaker sent it back to committee, which led to the speculation that she didn't have enough votes within her caucus to pass it out in the current form.

Several of the votes during the last two weeks were "not to concur" in Senate amendments to previously passed House bills. HB 3310, which included the Beaverton Walmart amendment, is one that is still hung up in conference committee. Senator Ringo is trying hard to get it out of the conference committee, but the business lobby is keeping the Republican leadership of the House firm against the amendment. SB 887, which was sent to conference committee when the Senate refused to accept the House amendments, remains fully engaged in battle over the NIKE amendment. Rumor has it that NIKE lobbyists are insisting on the 2040 date for protection from annexation, and further are insisting that the other three companies be taken out of the bill. The fury of this battle is shaking the Capitol, with the raw power of big-money lobbyists on clear display. It is not a pretty sight and it isn't clear that the interests of the citizens are being taken into account.

This period was a very good one for my legislative agenda with HB 2507, the air bag disposal bill, and HB 2706, the HIV testing bill, both passing the Senate Rules Committee and the Senate itself. They are both on their way to the Governor's desk for signature. That makes a total of seven bills of which I was the sponsor or chief co-sponsor moved to the Governor. That is a very good record for a minority member and there is still a glimmer of hope for a couple of others. I'll review the bills I passed in my session-end message, which still may be a while away.

The other very big event this period is that we received the official ballot-title and summary for the HOPE for Oregon Families initiative to put the right to access to affordable and effective health care into the Oregon constitution. If the title isn't challenged in the Supreme Court by a week from Monday we'll be ready to start gathering signatures by July 20. If it is challenged we'll be delayed by a couple of months.

The email traffic this last period included continuing mail on SB 1000, the civil union bill. I strongly support civil unions, which many backers of Measure 36 also supported during the Measure 36 debate and even President Bush supported during discussions of a constitutional amendment opposing gay marriage. I do not believe it is appropriate to treat committed, loving couples differently under the law. Since Measure 36 passed, I believe we have a constitutional requirement under the Equal Protection Clause of the U.S. Constitution to provide the legal benefits of marriage to couples we prohibit from marrying. The Senate passed SB 1000 yesterday, and perhaps the battle will heat up in the House. But I do not believe there is any chance the Republican leadership in the House will allow the bill to get to the floor.

I have also received a great deal of mail on HB 3481, the biofuels bill that came to the House this week. A very odd couple, Rep. Jackie Dingfelder, a liberal Portland Democrat and Rep. Jeff Kropf, a conservative rural Republican, sponsored the bill. The bill started out as a very good bill, but morphed into a bill with some very bad elements, including a long continuation of the useless pollution tax credit. That credit gives away millions of dollars to corporations for doing what they need to do under law and even provides tax credits to people buying garden wood chippers. We had a minority report that was defeated along party lines and I ended up voting against the bill in the form we faced. I also continue to receive mail urging me to support SB 329, the bill to expand the Oregon Prescription Purchasing Plan. I usually point out that I'm likely to support the bill, since it is my bill, but the House Republican leadership is holding it hostage for the moment.

While the email load is getting lighter as the end of the session nears, I always welcome it.

The MitchMessage
July 23, 2005

We're on another three-day break, but this one looks a little more reasonable than the two earlier ones did. Those two were clearly ridiculous. At least this time the leadership seems to be in negotiations that should lead to a budget deal. I heard last night that the negotiators were going to meet all night to move the process. We'll see. The truth is there isn't all that much more that needs to be done, and the only thing that seems to be holding things up is partisan bickering and stubbornness on the part of a couple of leaders.

But the week was a wonderful week for the HOPE for Oregon Families initiative campaign, sponsored by Senators Bates and Westlund, and me. This week we received our final ballot title and summary and received approval to begin gathering signatures.

On the legislative front, as we are moving toward the final days of the session we have had some interesting issues emerging and my email has been following these issues. One of the hot topics I've been hearing about is that of funding the pesticide reporting system. And it continues to look like the Republican leadership in the House will keep its funding out of the budget this year, once again.

That reminds me to comment on what has felt to some like partisanship in my comments in the last few *MitchMessages*. I want to make very clear what I'm saying. I have been very critical of the House leadership, and by that I mean Speaker Karen Minnis and Majority Leader Wayne Scott. I have many good friends among the Republican membership of the House and of the Senate. And I value those friendships. Most of the bills I've passed have at least one Republican included in the sponsorship. And, in fact, I like Speaker Minnis. But this session has had more than some frustrating moments because the Republican leadership has chosen to make things far more partisan than is necessary. The Speaker is the Speaker of the whole House. But more and more of her decisions have been clearly partisan decisions.

The model this year is not to hear any bills that would cause an embarrassing vote among her caucus members. Decisions seem to be about how things will look during the next election. Eventually however, the Democrats will take the leadership of the House, since the pendulum always swings, and especially so since there are 70,000 more registered Democrats than Republicans in Oregon. When that happens I'm going to be fighting very hard to create a legislature that is much less partisan and more structured to protect the rights of the minority. Three things come immediately to mind. First, I believe the minority should name the minority members of each committee. It is not done that way now. The Speaker names all members of committees. Second, I believe whether or not a bill is heard in a committee should be determined by the merits of the bill. It is not always that way now. Frequently the bills get a political rating, rather than a merit rating. And finally, I believe that the minority should have some power to bring bills to the floor for an up and down vote. This session any time a minority member has moved to bring a bill out of committee it has failed on the floor by a straight party vote. I think that is wrong. So that is where I am coming from when I talk about the Republican leadership blocking a bill from coming to the floor, or pulling some trick in committee.

We did have a totally bipartisan debate this week and that was the debate on the meth package that has been worked on by Sen. Ginny Burdick (D) and Rep. Wayne Krieger (R), the chairs of the two Judiciary Committees. I think it was the longest debate of the session, but it wasn't really a debate. It was a forum where almost everybody (but me) explained how important the package was and how his or her constituents were going to hate it. I have been taking a bit of heat on that bill, but I voted for it. And it passed the House on a 55–4 vote. My vote was really an easy one for me. I'm a health-care researcher and I understand the issues of moving pseudoephedrine and similar products to prescription-only status. But my decision is based on two things. First, I believe there are products on the market that are almost as effective, and new ones are coming along quickly.

But equally important was my experience on the subcommittee studying child welfare and child protective services. I understand making it more difficult to get meth ingredients won't stop the flow of meth onto the streets. I know 80 percent of the meth supply comes from Mexico and other places. But HB 2485 will put a dent in cooking meth in Oregon and that is extremely important. The cooking of meth creates dangerous conditions, and especially dangerous conditions for kids. Kids living in a home where meth is being cooked absorb 5mg. of meth per hour from the environment. That situation must be stopped, or at least slowed. Making it more difficult to "smurf" Sudafed is a beginning and one I'm willing to support.

Working on that child welfare subcommittee provided another leadership disappointment for me. After a great deal of work, Rep. Billy Dalto (subcommittee chair) and I produced a bill to improve the child welfare system. After we introduced HB 3501, the Speaker decided we weren't going to hear the bill this year, apparently because she was angry about something or other. That bill would have been improved and, if passed, would have had a chance to greatly improve the safety of children in Oregon.

I think the thing I've received the most email about this last two weeks was still SB 1000, the civil union bill. The email from constituents continues to run about 10–1 in favor of the measure, although we continue to get dozens of phone calls on both sides of the issue from people who aren't willing to identify themselves. I don't pay too much attention to those. Rep. Dalto told me he has received 2000 phone and email messages about SB 1000. The Speaker pulled a neat parliamentary trick this week, by bringing SB 1000 to a hearing in the House Committee on State and Federal Affairs (the graveyard committee) on 37 minutes notice, gutting it and stuffing it with a House bill on reciprocal benefits. Those are benefits that any two people (think brother and sister) can arrange. The bill was then sent to the Special Committee on Budget. The reason this move was so slick is that there are only two ways the minority can get a bill to the floor. One is a minority report on a bill coming from committee. But the Special Committee on Budget is structured so it's not possible to get a minority report. And the second point is that if the minority tries to get the bill to the floor via a motion to remove from committee, the bill that would be removed would not be the original SB 1000, but rather the newly minted and obnoxious version created in committee.

We've had a few other interesting debates this period. HB 2157 is a bill that clarifies when an agency or a licensing board can obtain fingerprints to use in an FBI nationwide background check. More and more, and for good reasons, the state is gathering fingerprints and passing them on to the FBI. The process is to put the fingerprints onto a card, use the card to digitize the fingerprints and send the digitized image to the FBI. The protocol is to destroy the card. But during hearings I asked over and over if the State Police had heard from the FBI about whether they put the fingerprints permanently into their records. And the FBI declined to answer that question. That caused me to become very worried about sending tens of thousands of fingerprints on people whose only crime is to want to work in Oregon. While criminal background checks are more than appropriate for many occupations, I wanted to see some limits on when and how the decision would be made to require fingerprints.

I've lived for a long time and I'm a generally trusting fellow. But over my lifetime I've seen so many abuses of governmental power that I've become very cautious. Consequently, I took the floor and spoke about the dangers of this bill and tried to caution about putting clear sideboards on the process. I found it interesting that it became a debate on terrorism, rather than on state occupational licensing. I was particularly worried when the carrier of the bill, in his closing statement said that safety should be all of our first concerns. I must be a bit odd, but I think American freedom should be our first concern.

The bill passed with four no votes, with Rep. Shields, Dingfelder, and Wirth joining in my objection.

The Governor has vetoed two public power bills. I voted for SB 1008, Sen. Deckert's bill creating a state public power board that the Governor could call into force to take over PGE if Portland was successful in buying it. But I voted against SB 671 that would have created a mutual company to bid on PGE. I talked to Sen. Deckert last night and he isn't very happy with the Governor. On the other hand, I was delighted when the Governor vetoed HB 2480, a very bad bill sponsored by one drug company to help keep a monopoly for their hepatitis C treatment. I've promised the Governor that I would work hard to make sure his veto of HB 2480 would be upheld. Those are the only three bills he has vetoed so far.

We're still getting some very bad budget bills. For example, I voted against SB 5583, the budget for district attorneys and their deputies. That budget not only provided less than the Governor's budget, but also provided $400,000 less than is provided in the current budget period. And we're still fighting over HB 3502, the bill that would make the State Fair a park and fund its deficit using Measure 66 funds dedicated to parks and salmon recovery. We also passed a terrible bill on adoptions that sounds quite reasonable (HB 2009), but isn't. The bill would give grandparents first refusal on adopting a child who has been in other people's custody. As a grandparent the idea sounds good, but in fact it is clear that sometimes other arrangements have been working very well and the grandparents have not been in the picture. We need to be clear that the child's best interest is taken into account, rather than that of the grandparents.

And finally, I want to report a local victory for a group of my constituents and to thank Portland City Councilor Sam Adams for his efforts. I have been concerned about the intersections of West Burnside and Skyline, both SW and NW. Brant Williams, recently replaced as city transportation director, has worked with me and arranged to widen the turn lanes from NW Skyline onto Burnside so there is now a right and a left turn lane. But it hadn't been striped yet and Mr. Adams helped get that work done. The intersection works much better now, but I still haven't given up my hope for a signal light there.

Finally, our plans for the HOPE for Oregon Families initiative are emerging. That initiative would put in the constitution that access to affordable and effective health care is a right of all Oregonians and would give the legislature four years to create a pragmatic, incremental plan to begin moving in that direction. There are currently 610,000 Oregonians without access to health insurance and the rest of us are paying the tab for the lousy and expensive care they receive. We will need to gather about 125,000 signatures and we're hoping to get commitments from various groups to gather perhaps 50,000 of those signatures. And we also need to raise a great deal of money to put this on the

November 2006 ballot. If you would like to help in any way, or if you would like a copy of the proposed amendment, please let me know.

I'm hoping the next *MitchMessage* will come after the session is over. Keep in touch.

 ## The MitchMessage
August 10, 2005

This is the first of two end-of-session *MitchMessages*. In this message I'll focus on the events between the last *MitchMessage* and the session's end. About two weeks from now I'll send out a *MitchMessage* reviewing the whole session. I've delayed this message longer than I had intended, because it's taken me some time to get a bit of distance from what happened during the last few days of the session. I'm still quite angry over the abusive process and over the Republican House leadership's unwillingness to allow several good bills to come to a floor vote, including SB 1000 (the civil union bill) and several important health-care bills.

As you may know we adjourned *sine die* at 6:21am on Friday, August 5 after a marathon session that had begun nearly 20 hours earlier. It was a brutal experience and a totally dysfunctional approach to completing the work of the 73rd Legislative Session. After taking two three-day holidays during the last couple of weeks, the Speaker insisted on keeping us in session all night, rather than adjourning late in the evening and returning the next morning to finish in daylight and with due deliberation.

And, of course, crazy things happened. For example, an important conference committee met at 2:30am with no one around to observe what was happening. I'll talk about that conference below, as it was important in a different context. But the main thing that was going on was continued mad negotiations between the House Republican leadership and the Democratic Senate leadership. The Democrats seemed to be at a disadvantage because they appeared committed to making something happen and the House Republicans seemed committed to making sure nothing good happened. The process is particularly aversive to the 83 members of the legislature who weren't really in the discussion about most issues, simply being passive (albeit very sleepy) observers to what was going on "above their pay-grade." I was impressed with the articles in *The Oregonian* last Saturday and Sunday, because they nailed it exactly. And certainly their Sunday editorial was also right on. If you haven't read those articles they are available on Oregonlive.com.

Some useful things happened during the last two weeks of the session, along with some terrible things. We amended the pedestrian crosswalk bill we had passed in the last session. That was particularly important to the cities. Under current law a car can't move in the crosswalk until a pedestrian is completely out of the crosswalk. Now (because of SB 591) it will be possible to proceed when a pedestrian is six feet out of the lane of travel of the car. After a great deal of struggle, the House leadership relented and allowed funding to go forward for the new terminal at the North Bend Airport. Funding was stopped because the Republican leadership was mad at Rep. Arnie Roblin because he helped force a vote in the House on a decent school budget (which all Republicans were forced to vote against by their leadership). We were able (Rep. Boone and myself) to slip one past the Speaker, with an amendment to SB 782 that rescinded the requirement that the very poorest (less than $50 per month income) people on the Oregon Health Plan needed to pay a part of their premium. This bill addressed some other aspects of OHP, and we also added a six-month grace period for all OHP members who had trouble paying their share of the premium. And we passed a bill that requires Beaverton to post notice of photo red light cameras or photo mobile radar before the affected area, not 400 yards after it, as is their current practice.

During this period, the House leadership stopped every bill attempting to deal with the childhood obesity epidemic. The most aggravating one for me was their rejection of SB 1076, which would have simply required the Oregon Health Policy Commission to do a study of childhood obesity and make recommendations to the legislature. I understand agri-business and the food and restaurant lobby stopping all of our bills about food in the schools, but the House leadership killed a bill to add P.E. time in schools in 2017. Yes, that says 2017. That bill was stopped because Senate President Courtney favored it. I couldn't even get a hearing on one of my bills, which would only have directed the State Department of Education to develop a policy on the health of school children.

During this two-week period I got to vote against a set of budget bills (that passed anyway). I voted against the K–12 funding bill, as I have been saying I would do with any budget less than $5.4 billion. $5.24 billion didn't meet that test. I voted against the higher education budget, which had a couple of good things in it, because it was much too low generally and continued a long trend of denying proper support for our university system. I voted against the Department of Forestry budget because the House leadership insisted on a budget note requiring higher cutting yields in the Tillamook Forest. I voted against the Department of Education budget because it didn't fund Headstart at a level that would allow 100 percent of eligible kids to attend. And I voted against the Secretary of State's budget because the House Republicans killed several audit positions in an attempt to move the audit function (unconstitutionally) from the Secretary of State to the legislature. I can't imagine a worse proposal. I voted against the budget for the State Commission on Children and Families because it cut 1/3 out of the Healthy Start program. And I voted against the budget for the Department of Human Services which cut funds from general assistance and cut a great deal of money for smoking cessation programs that were approved by the voters. Regrettably the Senate Dems went along with several of these things as a part of the overall budget deal. Otherwise I guess we'd still be in Salem.

Things were happening on land use during the last period as well. The House leadership stripped Senator Ringo's Walmart amendment out of HB 3310 and the bill passed without that amendment. The nearly full version of SB 887 passed out of the Senate and the House concurred (43–15) with the amendments made in the Conference Committee. The bill provides a two-year moratorium on any involuntary annexations by Beaverton and establishes a task force to review the whole annexation situation. But it also protects NIKE, Columbia Sportswear, ESI, and Tektronix from involuntary annexation to Beaverton until 2035. I felt protecting my constituents was sufficient reason for me to become chief co-sponsor on the bill and to support it as it went through a crazy passage. The attempt to make a little sense out of implementing Measure 37 failed. The Senate passed SB 1037, which provided a tract of record system and clarified the appeals system for Measure 37 claims. Then the House Leadership added a section to provide for transferability of claims. That was a poison pill for the Senate and they refused to concur on the amendments, killing the bill, and any hope of clarifying Measure 37. Perhaps next session.... But there was a ray of hope in land use as one part of the final budget deal was the approval of funds for the Department of Land Conservation and Development to guide a systematic review of Oregon's land-use system.

A few of us fought a hard, but fruitless battle against further government intervention in the lives of Oregonians. I mentioned earlier the bill that will increase by thousands the number of fingerprints state agencies will put into the FBI's fingerprint files. But last week we also approved (over my objections) a bill to direct the Department of Transportation to begin gathering biometric data for their records. SB 640 is a bill that requires digitizing facial scans and the use of pattern-recognition software in an attempt to prevent the same person getting driver licenses under different names. I objected to the bill on freedom principles, but I was equally concerned that by the firm's own data that accuracy would be about 53 percent with a database as large as DMV's. That is about as good as flipping a coin. What a waste!

The most disturbing move that happened on the last day was the House treatment of a bill that included a provision allowing the Portland Public Schools to continue to collect about $15 million in taxes it already collects. The Speaker committed to supporting this bill, HB 2070. When the bill came to the floor on Wednesday, I was watching it for PPS, although the Republican chair of the House Education Committee (Rep. Flores) was carrying it on the floor. As the bill came to a vote the reader board recorded 32 positive votes for the bill, including Speaker Minnis. But there were also three Democrats off the floor. The Speaker Pro-tem was at the podium and didn't bring down the gavel, which gave Majority Leader Wayne Scott time to go among the Republicans and one-by-one get them to change their votes from yes to no. After four did that I changed my vote from yes to no and announced I would bring the bill back for reconsideration the next day. I did that because I still believed the Speaker when she said that she supported the bill and if she did follow through it would pass when everybody was on the floor. When I came on the floor the last day, Rep. Scott told me the bill was dead and that he had locked down the Republicans against the bill. I told him I was going to rerun the bill and force a vote anyway. Later in the day the Speaker told me she would name a conference committee to consider the bill if I didn't run the reconsideration vote. Since that appeared to be the only chance to keep the bill alive, and after conferring with the PPS folks, I agreed to that deal. That was the conference committee that was held at 2:30am and quietly killed the bill since the Speaker refused to let it come back for a vote.

But to end this message on an upbeat note, there were two very important bills that passed during the last week. The first was SB 71, the Governor's Connect Oregon Plan that authorized the issuance of lottery bonds to establish a Multimodal Transportation Fund to finance infrastructure developments in public transit, air, marine and rail facilities. That is a very important bill, and a nice companion to the ODOT budget bill that included funding for both passenger trains. It is also a significant jobs bill. And secondly, we finally passed SB 1, the mental health parity bill that was also a piece of the end-game deal. So many people have fought hard for that bill and it is very satisfying to see them enjoy that victory after probably eight or more years of trying.

In a couple of weeks I expect to get enough perspective to review the whole legislative session. I'll be back with you then. In the meantime, it is full speed ahead on my HOPE for Oregon Families initiative to improve access to health care for all Oregonians. We continue to look for help with that initiative, both financial and help in organizing signature gathering. Please join in by return email.

The MitchMessage
August 25, 2005

"It was the best of times, it was the worst of times" does **not** begin to describe the recently ended 73rd Legislative Assembly. In my first *MitchMessage*

back before the session began I said that the real question will be the extent to which the Republican majority in the House and the Democratic majority in the Senate can find ways to work together for the good of the citizens of Oregon. I was somewhat hopeful and I looked forward to a shorter (over by early July) but perhaps productive session. I said I certainly intended to do my part to make that happen. Other than me doing my part, none of that came to pass. Consequently, the session did very little that will make a great deal of difference for Oregon's citizens. On the other hand, not too many disasters happened either. In summary — it was a mediocre session.

Personally, I had a pretty good session; passing eight bills of which I was the sponsor or the chief co-sponsor. The Governor has signed seven and told me he will sign the eighth. I don't think anybody else in the minority of either body did that well. But some of the most important items on my legislative agenda didn't get out of the Republican-controlled House.

From the perspective of a Democratic or a moderate Republican House member, this session was about as partisan as it could possibly get. Far more often than was necessary, the House Leadership locked votes down, causing all of their caucus members to vote as a block. This was different in the 2003 session, when a strong minority of moderate Republicans acted independently of their caucus to vote their conscience on many bills. Further, this year the Speaker prevented many bills from even being heard in committee. That triggered a strong reaction from the minority, trying to get ideas on to the floor using minority reports out of committee and other parliamentary procedures to attempt to force bills out of committee for a floor debate and vote. That angered the Republican leadership so much that they changed the House rules in the middle of the session to further restrict the ability of the minority to get votes on the floor for any bill the Republican leadership did not want considered. Many of these bills would have passed on a straight up and down vote.

From the perspective of the overall legislature, the worst day of the legislative session was the day, very early in the session, when the two leaderships agreed upon the total budget spending number of $12.393 billion. The Senate leadership agreed to that because of the Republican threat to split the Joint Ways and Means process if they didn't agree. This was done prior to the final two revenue forecasts and was totally premature. Of course, the Republican leadership quickly split the Ways and Means process anyway, creating special House budget committees that they could easily control. Those committees were structured to prevent minority reports on their bills. Newspaper reports indicated that Speaker Minnis and Majority Leader Scott were so proud of outsmarting the Democratic Leadership of the Senate that they have that agreement framed on the walls of their offices.

The significance of the agreement was that far less money was put into necessary services than there was actual revenue to support. The K–12 budget was inadequate, as were the higher education, Children Protective Services, Oregon Health Plan, senior services, alcohol and drug treatment, tobacco use reduction, and state police budgets. And I voted against all of those budgets. The only budget that fared well was the Department of Corrections budget, getting an increase of $300 million, to a new budget of $1.2 billion. As I thought about these budgets it became clear to me how two initiatives passed a decade ago led to Oregon's current fiscal problems. The two initiatives were Measure 5, moving funding of schools from local funds to the state budget without producing any new state funds, and Measure 11, causing mandatory minimum sentences for various criminal offenses. Before Measure 11 we had about 2000 employees in corrections. We have about 8000 currently. Furthermore there was one attempt after another in this session to increase mandatory minimum sentences or add capital punishment to crimes that currently do not carry execution as a penalty. We used to think the corrections system focused on rehabilitation and public safety. We've now moved to a complete focus on vengeance. That may feel good, but it doesn't make us any safer.

The legislature passed two landmark measures this year, SB 1 and SB 71. SB 1 is the mental health parity bill, requiring health insurance companies to provide coverage for the treatment of mental illness on the same basis as the treatment of physical illness. Mental health advocates have been struggling to make that happen for more than a decade. I was pleased when it passed, but my thoughts kept coming back to the fact that 625,000 people with no health insurance at all won't be helped by the measure. The second major bill of this session was SB 71, the Governor's Connect Oregon Plan that authorized the issuance of lottery bonds to establish a Multimodal Transportation Fund to finance infrastructure developments in public transit, air, marine and rail facilities. That is a very important bill and a nice companion to the ODOT budget bill, which included funding for both passenger trains. It is a significant jobs bill.

And, of course, the legislature passed nearly 2000 other bills, many of which were important to many people. Included in that number was the restructuring of the school zone speed law that had angered so many Oregonians. The new law will apply a 20-mph speed limit in all school zones from 7am to 5pm on school days only, unless a sign with flashing yellow lights requires something else. More than 50 percent of my constituents live in unincorporated Washington County and were threatened by Beaverton's aggressive annexation moves. So I made annexation a major issue and passed three significant annexation bills, HB 2484, HB 2722, and SB 887. HB 2722 was the most fun. It eliminated cities' ability to veto the formation of any other city within three miles of its borders. Beaverton's position that no area in my district could even make a case for creation of a new city really annoyed my constituents. It really doesn't seem feasible to form another city from the 190,000 people who live within urban unincorporated Washington County. But it certainly seems appropriate for them to be able to study the possibility without the threat of an arbitrary veto from Portland, Beaverton, North Plains, or Hillsboro. SB 887 was a very difficult bill, because it not only prevented Beaverton from forced annexation for the next two years while annexation policy is being studied, but gave NIKE, Columbia Sportswear, ESI, and Tektronix long-term protection from annexation into Beaverton.

Among the other successful bills I sponsored or was chief co-sponsor for were HB 2426 (expanding dental hygiene services to poverty populations), HB 2518 and HB 2755 (two technical bills). My two favorite bills of the session were HB 2507 and HB 2706. The idea for HB 2706 was brought to me by two OHSU family medicine residents (Drs. Abbas Hyderi and Michelle Adler). This bill will make it more likely that pregnant women are tested for HIV as a part of their first obstetrical visit. The medical, public health, and HIV/AIDS communities supported the bill. With HB 2507 Oregon becomes the first state in the Union to institutionalize the proper treatment of airbags containing sodium azide when a car is dismantled. I read a mystery novel (*Partners in Crime* by J.A. Jance) in which the victims were murdered by the ingestion of sodium azide, which is a deadly poison. Sodium azide has some other very nasty characteristics, but is completely neutralized when an airbag is simply blown when a car is dismantled. Ms. Jance, in an afterword in the book, remarked that she hoped a legislator somewhere would act to make us safer by helping auto dismantlers treat air bags properly. I introduced the bill and worked out total consensus among auto wreckers and other concerned parties to create the method for treating air bags safely. The bill passed overwhelmingly and was signed by the Governor with the book prominently in place at the ceremony.

On the other hand, three of my most important bills (I started with 45 in my legislative agenda) didn't make it out of the House. My take-home bill was HB 2560, which proposed the ultimate merger of OHSU and PSU. It passed out of the House Education Committee, but died in the House Budget Committee. HB 2704, my Forest Park protection bill passed out of the House Land Use Committee, but was sent to the House Agriculture and Natural Resources Committee (because it had forest in its name), where it died. And SB 329, which I co-sponsored with Sen. Bill Morrisette, passed the Senate and passed out of the House Health and Human Services Committee, but died in the House Budget Committee. SB 329 would have expanded the Oregon Drug Purchasing Plan, which Morrisette and I had founded last session with SB 875. We tried every which way to work out some compromise with the drug company lobbyists, but they weren't willing to compromise at all. So the bill died.

In addition, I introduced HJR 6, which would have referred a constitutional amendment to the voters that declared that all Oregonians have a right to access to affordable and effective health care and it's the obligation of the state to ensure that happens. I didn't even get a hearing on the resolution, for the second session in a row. Since that time, I have introduced, with Senators Bates and Westlund, the HOPE for Oregon Families Initiative and we are gathering signatures to get it on the ballot. When approved in the November 2006 election it will put that principle into the Oregon constitution and give the legislature two sessions to create an incremental and practical plan to achieve that.

There were several other great bills that the Republican House Leadership killed. These included HB 2940 (reinstating the ten cent cigarette tax), HB 2817 (requiring disclosure of drug company gifts to doctors), SB 1011 (which would have allowed victims of Vioxx to sue drug companies), SB 849 (requiring the availability of emergency contraception for sexual-assault victims), SB 545 (which would have reined in predatory payday lending practices), HB 2837 (which provided health insurance rate regulation), SB 931 and HB 2942 (allowing only fire-safe cigarettes to be sold in Oregon), and many, many others. All of the Senate bills passed the Senate, usually with strong bipartisan support, but never got a vote in the House. The House bills didn't even get out of the House committee.

And, of course, there were SB 1037 and SB 1000. SB 1037 was the Senate's attempt, led by Sen. Charlie Ringo, to provide some sense to Measure 37 that was passed by the voters. It passed the Senate after a great deal of debate. But when it got to the House the Speaker required that a section be added that provided nearly unlimited transfer of development rights after a successful Measure 37 claim. Transferability is clearly not provided in the version of the statute passed by the voters. This turned out to be a poison pill, which the Senate refused to swallow. The bill died in conference committee.

SB 1000, which would have provided for civil unions also died an unceremonious death in the House. People have asked me for the story behind the death of SB 1000 in the House. But there isn't really anything to tell. Had the bill come to the floor it probably would have passed. But there was zero chance that the Speaker would ever have let that bill out of committee. The religious-right lobby, led by ex-Rep. Tootie Smith, was there every day keeping the pressure on. Consequently, the Republican leadership simply didn't want their caucus members to have to vote, one way or the other, on SB 1000. It was quite clear the bill was DOA when it arrived in the House.

And finally, there was HB 2070, which would have provided the ability of Portland Public Schools to continue to receive $15 million a year in local taxes.

The Speaker assured everybody that she was supporting the bill. I was monitoring HB 2070 for PPS during its floor debate the day before adjournment. At the vote 32 members voted yes, including Speaker Minnis. The Speaker Pro-tem delayed bringing down the gavel (which would have passed the bill), while Majority Leader Wayne Scott moved among the Republicans and instructed three of them to change their votes from yes to no. I then changed my vote to no so that I could move for reconsideration the next day. At that point I still believed the Speaker supported the bill.

The next day, Rep. Scott told me the reconsideration motion was dead as the Republicans were locked down against it. The Speaker then told me she would name a conference committee if I didn't move reconsideration. I reluctantly agreed. She convened the conference committee at 2:30am and then sent a staff member down to ensure the bill was quietly killed. Since this story was told in a letter to the editor published in *The Oregonian* last Wednesday, the Speaker called to assure me she had done nothing wrong in the process of this bill being killed. And perhaps she didn't. On the other hand, if she had wanted the bill passed, it would have passed. And the amazing thing to me is that word from the PPS administration is that they still believe Speaker Minnis is their only friend in the House.

This kind of thing happened time and time again this session. While I'm a trusting and optimistic person and always give people around me the benefit of the doubt, this session really left a bad taste in my mouth. When the Democrats take control of the House, and that will happen one of these days soon, I'm going to be there fighting for the return of bipartisanship and for ensuring that the minority party has much better access to the process. That will strengthen the institution and provide a framework for citizens to regain their lost confidence in the legislative process. □

A WHOLE NEW WORLD— A SLIM MAJORITY

OREGON HOUSE OF REPRESENTATIVES, 2007–2008

THE CONTEXT

The environment changed dramatically in the Oregon Legislature when the Democrats took control of the House after sixteen years of Republican control. The change in control of the House is only one of several differences that characterized the 74th Legislative Session; perhaps the most notable of which is that we explored the value of having a short session in the second year of the biennium.

The shift to Democratic leadership represented a sea change for me, as I transitioned from life as a minority backbencher to a new role as a relatively senior committee chair. The tone and the content of the *MitchMessage* changed as I matured in experience, moved up in seniority, and grew in influence, especially in the health-care arena. This is relevant because the agenda of the Democratic House Caucus included a focus on health-care reform that previously had been carried by the Senate Democratic Caucus, especially by Senators Alan Bates and Ben Westlund. We continued moving forward in this session.

The session had some special personal health challenges for me. In the final days of the 2005 session I announced that I had been diagnosed with mantle-cell lymphoma and had begun both chemotherapy and behavioral therapy. The treatments had been successful and I went into remission by December 2005 and have remained in remission. Then on December 27, 2006 I fell leaving a Trail Blazer game and knocked the quadriceps muscles off both knees, requiring bilateral knee surgery to repair the damage. That happened just a few days before the opening of the legislative session. While I did need to come to the opening session in an ambulance to cast the deciding

101

vote for current U.S. Senator Jeff Merkley to be elected Speaker, I did not miss a single meeting of my committee. That required organizing a whole new living arrangement, including creating a hospital room in a Salem motel and arranging wheelchair transit back and forth to the Capitol. The House staff made some heroic accommodations to facilitate my ability to function, including putting a hospital bed in my Capitol office and allowing me to wear short pants over my leg braces on the floor of the House.

Many of the messages in this chapter illustrate the committee function in the Oregon Legislature. The committees are central to the legislative process in Oregon because of the strong role of the committee chair and because bills may not be amended on the floor. That means that much of the action takes place (or does not take place) under the purview of the committee chairs. Consequently, there is a great deal of discussion about how committee chairs guide their agendas, including how they function to create consensus whenever that is possible.

More about the infrastructure of the legislative process is highlighted with comments about the use of such things as the consent calendar and courtesy "yes" votes in committee, given to help the chair get measures to the floor of the House for a vote. In addition, this was the session during which the relationship between lobbyists and members came to the forefront, stimulating the development of ethics rules to regulate the extent to which legislators could accept gifts or other benefits from lobbyists. It would be wonderful to say that the legislators spontaneously sprouted a conscience. But the sad truth is that a series of damning articles in the local press brought to the fore some very questionable practices, such as a lobbyist who provided all-expense trips to Hawaii for certain legislators.

The messages also reflect the changing nature of the agenda in the House with the change in leadership, including many examples of progressive bills that were brought to the floor and passed; bills that had been blocked by the past leadership of the House. In many of these examples, the bills would have garnered thirty-one votes in past sessions had they been brought to the floor. In that same light, the messages reflect upon some very interesting and entertaining floor debates, including the debate on the resolution to refer to the voters a constitutional amendment proclaiming the right to health care. That debate featured what I believe is the best floor speech I have given in my several terms in the legislature. (That speech is reproduced at the end of this book.) And the messages feature a most interesting, but painful, story about the fate of that measure.

Several continuing agenda items return this session and a series of new ones emerge. The continuing saga of Measure 37 gets attention, with the apparently successful development of a proposal to take to the voters that would clarify the measure. There is the return of Governor Kulongoski's proposal to provide health insurance for the uninsured children of Oregon. The expansion of the bottle bill reemerged, and the fight to increase the number of children who get the benefit of drinking fluoridated water continued.

The messages report the occurrence of several battles that touched on things that citizens considered matters of ideological, moral or ethical concern. Certainly, the fluoridation debate turned into that kind of a fight, but so did other issues. That category included the struggle on a proposal to stimulate research in Oregon using embryonic stem cells. The proposal to create a system of "real ID" in our driver license system triggered both sides of the immigration question and led to a debate characterized by a great deal of heat, but not much light. Several other new issues emerged as the Democratic agenda surfaced. The new issues included a proposal to encourage the use of alternative energy sources, such as biofuel. This topic would become a standard part of Oregon's legislative agenda. The difficult economic cycles in Oregon stimulated a new interest in improving our rainy-day fund to provide a budgetary cushion when we face declining revenues.

The experimentation with a short session during February 2008 is documented in the messages as a part of the 74th Legislative Session. It was an intense session, but one that produced the consensus that it was an idea worth taking to the voters.

And for one more session, my proposals on Forest Park and on PSU/OHSU went nowhere. But we live to fight another year.

The MitchMessage
January 28, 2007

I'm sorry that my first *MitchMessage* of the session has been delayed. I had an accident on December 27 and have been working confined to a wheelchair. (For more information you might check Harry Esteve's *Inside the Capitol* column "Health care is no issue; it's real life" in *The Oregonian* on Friday, January 26. You can find it on www.oregonlive.com). This is my first weekend home in Portland since I had bilateral knee surgery on December 28.

Notwithstanding the health events, the session has been very exciting for me. Since the Democrats have only a 31–29 majority it was necessary for me to leave the hospital on January 8 to cast my vote, the 31st vote, to elect Jeff Merkley as Speaker of the House. A controversy developed in the opening session and the vote on the rules of the House was delayed until 2:30pm. I was scheduled to leave after the morning session and get back to the hospital, but the Republican leadership refused to assure they would provide a courtesy vote so I could get back to my hospital bed. Consequently I stayed until 4pm to cast a vote for the proposed rules. The final vote was 56–4, so it really would have been no problem for them to let me off the hook.

The big fight that slowed the rules voting was a controversy over a new set of ethics rules that Speaker Merkley had proposed; the battle seemed to me to be totally artificial. After making no headway over the past four years in restricting what legislators could receive from lobbyists, most of the Democratic candidates campaigned on ethics reforms. After *The Oregonian* reported on several trips that legislators had taken courtesy of Paul Romain, a beer and wine lobbyist, the issue became central in at least two campaigns. Merkley's ethics proposal, which banned such free trips, also banned gifts with a value greater than $10. The minority leadership, apparently driven into an ethical frenzy after blocking reform for several years, decided that $10 was too high a limit and began to fight for a total gift ban. They presented that argument despite the fact that they were included in the group developing the new rules and had approved them the previous week.

It seemed a shame to mar the opening day of session with partisan bickering. The new leadership is working to create a bipartisan spirit in the House, changing a set of rules and behaviors that had led to a significant reduction in rights for the minority party over the last several years. One important inclusion in the rules returned the House to proportional representation on all committees, with a minority vice-chair on all committees. In the prior session Speaker Minnis had named seven Rs and two Ds to the Emergency Board. That will be five and four under the new rules. It does seem that a bipartisan spirit is beginning to emerge. It is, however, a very fragile thing. The Republicans seem really bruised, losing control of the House after sixteen years. It may be their plan to focus on the next election, rather than to tackle the difficult problems we face in a bipartisan way. But I hope not.

I'm thrilled to have the opportunity to chair the House Committee on Health Care this session. That, of course, has been my dream since I began to run for the legislature in 1999. The other Democratic members on the committee comprise four wonderful freshman members, including Rep. Tina Kotek, one of the vice chairs and Rep. Suzanne Bonamici, who replaced Brad Avakian when he moved on to the Senate.

I was released from the hospital on January 12, just in time to gavel in the first meeting of the committee — well, only fifteen minutes late. We immediately began to work on several critical issues, the first of which is Governor Kulongoski's Healthy Kids proposal (HB 2201), which would use an 84-cents-a-pack increase in cigarette taxes to help all kids in Oregon to get health insurance. We held joint hearings with our sister Senate committee on the bill, Monday, Wednesday, and Friday this past week, a total of seven hours of hearings. Then the House committee moved into a work session at 4:30pm Friday, and passed the bill out. We had a bit of debate on the bill and on two amendments offered by Vice Chair Richardson. I tried to work out a compromise on one of those issues, but it appears that the Republican caucus isn't ready to compromise yet and preferred to have the amendments fail. Consequently, the bill passed by a 5–4 vote, along straight party lines.

The bill is now on its way to the House Revenue Committee and ultimately to the Committee on Ways and Means before it gets to the House floor. I hope that we can work out a compromise so we can move forward to provide health insurance to the 117,000 uninsured kids in Oregon.

Next we will begin to work the bill to further expand the prescription bulk-purchasing pool that the voters expanded during the last election. Sen. Bill Morrisette and I started that program with SB 875 that we passed in the 2003 session.

Being in the majority creates a very different set of pressures for me than I faced as a member of the minority. First, I find being a committee chair takes an enormous amount of time. I meet several times each week with the committee administrator and with both vice chairs. Second, every group with a bill that could be referred to the committee wants to meet with me. It turns out that the committee chair has some very strong powers, including the ability to hear or to kill a bill without a hearing. It is certainly my plan to hear bills that have a chance to get out of committee, and probably many other bills as well. But it has the proponents very concerned to talk to me early.

In the past two sessions I worked a very large legislative agenda, perhaps as many as 40 bills in each session. And I was relatively successful as a member of the minority. The irony is that this session, with a better chance of passing bills, I need to narrow my personal legislative agenda. Rather than pushing some of the bills I have in the past, I've signed on to bills sponsored by other members to do the same thing. I'll focus on passing the health agenda, working on significant health-care reform, and attending to a smaller set of bills, such as my plan for PSU/OHSU. I'll work with Tom Powers, my new legislative assistant, to keep track of other bills. I'll discuss key items from my legislative agenda in my next *MitchMessage*. And in future *MitchMessages* I'll fill you in on the progress of things like the biofuels and Measure 37 reform.

During the second week of the session we passed a bipartisan resolution that signaled our intention of experimenting with a short session during the second year of the biennium. This follows the recommendation of the Commission on the Legislature. As part of that plan we also adopted a very strict legislative calendar that moves toward ending this year's session by June 28. If we can achieve that schedule it would mean the combined length of the two sessions would be about ten days shorter than the average of the sessions held during the last 20 years. That tight schedule is already having an effect. Monday is the deadline for us to submit bills to be drafted. And the end of February is the deadline for us to introduce a bill. It will be a political and a management challenge to keep to that schedule.

Please keep an eye out for the *MitchMessage* to look a bit different. The system I use to email it is both antiquated and cumbersome… and we're exploring a new system. I hope you will continue to find it useful, even if it looks a bit slicker.

The MitchMessage
February 13, 2007

It is hard to believe that we have been in session more than a month. But things have begun to roll. The committees are hearing bills and moving them out. Some bills are moved to other committees (such as Ways and Means) for further work, and some bills have begun to move to the floor for consideration. We voted on the first batch of bills last week and more are on the way for this week. There has been a major bottleneck in getting bills drafted, however. Lawyers in the Office of Legislative Counsel draft all bills. Last Monday was the last day we could request bills to be drafted and the office received about 1000 requests in the day or two before the deadline. It has created some degree of chaos.

There are several hot topics in the House, complete with bills moving along. I reported that the Healthy Kids proposal, designed to ensure that all children in Oregon are covered by health insurance, had moved out of my committee. The bill is currently in the Committee on Revenue because the program is funded by an increase in the cigarette tax. But at the same time there have been active negotiations between the Democratic and the Republican leadership to try to craft a bill that could be supported by at least some members of each caucus. We'll see how that works out in the next week or so.

An alternative fuels package is also working its way through the House with strong bipartisan support. There are some critical elements of this bill that will be supported by members of both parties. The bill will foster alternative, clean energy sources and will also stimulate economic activity in the rural areas as bio-fuel energy resources are developed.

A set of proposals to reform the personal lending industry comes to the House this week, following on the payday lending reforms of the 2006 one-day special session. I expect they will all pass.

There is bipartisan interest in the development of a rainy day fund, although the parties differ somewhat on how to create it. The business community seems willing to eliminate the upcoming corporate kicker as one of the sources of the rainy day fund. There seems to be some interest in increasing the minimum business tax as another source of money for the rainy day fund. We'll see how that plays out in the next week or so. It will take a vote of the people if we decide to try to eliminate the corporate kicker permanently.

Finally, there is Measure 37, the topic that has stimulated the most email during the last two weeks. I'm hearing that the voters voted for Measure 37 and consequently the legislature shouldn't screw around with the "will of the voters." At the same time, I'm getting a ton of email saying that the people didn't intend Measure 37 to completely destroy Oregon's livability, so the legislature must do something to stop Measure 37. I think we need a solution somewhere in the middle. Measure 37 as passed can't actually be implemented. So the legislature must do something. I hope we can do something that implements the spirit of Measure 37, but mitigates some of the potentially terrible elements of the measure. There is a joint House/Senate committee working on short- and long-term solutions.

I said in the last message that I would begin to report on my legislative agenda this week. Of course, given the bottleneck in the Legislative Counsel's office, many of my bills have not yet emerged. As I said in the last message, I'm still committed to moving the bill to eventually integrate PSU and OHSU. I just heard that the Oregon University System has actually begun a formal study of the feasibility of integrating the two institutions.

Many of you helped us in the unsuccessful attempt to get the HOPE initiative on the November ballot. HOPE would have put the right to health care into the Oregon Constitution. Unfortunately, we were only able to obtain about 125,000 signatures, when we needed more than 140,000. I have now proposed HOPE as a referral from the legislature. HJR 18 would automatically put the proposal onto the ballot, if we can pass it out of the legislature. The Oregon Nurses Association is very supportive of HJR18. Today the bill was assigned to my Health Care Committee.

I have another annexation bill in this session in HB 2638. This bill proposes changing the island annexation component of ORS 222.750 to prevent a city from annexing an area simply by annexing streets around the area. I continue to believe that people should have a say in how they are governed. Since there isn't a land-use committee this year the bill has been referred to the Committee on Natural Resources, which will be considering most land-use issues, except Measure 37.

I'm also working on several health-care measures, including bills to expand the bulk-purchasing pool established by SB 875 in the 2003 session and expanded by an initiative in the November election. We have already held a joint hearing on the measure with the Senate committee. I am also working on a bill to require hospitals to report on hospital-acquired infections (HB 2524) and a bill to safeguard patient data in health-care systems. And I'm working on a pair of bills to restrict the ability of drug companies to give gifts to doctors (HB 2523 and HB 2648).

And finally, since I'm getting many inquires about my health status, a word about that. I can say that I'm getting stronger each day. I'm now six weeks from surgery and will get my braces off in another three weeks. I am walking (with a walker) more and more and spending less time in a wheelchair. This has been a very interesting experience.

Finally, keep the email coming. It is very useful for me to hear what is on your mind.

The MitchMessage
March 4, 2007

The pace continues to pick up in the Capitol, as the leadership is determined to adjourn by the end of June. We are able to address issues that were totally blocked by the previous leadership of the House. A great example of that occurred as the House debated (and passed overwhelmingly) HB 2163. That bill requires cigarette manufacturers to sell only fire-safe (reduced ignition propensity) cigarettes in Oregon. Canada, New York and six other states already limit sales to fire-safe cigarettes. Last session a similar bill passed in the Senate, but was never heard in the House. I introduced a similar bill during the last two sessions and wasn't able to get a hearing on either of them. It turns out that some (but not all) of the tobacco lobbyists, when faced with a Democratic majority, decided to cooperate with the proponents, including the State Fire Marshal, and get a bill with which they could live.

The big news during the past two weeks was the debate on HB 2707, a bill to establish a rainy day fund in Oregon. The bill, backed by the major business groups of the state, would eliminate the upcoming corporate kicker, take money from the biennium ending-fund balance, and create a rainy day fund not to exceed 10 percent of the prior biennium general fund revenue. It also established the rules under which the fund could be tapped. The debate raged, with a vote on both a minority report and a majority report out of the revenue committee. The battle lines were drawn along party lines, even though there wasn't a great deal of difference between the two reports. But it did turn into a partisan battle and, because the bill took the corporate kicker away, 40 affirmative votes were required for passage. The ultimate outcome was that the bill got the 31 Democratic votes and no Republican votes. I was sad after the vote, because it seemed there was so much opportunity for a real compromise.

Two things happened the next day. First radio and mail ads flooded the districts of five Democrats, including David Edwards and Chuck Riley in Hillsboro, announcing that they had voted for a $1 billion tax increase. The Republican leadership denied having anything to do with the ads, although they acknowledged the Republican House election committee financed the ads. But, more importantly, the House and Senate leadership of both parties sat down and began to negotiate a compromise on HB 2707. By 5pm that day they jointly announced a deal including both the creation of a rainy day fund and the implementation of a corporate minimum income tax. We'll vote on those bills next week and I certainly hope this situation foreshadows how we can work together the rest of the session.

As I was preparing to write this message I was struck by how many of the bills we pass in the House move as a part of the consent calendar. When a committee passes a bill, if it decides there is no need to debate the bill, it has the option of bringing it to the floor as a part of the consent calendar. That means that unless a member asks for its removal from the consent calendar, it will be read into the record and voted on without debate. For example, my committee passed out a bill that allows for a school district to transfer an employee's sick-day account when hiring an employee of the State Department of Education into the district. Since this bill only allowed a district to do that, but didn't require it, there didn't seem a need for debate. Perhaps 30–40 percent of the bills on the House agenda are, or should be, on the consent calendar.

In past messages I've commented on the various ways an idea gets transformed into a bill. HJR 4 is an interesting case in point. The Grant High School Constitution Team, which has won many district and state titles and recently finished second in the country, noticed an anomaly as they studied the Oregon Constitution. They noticed that while 18-year-old citizens could vote in Oregon, there was a special section of the constitution relating to voting on school measures. That section requires voters on school measures to have six months residency in Oregon, to be 21 years of age, and to demonstrate the ability to read and write. HJR 4 will refer the repeal of this section to the Oregon voters in the November 2008 general election.

We passed another significant bill last week — HB 2204. This bill put interest limits (36 percent annually) on companies that provide title loans. This expands the regulations we put on payday loans during the special session last year. This was another measure we were not even allowed to debate in prior sessions and these companies were charging interest rates above 300 percent. I expect this bill will quickly pass the Senate and be signed by the Governor.

Next week we should have an interesting debate on HB 2170. This bill would expand the authority of the Oregon Liquor Control Commission in two ways. Currently, the OLCC can allow an establishment to have a temporary permit to sell beer and wine for 90 days while the Commission processes a regular permit application for the establishment. HB 2170 expands the Commission's authority in two ways. First it expands the time to 180 days. And more distressingly, it also allows OLCC to grant temporary permits for the sale of hard liquor under those same conditions. The bill passed out of committee with a five-to-two vote, with one D and one R voting no. I'm joining with Representatives from the north and northeast neighborhoods to fight the bill on the floor and I think we might have a chance to stop it in the House. If not, the battle will continue in the Senate.

The mass emails I've been receiving during the last two weeks continue around Measure 37, the Iraq War resolution, and hospital-acquired infections. I think you all know my position on Measure 37, since I've discussed it many times in these messages. It's a mess and we need to do something about it, including supporting SB505, which will slow the process while we can figure out what to do. I'm a co-sponsor of the resolution opposing sending more troops to Iraq. And I'm the chief co-sponsor of the hospital-acquired infection bill. I will pass some form of this bill out of my committee.

Please keep the email coming, but if you already know my position on a measure, you probably don't need to join the flood when you get a request from Consumers' Union, OSPIRG, 1000 Friends of Oregon, NARAL, BRO, or other organizations.

And finally — a health report. As of Friday I'm out of my braces and now back to wearing long pants. I will need to use a walker for another month, but I'm feeling that I'm improving my physical functioning in many ways. Keep sending those good wishes.

The MitchMessage
March 18, 2007

The legislative session has begun moving at a faster pace since the last *MitchMessage*. During this period we passed several significant pieces of legislation among the dozens of bills that passed the House. For example, we passed HB 2589, a bill that prohibits members of the legislature from taking a job as a lobbyist until a full legislative session has passed. We frequently heard complaints that legislators moving directly from the legislature to a lobbying job didn't pass the smell test.

Perhaps the most significant legislation we passed was a pair of bills that created a rainy day fund for Oregon. This pair of bills (HB 2031 and HB 2707) did not get through the process easily. The leaders of the House and the Senate announced a deal had been reached that included the suspension of the corporate kicker for the coming year to feed the fund, the inclusion of money from each biennial budget to add to the fund, an increase in the corporate minimum income tax, and an increase in the exemption from the estate and inheritance tax from $1,000,000 to $2,000,000. It looked like a completely done deal.

We walked into the House chamber prepared to pass both bills. Suspending the corporate kicker takes 40 votes in the House (20 in the Senate). Increasing the corporate minimum takes 36 votes in the House. I assumed it would be an easy vote since we had a deal on how many Republican and Democratic votes there would be on each bill. As the session began the Republican leadership asked for a brief recess. After several hours of recesses and conferences it turned out that the deal had fallen apart. A key part of the deal had been Republican insistence that the increase in the corporate minimum be a part of the plan. But the bill to implement the corporate minimum caused a firestorm of protests about unintended consequences. Once the nature of the problem was clear it only took about 24 hours to come to resolution. The Republican caucus demanded the removal of the two things they had demanded be put in as a part of the deal. The corporate minimum and the increase in the exemption for the estate tax were stripped out of HB 2031 and both bills passed by an overwhelming majority. I expect we will try to craft a new corporate minimum tax before the end of the session.

The other two major bills of the last couple of weeks had a much smoother journey. SB 426 establishes the Oregon Educators' Benefits Board, which will oversee the creation of a purchasing pool for health insurance for school employees statewide. It is something many of us have campaigned on for several sessions, because it has the potential to reduce the cost of health insurance for many school districts. The battle turned bitter because currently the Oregon School Boards Association provides health insurance for many school districts and along the way receives millions of dollars in "commissions" for providing that service. OSBA lobbied the individual school boards to lean on their legislators. And some of the school boards responded. For example, I received several emails from employees of the Hillsboro School District urging me to vote against the bill. On the day of the vote Wayne Scott, the minority leader, issued a letter listing the OEA contributions to all the House members. I assume that was an attempt to get the message across that our votes were purchased by OEA. But the ultimate vote in the House was 36–20, with five Republicans voting with all the Democrats to pass the bill.

And on last Wednesday we passed HB 2700 the contraception equity bill, which requires health insurance companies that provide prescription coverage to cover contraception. The bill also requires hospitals to inform victims of sexual assault of the options available for emergency contraception. This was a bill we have not even been able to consider for the last ten years. It came to the floor this time and passed overwhelmingly (49–9). It caused a spontaneous celebration on the floor and in the gallery. Celebrations are not allowed in the House and there was considerable consternation about the breakdown of decorum.

We didn't win them all. HB 2170 is a bill to allow the Oregon Liquor Control Commission to grant temporary permits to sell booze for up to six months. This represents a large increase in authority and was fought by several neighborhood associations in Portland and other cities. We had a spirited floor fight on the bill, but it passed 37–21, with 14 Democrats (including me) and 7 Republicans voting no. We hope the Senate will pick up the fight, with a chance of turning the bad decision around.

Folks have asked me to comment on the state of health-care reform. The most important pending bill is HB 2101, the Healthy Kids Act, which I discussed in an earlier message. We have not yet been able to put the agreement back together on HB 2101, but I expect we will do so. If not, we do have the votes to refer the program to the voters and there is every indication it will pass in a general election. But even when we do get Healthy Kids there will still be 475,000 adults without access to health care.

There are three main groups that have been working on creating a system to provide affordable and effective health care to all Oregonians. Ex-Governor John Kitzhaber has formed the Archimedes Movement to help him develop a more rational plan for health care in the United States. The Kitzhaber plan calls for a request that the federal government give Oregon the authority to revamp Medicare, Medicaid, and private health insurance (including the income-tax deductibility of employer-paid health insurance). His plan has been introduced as SB 27, which would order Governor Kulongoski to seek the federal waivers and would create a commission to design how the health-care system would be organized if the waivers were to be granted.

Senator Alan Bates and Senator Ben Westlund have been working very hard for more than a year to create their own plan, which was introduced as SB 329. Bates and Westlund co-chaired an interim Senate commission on health-care reform, on which they invited me to serve and are currently co-chairs of the Senate Special Committee on Health Care Reform. My Sub-committee on Health Care Access has been meeting with the Special Committee two evenings a week to help (or perhaps obstruct) the process. SB 329 also creates a form of permanent entity (perhaps commission) that would be endowed with broad powers to regulate health care and would be charged with creating the plan for universal access that would be brought back to the legislature for final approval. Senators Bates and Westlund have embarked on a 15-city tour of Oregon explaining what they hope to achieve with SB 329.

After a series of meetings (which I hosted) Bates, Westlund, and Kitzhaber agreed to merge their two bills and create a common effort to pass them through the legislature. This agreement was announced at a rally on Wednesday on the steps of the State Capitol. We hope an integrated bill will emerge from the Legislative Counsel's office very soon.

The third body working on the creation of a universal health plan for Oregon is the Oregon Health Policy Commission, of which both Senator Westlund and I are members. The Commission released a draft report and I asked Legislative Counsel to draft a bill based on that report. That bill is HB 3368, of which I'm the sponsor. It proposes creating a plan including both an individual mandate to purchase affordable health insurance and a kind of employer mandate. HB 3368 also includes a full expansion of the Oregon Health Plan and proposes a form of payroll tax to finance parts of the coverage. The current agreed-upon strategy is to give the Bates-Westlund-Kitzhaber combined bill a chance to make it through the Senate, before attempting to move an independent approach through the House.

Several other critical health-care bills will begin moving through the House very soon. SB 362, which calls for another expansion of the Oregon Prescription Drug Program, passed the Senate last week (21–6) and will be coming to my House Health Care Committee. I expect we will pass it easily in the House. HJR 18, the HOPE amendment referral bill, is also ready to begin moving after we finished polling different forms of the constitutional amendment. We passed a bill out of the House Health Care Committee to increase transparency in charges under health insurance. And I expect to have a bill ready to move shortly on reporting of hospital-acquired infections. The pace is really picking up.

My health continues to improve, as I get more mobile each day. I really appreciate all of the kind thoughts you have sent along. And keep the email coming, especially email that isn't a part of a mass mail campaign.

The MitchMessage
April 1, 2007

Things got a bit unruly in the Oregon House these past two weeks. But we managed to pass some major (and a lot of minor) legislation. It really has begun to look as if the session will end near July 1 and that is putting a great

deal of pressure on the process and on the members. The period began with
a spirited debate on HJM 9, a non-binding resolution urging the President to
begin withdrawing U.S. forces from Iraq as soon as possible, but not later
than December, 2007. As you can imagine, the debate became very heated.
A key debater, speaking in favor of the resolution, was Rep. Brian Boquist, a
Republican who has served several tours of duty in Iraq.

I found myself joining the debate. I try hard to limit the number of floor
speeches I give. During my first session I noticed some members feel the
need to comment on everything. And when they get up to speak, the members turn off. Consequently, I restrict my floor speeches to measures about
which I believe I have something unique to say. Rep. Gene Whisnant, also
a Republican veteran military officer, attacked the resolution by reading off
the names of the Oregonians who had died in Iraq. I then decided I needed
to speak in favor of the resolution as a matter of conscience. After a long
debate, the resolution passed — largely, but not entirely, along party lines.

Good manners broke down later in the week when we prepared to debate
SB 400, a bill that would allow public safety officers (police officers and
firefighters particularly) to discuss safety issues as a part of their collective bargaining. This bill has been a major objective of all the public safety
unions for several years and hasn't even been debated under Republican
leadership. About 400 firefighters bused in to watch the debate. Because it
is a Senate bill it was scheduled at the very end of the agenda, but common
practice under these circumstances is to request consent to move the item up
in the agenda. The Republican leadership refused to grant their consent. We
worked through lunch to get through the agenda so we could debate SB 400
while the firefighters were still in the gallery. They sat through four hours
of debate on other bills before watching the bill go down to defeat. (It was
eventually sent back to committee and a version will emerge that will pass.)

We had a similar dust-up this week over HB 2372A, a bill that requires
employers to provide unpaid rest periods to employees to express breast
milk if it does not cause undue hardship to business operations. This is a bill
that seems completely reasonable, but the Associated Oregon Industries has
fought it forever. Consequently we never debated it before. Similar to the SB
400 debate many advocates for nursing mothers came to the Capitol to watch
the debate. And similar to the earlier situation, the Republican leadership
refused to allow a suspension of the rules to move the bill up the agenda.
The bill was debated well after lunch, with the pro side of the debate led by
a Republican woman, Rep. Vicki Berger. HB 2372A passed easily, but long
after most of the advocates had left because of other commitments.

One of the interesting things about this session is that bills are being
allowed to come to the floor without a clear-cut determination that they have

the votes necessary to pass. SB 400 was one example of that. In another debate last week a bill to require helmets while driving an all-terrain vehicle (ATV) came to the floor and after a spirited debate was soundly defeated. There seems to be a willingness to actually listen to the debate and decide how to vote. I think this is a very good sign.

It is very different serving in the majority than serving in the minority. Being in the majority clearly entails more work and much more responsibility. But it is also much more rewarding. When I was in the minority I had the time to focus on my own legislative agenda. Now two things are different. My vote on the floor counts in a different way. And being a committee chair brings a whole different level of activity. Everybody needs to talk to me about any number of different bills. And there is less time to meet with lobbyists and other interested parties. My typical day includes floor session from 10:45 to about 12:30, followed by a caucus meeting until at least 1pm. On most days I have an education sub-committee or full committee meeting from 1:00 to 3:00pm and on all days I have a health-care sub-committee or full committee meeting that runs from 3:00 to 5:00. On two days a week I have a health-care reform committee meeting that lasts from 5:00 to 6:30.

In addition, I need to meet daily with my committee administrator and frequently with my two vice-chairs Rep. Richardson (R) and Rep. Kotek (D). And I meet daily with my legislative aide (Tom Powers) who monitors my legislative agenda. I have also been testifying about three times a week in hearings on the bills of which I'm the sponsor. That leaves Harriet frantically filling up every other 15-minute slot on my calendar with someone from the long line of people in my outer office looking to urgently meet with me because they have a bill coming up in my committee. Then Harriet also is certain to pop in after 15 minutes to remind me that my next appointment is waiting and I'm already 20 minutes behind because I talk too much.

Being a committee chair has brought me much closer to how the legislative process works. It turns out that the committee chair has nearly absolute power to decide which bills are heard in committee and which bills are moved along in the process. (I try to hear most of the bills assigned to my committee.) The committee chair also has the power to create a working group to improve a bill to the point that it achieves consensus, which is usually the objective. An interesting example of the process was in the flow of HB 2213 through the House. The Department of Consumer and Business Services suggested this bill. DCBS is the agency that regulates health insurance. The bill requires insurers to provide a reasonable estimate to their enrollees of the cost of procedures and services for which enrollees will be responsible. The bill was supported by consumer advocates and fit into the

Democratic Caucus Roadmap agenda promising more transparency in the
health-care field.

But the insurance industry said the bill, as written, would be impossible
to implement. I asked Rep. Ben Cannon, the vice-chair of the Health Care
Access sub-committee to lead a work group to produce a version of the bill
to which all parties could agree. I also asked Rep. Dennis Richardson, the
Republican vice-chair of the sub-committee, to join the group. I asked a
small number of representatives of insurance companies, DCBS, and the consumer advocacy movement to form the work group. The committee administrator volunteered to staff the group. And I gave them three weeks to come
in with a perfected bill. Under Rep. Cannon's leadership they did their job
ahead of schedule, bringing back a bill that all parties supported. It wasn't
a perfect bill in the eyes of any of the parties, but they all agreed it made an
important beginning and was achievable. The bill passed easily out of the
sub-committee, the full committee and passed the House without a single no
vote. It's now on to the Senate, where the process will begin anew.

If the Senate passes the bill without change it would be on to the Governor's desk for his signature. If the Senate amends the bill it will be up to me
to decide whether to recommend the House concur with the Senate amendments. If the House agrees to concur, the concurrence vote moves the bill to
the Governor's desk. If the House refuses to concur a conference committee
will be named to try to reach agreement on one version of the bill. If they
reach agreement it might be on the House version, on the Senate version,
or on some new version created by the conference committee. Then both
the House and the Senate need to approve the conference committee report
before it goes to the Governor.

Not all bills work out so easily. We received a bill in committee that I
sponsored with Rep. Carolyn Tomei to require hospitals to report on hospital-
acquired infections (HB 2524). The hospitals objected to the original form,
but agreed to work on an amendment. Tom Powers worked with them and
with the state agency that has responsibility to report on the data provided
by the hospitals. After a couple of weeks they produced an amendment that
all could agree upon that would really begin the process in a great way. But
when we heard the bill in committee and accepted the new amendment, the
agency reported there would be a $300,000 fiscal statement, signifying it
would cost $300,000 more per biennium to do the reporting than was in the
Governor's budget. If that turns out to be true we can't send the bill directly
to the House floor for a vote, but need to refer it to the Ways and Means
Committee to look for the money in an already over-committed budget. It's
not too likely to escape from Ways and Means unless the fiscal is reduced or
we can get some substantial power to push for it.

I continue to hear from my constituents and on most days that is very welcome, even when I get 50 of the same messages triggered by one organization or another. I did receive many messages urging a yes vote on HJM 9. I'm also getting a great deal of anti-fluoridation email, but most of it is not from constituents. And the mail is beginning to arrive on the anti-discrimination measures. Keep in touch.

The MitchMessage
April 15, 2007

It seems to me that there is a significant change in the nature of the issues we began facing in the House and in the Health Care Committee these last two weeks. During the early part of the session we did face some difficult and contentious issues, and generally worked out compromises that marginally satisfied both sides. We passed SB 362B, expanding the Oregon Prescription Drug Program. In the Health Care Committee we moderated battles between hospitals and consumers, between physical therapists and chiropractors (round two is going on now), between consumers and insurance companies, and between public health professionals and school food services directors. (We passed HB 2650A, which sets minimum standards for food and beverages sold in the public schools.) These things just took time, patience, and a bit of leadership. These were important issues, but only required technical fixes.

We have begun facing "this I believe" issues and the going has gotten tougher. We are dealing with two bills in the Health Care Committee that are perfect examples of this kind of bill. And in the next week or two we will be voting on two more of them on the House floor. In the Committee we are dealing with HB 2801 and with HB 3099. HB 2801 is a bill to foster the development of embryonic stem cell research in Oregon and HB 3099 is a bill to extend the fluoridation of community water systems in communities with more than 10,000 people. You would think that the question of whether Oregon should join the other 47 states with widespread fluoridation in their public water systems is one that could be answered by simple scientific analysis. But it isn't.

It is an odd debating line-up. On the pro-side of the issue are almost all of the dentists and dental organizations, virtually all of the public health scientists, and the army of public health advocates. In opposition are those who are cautious about the government interfering in individual lives and most of the environmental community. It is clear to me as a health researcher that the scientific data gathered over the past 50 years overwhelmingly points to the safety and effectiveness of fluoridating public water supplies. But the opposition brings scattered data to argue against imposing fluoride in drinking water when there are other ways to get fluoride to kids. Some of their arguments have merit and some are of the variety "if the EPA issues a bulletin recommending fluoride in the water supply be kept under five parts per million it must be an indication that it *might* be dangerous at one part per million." After listening to the debate it has become obvious that it is no longer about scientific evidence for most of us — it has become a "this I believe" issue and there doesn't seem room for compromise, nor would it be fruitful to produce much more scientific evidence.

HB 2801 seems to produce even more in the way of pre-fixed positions. The opposition is clearly from the right-to-life community. The strongest support comes from the medical science community and from advocates for research for diseases that seem most likely to benefit from embryonic stem cell research — Parkinson's disease, diabetes, muscular dystrophy, MS, ALS, and spinal cord injury. Embryonic stem cell research requires using blastocysts as donor cells to produce some stem cells to grow. Embryonic stem cells are important because they have the potential to turn into any other cell. I found it ironic that we had a great deal of testimony earlier in the week about the wonder of donating organs after one dies. The ability to produce good after death was viewed as a wonderful option, giving one a bit of immortality after death. But nobody talked about the wonder of using material from a five-day-old embryo to potentially save many lives before the embryo is destroyed.

We heard extraordinary testimony from a wife about how her husband was saved from a totally hopeless diagnosis for a blood disease. What saved him was a treatment resulting from years of research at OHSU on adult stem cells. Her final conclusion was that OHSU should not be allowed to do the research on embryonic stem cells, even if it saved the lives of men like her husband. Why? Because it is immoral. Not too much I can do with that kind of testimony, except cry with the story as I thought of the thousands who might be denied the same kind of miracle that saved her husband.

And this next period we are going to be facing the most controversial of "this I believe" questions when we vote on SB 2 and HB 2007. SB 2 includes gender preference within the statute that bans discrimination by membership in a class. HB 2007 provides some rights to committed same-sex couples that they are excluded from because they cannot marry. SB 2 has passed out of the Senate and both bills passed out of the House Committee on Rules, Elections, and Ethics last week. What goes with considering the "this I believe" issues, among other things, is a flood of email, phone calls (mostly anonymous), and letters.

When I began to run for the legislature I made a pledge to my future constituents. It included, among other things, the pledge that I would tell the truth (even if it wasn't what people wanted to hear), that I would listen to my constituents and that I would vote my conscience on the difficult issues. I have been careful in responding to my constituents email to report my position as explicitly as possible. Even when it gets a response like "I'll remember this vote and I'll never vote for you again." And some that seem a bit more intimidating.

I remember when Lyndon Johnson was at the lowest point of his popularity during the Viet Nam war his press secretary would announce how the opinions were running on the President's handling of the war. (Does that sound familiar?) One day his press secretary came out and announced it was the President's birthday and the telegrams were running 3–2 in favor of him having a happy birthday. I believe my constituents generally support my position on these difficult issues, although the statewide email is definitely not supportive. But not withstanding the support count, these are issues that will get my principled vote.

The two other issues that are drawing the most constituent email are the expansion of the bottle bill and Measure 37. I think the bottle bill expansion is about settled. I believe that plastic water bottles and a few other bottles will get deposits. I do not think we have the votes to increase the deposit to ten cents, although I definitely support doing so. Measure 37 is a more complicated situation. We have a bipartisan committee trying to work out a compromise. They have seemed close to getting a consensus bill out several times and each time the compromise came apart. I hear they are going to announce something this week, but I'll believe it when I see it.

And finally, there is the budget. Minor agency bills are coming out, but there is wide dissatisfaction with the co-chairs' proposed higher education budget and with several other elements of the budget. Changing the budget numbers is a somewhat mystical process for any of us who are not on the Ways and Means Committee. But I remain hopeful that better numbers will emerge.

The MitchMessage
April 29, 2007

When I first ran for office I asked a veteran lobbyist what he expected of me in return for the campaign contribution I was soliciting. He said he expected two things. First, when he requested a meeting with me I would meet with him. And second, when I told him how I was going to vote on a bill, I would either vote that way or let him know I had changed my mind.

He said it was very embarrassing to tell a client how a bill was going to come out and then find it wasn't going to come out that way. I learned it is perfectly fine to tell a lobbyist you are undecided or you are a "soft" yes, which means you might change. But a yes means yes and a no means no.

This came into play this week for me as I was working to get HB 3099, the water fluoridation bill, out of the Health Care Committee and on to the House floor. The lobbyist for the Oregon Dental Association, the main proponent of the fluoride bill, assured me that I had the five votes I needed to move the bill, and that there were 32 firm yes votes in the House. But I was frankly worried that one of the "sure" yes votes in committee might not turn out to be a yes.

Another quaint custom I learned early in my first session was the "courtesy" yes vote in committee. A courtesy yes vote comes when a committee member, who will likely vote no on the House floor, agrees to vote yes in committee to allow a bill to move to the House floor for debate. This usually happens when a member is planning on voting no, but doesn't have a problem with the bill being debated on the floor and acted upon by the full body. A courtesy yes played an important part in the committee action on HB 3099.

Since I supposedly had five sure yes votes I was prepared to move the bill. But I asked a member of the committee, who was an announced no vote, if the member would provide a courtesy yes, if the sure yes vote went south. The member agreed to do so, if the motion took a certain form. As it came to pass, the member who was a sure yes, steamed out of the committee room as the bill was being debated and didn't return until after the vote. The committee voted to move the bill to the House floor, on a 5–3 vote. There is a fabric of trust among members of the House and courtesy votes strengthen that fabric, while a "sure" vote that disappears, weakens that fabric.

A member who refused to vote on the House floor Thursday triggered the strangest floor session I've observed during my three terms in the House. I carried HB 2201, the Healthy Kids act, on the House floor Thursday. The bill would provide health insurance for all of the uninsured children of Oregon, some 120,000 kids. Since the program would be financed by an increase in the tobacco tax, it required a 3/5 majority to pass. We had a very spirited debate on the measure, which began to deteriorate into a series of parliamentary moves, intended to delay or avoid a vote. There were many members, mostly in the minority party, who did not want to vote for a tax increase, but also did not want to vote against a great plan to get health insurance to children.

Finally, there was a call of the House, which requires members to remain on the floor. Then there was a motion to end debate (after about two hours), and the vote on the bill began. All of the members voted except one member and the bill was not going to get the required 36 vote majority, having only 32 yes votes. But that member, Rep. John Lim, refused to vote. Rep. Lim announced he was not going to vote at this time, since debate had been cut off. The House rules require each member on the floor to vote, but they don't say what to do if one refuses to vote. Since we were under a call of the House nobody could leave the floor and since we were in the middle of a vote no other motion was in order. Consequently, the other 59 members of the House sat around waiting for the impasse to end. It was quite a zoo, until the speaker finally announced that Rep. Lim was in violation of the rules and announced the bill had failed to achieve the required 36 aye votes. The final vote was 32–27. Rep. Lim continued his protest by remaining at his desk on the House floor until the next morning.

Despite this odd session the House passed many important bills during the last two weeks. Perhaps the most controversial of them happened early in that period when the House passed SB 2 and HB 2007. As you can imagine, the debate was furious over creating the contractual relationship of domestic partnerships for same-sex couples and prohibiting discrimination based on sexual orientation. Both bills passed the House after amendments were added to HB 2007 giving churches and other religious organizations broad exemptions from the discrimination provisions. I got a great deal of very hostile email over my yes vote on these bills, although most of it was from outside my district.

We passed HB 2082, which reforms the signature-gathering process on initiative campaigns. I learned a great deal about this process as I worked to qualify the HOPE amendment to the constitution for the November 2006 ballot. I supported this bill, which passed the House easily.

We passed a modification of the Oregon Family Leave Act (HB 2485) to allow employees to use paid accrued sick leave when taking family leave. I received a great deal of supportive email on this bill.

We worked on several important bills, in committee and on the floor, relating to hospitals. For example, we moved a bill to the Ways and Means Committee that requires hospitals to report hospital-acquired infections. I believe that bill will survive the Ways and Means process and will get to the floor. And we passed HB 3290 on the floor, which requires hospitals to report on their contributions to charity care and other community benefit activities in a much clearer way.

And finally, we passed one of my favorite bills. One of my pet projects over the last couple of sessions relates to the Washington County commuter train that will begin running between Wilsonville and Beaverton in the fall of 2008. I have long believed that it is possible to extend that train line to allow it to operate between Beaverton and Salem. We passed HB 2472 that creates a task force to explore extending that rail service to Salem. If that task force begins work as soon as session is over, the earliest this extension could take place would be 2018. As I carried that bill on the floor I began the debate by blowing a train whistle, which certainly woke up the Body.

April 30 is the last day most of the House committees can work on House bills and most of the Senate committees can work on Senate bills. So we now move into the phase where we begin working seriously on bills from the other chamber. The leadership is really committed to adjourning by the end of June. We'll see.

The MitchMessage
May 13, 2007

Obviously I produce *the MitchMessage* to inform my constituents about the activities of the Oregon Legislature and, of course, to brag about my accomplishments. But there is another purpose for the message and that is to serve as my own diary of my reactions to what is happening in Salem. When I joined the legislature in January 2003 I thought I might want to write a book about my experiences in the House. And as an academic at heart I still haven't given up that idea. But it is not in my nature to keep a daily log. Consequently, the *MitchMessage* is my compromise. The reason I mention this is to explain why I sometimes get off into flights of speculation about the legislative process.

One of the readers asked me to comment in this edition about *The Oregonian* article discussing the strained relationship between Majority Leader Dave Hunt and Minority Leader Wayne Scott. That led me to consider the larger question of the relationship between the majority and the minority caucuses, which of course is, to a great extent, the framework within which the two leaders operate. Several random thoughts come immediately to mind. The first thought is that spending 16 years in the majority is lousy training for being in the minority. It is much easier to transition from the minority to the majority. It feels to me that much of the behavior of the minority caucus during the first three months of the session was triggered by the anger and frustration of losing four seats (and the majority) during the 2006 election. It was clearly not something that they expected. They seemed to discount the great candidates we fielded and the nearly flawless campaigns they ran, and blamed their disaster on national politics and on specific campaign mistakes they attributed to their leadership.

Another random thought that came to mind is that the creation of legislation is influenced by both policy and political factors. While that is obvious, it is easy to only consider how to achieve good policy and to forget what an important role politics plays. Or to think everything is politics. In truth, the members of the current Democratic and Republican caucuses have very different policy positions on a number of key issues, including the most important one, the role of state government. On balance Republicans feel the smaller the role state government plays the better. On balance, Democrats feel that we must decide what needs to be done by government and then we need to figure out how to get the resources to do those tasks as efficiently as possible. This becomes operational in discussing things that seem to require new taxes, such as the Healthy Kids Program, which clearly needs a new source of revenue. The Republican position is stated as "if it can't be funded within the current budget it shouldn't be done."

On the political side, it is true that both caucuses can't help but keep one eye on the effect of legislative activity on the next election. For most of us, we begin thinking about the next election the morning after the last election. Political norms and House rules keep a lot of that under control. But, for example, it doesn't stop the Republicans from hiring a photographer to roam the gallery of the House chamber looking for opportunities to get unflattering pictures of our members. And it doesn't stop the Republicans from hiring robo-calls against five of our members the morning after they took certain votes. Nasty campaign mail immediately also followed against these same legislators.

Finally, in the case of Hunt and Scott you have to look to personality differences. Wayne Scott is an extremely successful entrepreneur and is the owner of several very successful businesses. He is a straight A to B guy. He once told me how frustrated he was with the legislature. He said in his usual life three or four guys get together in a room, decide what needs to be done, and then go off and do it. Nothing like that happens in the legislature. Dave Hunt on the other hand is very comfortable working within collaborative relationships. He is a transportation policy specialist, a Sunday school teacher and past president of the American Baptist Convention. They don't always speak the same language. I did, however, come upon Hunt sitting at Scott's desk on the floor this week, with both chatting and smiling. I remarked to them I would have liked to see that picture in *The Oregonian*.

In the meantime, it was a busy week in the Salem version of Lake Woebegone. We passed HB 3540 and HB 3546, the bills aimed at correcting some of the problems of Measure 37. HB 3540 refers, for voter approval, changes to the implementation of Measure 37. It focuses on facilitating claims for building up to three houses on a tract of land and ultimately limits most development claims under Measure 37 to ten houses. HB 3546 extends by one year the period for government entities to review and act upon claims submitted under Measure 37. Oregonians in Action is not crazy about the bills and they passed pretty much on a party line vote.

We passed a long overdue bill (HB 2372B) that requires employers of 25 or more employees to provide unpaid rest periods and a private location to allow lactating mothers to express breast milk at work. This was an issue that couldn't even be brought to the floor under Republican leadership. I always felt it wasn't so much the opposition of Associated Oregon Industries that stopped the bill, but was rather the reluctance of Republican men to talk about breasts in public. An irony of the AOI opposition to the bill was that AOI made accommodations for the female lobbyist arguing against the bill to breast feed when she came back to work after delivering a child. The bill passed overwhelmingly and would have passed overwhelmingly had it come to the floor in previous sessions.

We also finally passed SB 400, a bill I've discussed before. SB 400 allows public safety officers to include safety issues under their collective bargaining process. The first time the bill came up the Republican caucus refused to allow it to be heard out of order, requiring dozens of firemen to wait four hours before the bill was sent back to committee after an hour of debate. The committee made modest changes in the bill that made it acceptable to a huge majority of House members and it passed quietly and easily later in the week.

The autism epidemic received recognition this week as well. Families with autistic kids had a bill introduced by Rep. Peter Buckley. The bill, HB 2918, passed this week after several hearings and much discussion. It, among other things, requires the Health Resources Commission to review evidence on the medical and behavioral treatments of autism and to report on the effectiveness of these treatments. In addition, in response to the hearings, Dr. Bruce Goldberg, the director of the Department of Human Services, and Susan Castillo, the Superintendent of Public Information, announced that they would form a joint task force to study the problems of dealing with autism in Oregon and make recommendations on how to deal with it. It was enlightening to find the large number of House members with autism in their family.

Several of my bills continue to move along the process, thanks largely to my legislative director Tom Powers. He keeps directing me to Senate hearings about my bills, which mostly take place when I'm supposed to be somewhere else. We passed two of them (HB 3267 and HB 2733) without opposition out of the House during the last two weeks. HB 3267, which was suggested by my friend Tony Biglan at the Oregon Research Institute, creates a task force on Coordination of Behavioral Science Research in Oregon. It is intended to facilitate the ability of social and behavioral scientists in Oregon to help the state, including our agencies, do its work better.

HB 2733 is a reaction to a couple of instances where health-care facilities had serious breaches in their data security systems. It requires health-care facilities to report on the state of their data security systems each year and further requires that the CEO of the facility (or health-care system) personally sign the report. That signature signifies the CEO is personally responsible for reviewing their data security systems and also certifies that they have reported any problems with their security systems to their board of directors.

Some of you have asked for an updated health report, which I'm happy to supply. Other than the fact that I've been struggling with bronchitis since March, including about five rounds of antibiotics, I'm doing very well. My knees continue to improve and I've now gone through all stages of transportation assists — wheelchair, walker, and cane and I'm walking unaided. I've learned the corollary to being there is 90 percent of the battle. It's the need to keep putting one foot in front of the other. Finally, recent tests continue to indicate that my lymphoma is in complete remission.

Keep the email coming, my friends.

The MitchMessage
June 3, 2007

We're marching toward the end of the 2007 Legislative Session. The House leadership continues to insist that we will be done by June 29. In aid of this schedule all policy committees were instructed to close down on May 31. That meant that the committees needed to complete work on their bills and send them to the floor, refer bills to one of the three remaining committees (Ways and Means, Rules, and Revenue), or let the bills die in committee.

One of my bills, HB 2733, was killed Thursday in the Senate Health Policy Committee. The bill required hospitals and health insurers to report annually on the state of the systems in place to guard the security of personal health information. It's my impression that the bill was killed because of the ego needs of one senator who has a bill in process to deal with the security of personal data generally. Even though his bill excludes health-care providers, he apparently viewed my bill as a threat. Sometimes weird things happen in the legislature.

I did manage to finish the work of my committee, although in the end I sent one bill to Ways and Means and one to Rules. But we refined most of the other bills and sent them to the House floor for action. The bill we sent to Ways and Means (SB 34) would create a statewide database that would include any prescription for a broad class of drugs, including such things as Ritalin and Vicodin. That data would then be available on a 24/7 basis to be checked by any doctor or pharmacist faced with prescribing any of these drugs. Several of us are worried about the security of that database. I was fascinated by the number of times database security and the general concern around the development of databases emerged during the last couple of weeks.

In addition to the two bills discussed above, there was a very interesting debate on the House floor Friday. HB 2827 has been sitting in a committee and the Democratic caucus moved it to the floor. The bill requires ODOT to take the first steps to move Oregon into compliance with the Federal "Real ID" act. The Real ID act requires each state to create a new way to provide driver licenses, including a requirement that each applicant provides proof of legal residence. A database is then created that includes name, address, social security number, a photograph, and copies of the documents used to prove legal status. And that data is then linked with the database information from all the other states. If a state doesn't comply by 2011 the Feds will not allow that state's driver licenses to be used as identification on an airplane or for entering a federal building. It is as close to a national identity card as you can get. All that is missing is a number tattooed on the arm.

There was a long and interesting debate on the floor, in which I took part. Anybody running for office in Oregon knows that illegal immigration is going to play a key role in the next election and also knows how their vote on this issue could affect the outcome of their next race. I thought that I was going to be alone in opposing the bill, but it turned out there were 16 no votes — 13 Democrats and 3 Republicans. I salute those 16 brave souls.

I raised the question of moral courage in a debate in the education committee this week as well. (I guess it was my week to be sanctimonious.) The bill being debated in the committee was one brought by Senator Margaret Carter. Currently, if a man or woman was ever convicted on a misdemeanor prostitution charge they could not ever get a teaching certificate. The bill would allow the Teachers Standards and Practices board to consider an application for a teaching certificate after a minimum of five years. It would not require them to provide a certificate. It would only allow them to consider the application. It was clear to me that most members of the committee thought this was a reasonable position, but that nobody, except me, was going to vote for it. That led me off on a riff about courage.

My rant included a statement something like "Everybody is afraid Lars Larson will attack them by saying they were voting for bringing prostitutes into the classroom." And then I said something like "It really shouldn't matter because Lars has one stupid statement after another on his show." I've since heard he played that clip several times on his show the next day, with a comment something like "who voted for this guy?"

While we got important things done since the last *MitchMessage*, the minority continues to try to slow the process down. The routine has been going something like this: we come into the session (scheduled from 10am to noon), take the roll, do the opening ceremony, take courtesies. Then the minority leader moves for a recess for the purpose of a Republican caucus. The speaker asks how long do they need and the answer is 15 to 30 minutes. We recess. The Republicans come back 45 minutes to an hour later.

The next order of business is Propositions and Motions. One of the Republicans asks to be recognized and moves that some obscure bill be removed from the Ways and Means (or Revenue) Committee and brought immediately to the floor. They have previously introduced a series of bills solely designed to make our more vulnerable members take bad votes. The motion to withdraw gives them an opportunity to force those bad votes. After a brief debate, it's time to vote. Another Republican asks for a call of the House (to force everybody to be there to vote) and finally requests a voice roll call. Generally, all Democrats vote against the motion. This takes up a great deal of time, and it is now about 11:30 and the session is largely wasted. But by the end of the afternoon, several of our members' districts are flooded with robo-calls telling the voters their Representative favors illegal immigration, votes against adding state troopers, or some other dumb thing.

Next week we move to morning and afternoon sessions, with the promise that evening sessions will follow if we can't make better headway on our bills.

Having said all of that we did manage to pass some critical legislation during this period. For example, we passed HB 2760, which is an omnibus bill to clean up annexations done under the "Island Annexation" process covered under ORS 222.750. Among the things it does is limit the extent to which street annexations can be used to create an island. Under HB 2760 no more that 25 percent of the boundary of land to be annexed can be a public right of way. That should stop a city from annexing streets and then claiming that an area is now an island and can be annexed without the consent of the residents of the area.

We passed SB 707, which expands the bottle bill to include water containers and does a few other things. Many of us were disappointed that we weren't able to increase the deposit to at least ten cents, but the bill also includes a task force to look at ways to improve the whole process. We passed SB 838 (Senator Avakian's bill), which directs the Department of Energy to create a renewable portfolio standard under which electric utilities must derive 25 percent of annual retail electricity sales from renewable energy resources by the year 2025. SB 517 passed the House. It prohibits school district employees or volunteers from selling, marketing, distributing, endorsing, or suggesting anabolic steroids or other performance-enhancing substances to students. And we passed SB 384, which prohibits school districts from entering into contracts with administrators that include a "golden parachute." No more paying people for not working.

Another important bill that passed was HB 2626, which establishes a statewide system for recycling electronic devices, including computers, monitors, and television sets. It requires manufacturers to participate in the recycling program. For those of us who have tried to figure out how to recycle a computer, this will be a terrific improvement when it gets into place. And we passed HB 3181, which gives childcare providers the right to collectively bargain with the State. And finally, there was the fluoride bill, which hit a little bump in the road. On the night before we were scheduled to debate the bill on the floor of the House we were assured there were 32 votes in favor. On the morning of the debate that number had been reduced to 25. Consequently the bill went back to the Ways and Means Committee for refining. We have developed amendments to the bill, which provide more flexibility to cities. I am assured that we now have the votes to pass the bill and we should act on it in the next couple of weeks.

One of the things that has been happening is that House bills that were amended and passed in the Senate are coming back for concurrence with the amendments. It is up to the chair of the original committee to decide whether to move to concur or not to concur. So far, every bill that has come back to us went to the floor with a recommendation to concur and re-pass the bill. If the vote is not to concur a conference committee is named to iron out the differences. When the Senate was in Democratic hands and the House under Republican control there were many conference committees, some of which did not reach consensus. Perhaps we'll get by without them.

I'm really looking forward to seeing if we can get out of Salem by July 1. But the major impediment to that schedule is that we have several budgets yet to pass. And we have a few very necessary bills that will require 36 votes. Neither will be easy.

The MitchMessage
June 11, 2007

I felt drained as I sat watching the thirty seconds tick away on the House vote tally board waiting for the final count on HJR 18. House Joint Resolution 18 is the bill to refer to the voters a constitutional amendment declaring that access to health care is a fundamental right of every legal resident of Oregon. HJR 18 is a referral version of the initiative measure (#40) we worked so hard to get to the ballot last year. This bill is, by far, the most important to me of all the bills I have ever sponsored.

The bill drew a ferocious debate, even though it was clear that I had the votes to pass it. The three members who had voted against the bill in committee spearheaded the Republican side of the debate. The debate went off in strange directions, beginning with a motion by Rep. Dennis Richardson to return the bill to committee for an amendment that would include food and shelter to the statement of rights. I could have supported that concept were it not completely disingenuous. That motion was defeated. The debate then went off into wilder flights of fancy, including claims that by sending the question to the people we would create a socialist, communist, or totalitarian state.

The House has quaint debating rules, aimed at keeping debate on a calm plane. Allowed in those rules is the right of a representative to ask a question of the carrier of the measure, or of anybody else for that matter. The opponents used that technique to ask ridiculous questions and I yielded to those questions from the first three speakers. When it became clear to me that the questions were mostly being used to stall the debate I refused to yield to questions from the fourth speaker, much to his surprise.

One of the flights of fancy of an opponent led him to quote the preamble to the United States Constitution, with regard to our God-given rights to life, liberty and the pursuit of happiness. That became the theme to my closing statement, with my assertion that a 21st century American cannot exercise the right to life without having access to health-care services. I ended the debate with a statement that I wouldn't be standing in that chamber without having access to health care during the last two years, nor would many other members of the body, whose access to health care had kept them alive to take part in this debate. The final vote tally was 32–27, with all the Democrats and one Republican (co-sponsor Rep. Bob Jensen) voting yes. The bill now goes to the Senate.

The debate on HJR 18 kicked off a very interesting morning, also highlighted by a debate on SB 571, which requires that employers provide smoke-free worksites, including restaurants, bars, and taverns. This included a vote on a minority report that would have allowed smoking at Portland Meadows and delayed the effective date for bingo halls. After a great deal of debate the minority report was defeated. The main bill was ultimately passed on a 38–21 vote with all Democrats and seven Republicans voting yes. The debate on the two bills took up almost all of the morning and ended just at noon. The timing was important because two members of the majority needed to leave the chamber around noon. One of the two was Rep. Ben Cannon, who came in for these two votes. Rep. Cannon and his wife Liz were busy dealing with the birth of their first child for a large part of the week. The second member was ill and was hanging in for these important votes before leaving for a sickbed.

We had action on several health-care bills during this period, including one more fruitless try to pass the Healthy Kids bill that would finance health care for children on the basis of an increase of the tax on cigarettes. This was an attempt to pass HB 2967, which is a statutory referral to the voters. The cigarette tax increase in the measure would provide sufficient money to buy health insurance for all poor kids, for the Tobacco Use Reduction program, and for several other health-care programs. The debate on the bill was preceded by several weeks of negotiations between the Democratic and the Republican leadership. That led to the apparent likelihood that the Republicans would provide the five votes, that when added to the 31 Democratic votes, would be the 36 votes needed to pass the bill. Any bill that raises taxes needs a 3/5 majority of each chamber to pass. However, the legislative counsel has asserted that a referral that asks the voters to raise taxes also requires a 3/5 majority. This is not true in the case of a constitutional amendment referral.

Of course, as I expected, the Republicans had no intention of providing the votes necessary to pass the bill. On the first day of debate, the bill only gained 35 votes. There was a move for reconsideration and on the second day, two Republicans dropped off the bill and two Republicans joined the bill. Again, 35 votes. We could see that as many times as the bill was debated the Republicans would provide enough votes to get to 35. In fact, rumor had it that we gained one vote at the last moment and had 36 votes. But as soon as that happened, a Republican member, who had assured the Speaker he would be a yes vote 15 minutes before the vote, became a no vote. However, the battle isn't over. The Senate is moving to the House a constitutional amendment to implement the cigarette tax increase and the Healthy Kids program. Since that only takes 31 votes to pass, I expect that several Republicans will jump on the bill now that it doesn't matter.

Another bruising political fight came over the passage of HB 3540, a bill to refer to the voters a fix needed to effectively implement Measure 37. This bill finally emerged from a bipartisan committee on a pure party-line vote after weeks of negotiation failed to craft a bipartisan compromise. It seemed that at three different times a compromise had emerged, only to have hopes crushed when the Republican members checked with their caucus. The measure passed in the House. The Senate added some amendments. This week the House concurred in the Senate amendments and the modification of Measure 37 will now go to the voters. Almost all of the key votes were strictly party-line votes.

Some of the readers of the *MitchMessage* suggest that I sometimes sound too partisan in my reporting on doings in the House. But after bruising fights that seem as if they are only political, and not policy-oriented, such as the debates I discuss above, it is hard not to feel like the tough issues usually turn into a win-lose battle and much of the tactics are related to the next election campaign and not related to the issues at hand.

On the other hand, I frequently don't report in the *MitchMessage* on the dozens of bills that passed over the last two weeks that weren't the least bit political and were simply technical bills or bills that were perfected in committee. One absolutely critical matter that could have turned political, but didn't, was the bill to provide the provider taxes used to fund what is left of the Oregon Health Plan. This week we passed, without dissent, HB 3057. This measure extends the sunset on taxes on hospitals, nursing homes, and managed care plans that support care for 24,000 Oregonians who are a part of OHP standard. What makes these taxes different is that the institutions taxed all agree on the system, which provides matching funds to get federal Medicaid money for services. The effect of the taxes, generally speaking, is for the institutions to pay $1.00 in taxes and get $1.60 returned to pay for services rendered.

We passed a bill (SB 863) limiting, although not eliminating, robo-calls. It had universal support in the House. We passed several important healthcare bills, such as one (SB 656) clarifying how optometrists may treat glaucoma. There were some important health insurance bills, such as our concurrence on HB 2214 requiring transparency about the amount people will be charged for co-payments when they receive services and SB 8 requiring health insurance plans covering chemo-therapy to cover oral chemo-therapy agents. And we moved SB 191, which includes some important reforms in the long-term care insurance market. None of these turned partisan.

And we passed important land-use measures and key education bills, including the best pre–K and the best K–12 budget we have had since I joined the House. It felt good to be able to vote for education budgets and feel we had done some good. I'm afraid I won't have that same feeling about the higher education budget and expect I will vote against that budget. Although an important difference in being in the majority is that you have to take more responsibility for the budget process. In the minority I could vote against any budget I felt was inadequate. In the majority I might need to provide the 31st vote for budgets that have been crafted by the Ways and Means process, even if I think the budgets are inadequate. More later on that issue.

The Health Care Committee struggled with several very difficult bills concerning professional licensing boards, such as the Board of Medical Examiners. It is my intention to spend some of the interim dealing with how these boards balance their obligation to protect the public with their need to protect individual professionals. This is not an easy balance. Last week the *Portland Tribune* published a story by Peter Korn, indicating a significant failure of the nursing licensing board to protect the public. I have gotten approval from the Speaker to reopen the Health Care Committee for an informational hearing on that situation, as the first step in examining how all of the health professional licensing boards do their difficult job.

I think we really will be done by June 29. That should make these next two weeks very exciting. Keep in touch.

The MitchMessage
July 8, 2007—Post-session Message

I was seated at my House floor desk watching the people streaming onto the House floor. The gavel had just dropped on the adoption of the resolution to adjourn *sine die* (without a day) and I sat stunned. It was just after noon on June 28, and we had worked the final two to three days in an orderly fashion. It was not like anything I had experienced during my prior two sessions in the House.

In my *MitchMessage* just after the 2005 session ended I wrote "As you must know we adjourned *sine die* at 6:21am on Friday, August 5 after a marathon session that had begun nearly 20 hours earlier. It was a brutal experience and a totally dysfunctional approach to completing the work of the 73rd Legislative Assembly. After taking two three-day holidays during the last couple of weeks, the Speaker insisted on keeping us in session all night, rather than adjourning late in the evening and returning the next morning to finish in daylight and with due deliberation." In a quieter adjournment the 2003 session adjourned on August 27.

This calm and orderly process was symbolic of the way the whole session went. We had our drama and our excitement, but mostly it was calm and orderly. This message will focus on the happenings of the final two weeks of the session. In a couple of weeks, when I get enough distance from it for a proper perspective, I'll send out an overall review of the session.

Speaker Merkley announced very early in the session that we would adjourn *sine die* on June 29. That seemed completely ridiculous to those of us who were accustomed to working until August. But the schedule was designed to adjourn at the end of June, and adjourn we did — one day ahead of schedule.

The period began a little slowly. For the first part of the week the Republicans came into the chamber with the opening call, went through preliminaries, and then asked permission for a recess for a Republican caucus. They then disappeared for an hour or so and got back to work after 11am. Then on several days they would make a motion to withdraw some bill or other from one of the committees. It seemed to be both a stalling tactic and an opportunity to get one of our vulnerable members on the record with a bad vote. (As I said in previous messages, robo-calls or mass mailings were sent out the day the votes were cast.) The debate on the vote to withdraw would begin and be relatively brief, since generally it was clear that they didn't have the 31 votes to succeed on the motion. They would do a call of the House, which brought committees meeting at the same time to a stop, and then would request a voice roll-call vote. This whole business would take about 45 minutes. If I remember correctly, they repeated the process five times one day. I think they only succeeded getting a bill to the floor twice during the period, but both of those bills, including one that would create the office of Lieutenant Governor, were referred back to committee or move to the Senate to die.

The Speaker stayed very calm during these shenanigans. He simply made clear that we were going to complete the day's agenda even if we needed afternoon, evening, and weekend sessions to do so. And after a couple of late evening sessions and a Saturday session, things pretty much got serious during the last week. Then the main problem was coordinating our agenda with the Senate leadership. The Senate leadership seemed determined to complete their business early and closed down the committees relatively early. One of my bills, HJR 18, got caught in this web. The bill to refer to the voters a constitutional amendment on the right to health care passed the House. But I was informed that it wasn't going to be moved out of the Senate Rules committee — even though I had the votes to pass it in the Senate. I had a bit of a meltdown over that news. HJR 18 was not only my key bill of this session; it felt like the key bill of my career. But with the help of the House caucus leadership a deal was struck that the bill would be moved during the February session. I got a memo, signed by the leadership of both chambers that they would do everything in their power to make sure that happened.

We did manage to pass several measures to the people for votes over the next two years. The most notable was SJR 4, which is the Healthy Kids plan. This will ask the voters to put the plan into the constitution, including an 84.5-cent per package increase in the cigarette tax. The new revenue would provide health insurance for most of the uninsured children who are legal residents of Oregon. I believe this will be voted upon in November 2007. We also passed HJR 15, which asks the voters to modify the double-majority voting requirement on property tax elections. It would allow a single majority at regular primary elections and regular general elections. It will be on the ballot in November 2008.

As usual we passed several key budgets during the final two weeks of the session. Both the higher education budget and the human services budget received large majorities in the House. Although both budgets provided large increases over the prior budget, I voted against both of them. They were, in fact, about as good as could have been achieved in this session and I would not have provided the vote to sink either of them. But our investment in both of those areas is pitiful compared to most of the progressive states in the Union. Our treatment of higher education over the last 20 years is particularly shameful. It's time we figured out a dedicated source of funding for higher education in Oregon.

On the positive side of the budgetary ledger we passed a great budget for the Oregon Student Assistance Commission. Funds are included in this budget to implement the Shared Responsibility Model, which changes the calculation for grants to include factors other than the cost of education. Now the Opportunity Grant Award will vary by income level and family size and will provide much more security about the total funds that will be available to the student over the full college experience. This new model passed out of the House Education Committee and was supported by the Oregon Student Association and by the Governor's office. In addition, we passed an adequate construction budget for both higher education and for the community colleges.

Other budgets had interesting twists included within them. For example, the budget for the Parks and Recreation Department included funds for the Capitol grounds to become a state park. That seemed completely appropriate since I consider the Capitol to be "the Peoples' building." The Capitol receives tens of thousands of visitors each year. The Government Standards and Practices Commission budget provided for an increase in staff that will allow the agency to do its difficult job. The name of the agency will be changed to the "Ethics Commission." That is going to be quite important because we increased the Commission's responsibilities with the passage of SB 10, which changes the legal standards for legislators and other public officials.

And finally, the budget allocation for the Office of Health Policy and Research included sufficient funds for the office to implement the Hospital Acquired Infection Reporting Program. This program was passed in HB 2524, which was sponsored by Rep. Carolyn Tomei and me. It passed out of the Senate during this last two-week period after passing easily in the House. It was one of our few bills that, having been sent to the Ways and Means Committee, actually escaped with a budget allocation. This was an important bill, supported by the hospital community and by consumer advocates alike.

As I think about the budgets we passed my frustration returns with the whole Ways and Means process, which seemed to me to have significant perverse elements within it. There are two powerful nexus of power in the legislature. The first is the official process headed by the President of the Senate and the Speaker of the House. This is the official structure of the legislature, including the four caucuses and the formal committee structure of the legislature. And then there is the Ways and Means process, headed by the Ways and Means co-chairs — this session Senator Kurt Schrader and Rep. Mary Nolan. The Ways and Means process seems almost like a shadow legislature. The main constitutional task of the legislature is to produce a balanced budget. Ways and Means does that difficult task admirably.

The budget process begins with the presentation of the Governor's budget. His budget is produced before the legislature comes into session, using as its base the most recent official state revenue forecast. The co-chairs go to work producing the co-chairs' budget, which includes policy change decisions they make unilaterally. That budget version, coming early in the session, takes into account the most recent revenue forecast. The several W&M sub-committees, guided by the co-chairs' budget, go to work crafting the dozens of agency-specific budgets that ultimately comprise the state's budget. The sub-committees seem to have a great deal of power in crafting these budgets, within the guidelines.

None of that is what I consider perverse. Here is the perverse element. While the W&M process is working, grinding out the budgets and spending most of the available money, the policy committees, such as the House Health Care Committee I chair, are hard at work producing policy-relevant bills. If those bills have no significant budgetary impact they flow on to the House and the Senate for a vote. The exception is if a bill has relevance to another policy committee. In that case, it goes to another committee for policy consideration and then on to the floor. But if a bill passed out of a committee is deemed to have a non-trivial budget impact, it is referred on to the Ways and Means Committee. This decision comes about after the Legislative Fiscal Office asks affected state agencies to estimate the impact of the bill on agency resources. If the estimate comes back more than $50,000 it is automatically sent to W&M. Sometimes, inexplicably, it goes to Ways and Means even if without a fiscal impact.

In Ways and Means, producing the budget has the first priority, and the budget bills spend most of the money available. So while that process is going on the bills referred to the committee begin to produce a logjam of bills waiting for action — action that isn't going to happen until the budgets are done. By the time the budget bills were produced, about the second week in June, there were about 250 bills waiting in line in the Ways and Means committee. While it wasn't clear what selection criteria were being used, some of them began to pop up in one or another of the sub-committees. Almost none of the discussions seemed to be about fiscal matters; rather it seemed the bills were getting fresh policy scrutiny. Some of the bills emerged and were passed during this last two weeks. Some, even some with zero fiscal impact, did not get a hearing. All of this led to my feeling that the system was perverse.

Several of my bills passed during the last two weeks. HB 3270 is a bill to create a process for systematically hand recounting a probability sample of ballots from each county during the regular November general election. It is a good bill, intended to give our citizens confidence in our vote counting machines. I also worked on SB 1040, which allows school children to self-medicate in cases of asthma and several allergies. It took a conference committee, but it finally passed.

Other important bills that passed included one that regulates the use of non-competing clauses, a bill to prevent selling gift cards with an expiration date, SB 1036 that allows school districts to tax new construction under certain circumstances, and a bill (HB 2263) eliminating the CIM and the CAM. SB 858 passed, providing collective bargaining rights to adult foster care home providers, as did HB 2082, reforming the signature-gathering process for initiatives. We managed to do some good work. It was overall a very successful session, and we have a special session coming up in February to clean up things that are left over.

The MitchMessage
January 27, 2008—February 2008 Special Session

Oregon's grand legislative experiment will begin on February 4 when the Oregon Legislature declares an "emergency" and calls itself back into session. This session, scheduled to adjourn no later than February 29, has been variously called an emergency session, an experimental session, and a special session. While it is, to some extent, all of those it represents the Legislature's attempt to bring Oregon's government into the 20th century (let alone the 21st century). It is an explicit test as to whether it will be possible for Oregon to become the 45th state to have annual legislative sessions.

It is clear that the world has become a bit more complex than it was in 1859 when the Oregon Constitution was written. And because of the rapid pace of society now it seems obvious to many, me included, that the idea of biennial legislative sessions no longer is a viable approach. The legislative leadership, Senate President Courtney and House Speaker Merkley, have established a very tight timeline for the session and are attempting to strictly limit the number of bills to be considered. House members were not allowed to introduce individual bills, although Senate members were each allowed a single bill. Each of the House committees, except Rules, Ways and Means, and Revenue, were allowed to introduce one bill. Priority is being given to bills that will have broad support in the body and to bills that are stimulated by events since the end of the 2007 session and are perceived to need work before the 2009 session. If a successful session can be produced we expect to consider, during the 2009 session, a referral to the voters of a constitutional amendment that would authorize annual sessions.

I'm really looking forward to the session, partly because I enjoy being in the Capitol during session, and partly because I'm excited about a couple of the health-care bills that will be considered. On the other hand, this is going to be a challenging session because both the House and the Senate wing of the Capitol are in the midst of a major renovation. That work is scheduled to be completed in November. Consequently, none of the members will have an office during February. The facilities people have put up 90 carrels in several offices throughout the central portion of the Capitol. My staff will be using a desk in what was the Secretary of State's Election Division office. Each space includes senators and representatives, Democrats and Republicans. If you are looking for me during the session, I expect to be using my desk in the House chamber as my office, just like in the good old days. There will be pages on duty all day, delivering messages to the members. And we will have good computer access on the floor.

On Friday my House Committee on Health Care approved two concepts to be introduced on the first day of the session, one of which was referred over from the Rules Committee. LC 62 is a slimmed down version of a bill that was introduced during the 2007 session. The bill includes a modest increase in the number of children covered under the Oregon Health Plan. Currently children covered under OHP need to be re-enrolled every six months. This bill would increase the enrollment period from six to twelve months and would require that the children maintain their coverage as long as they remain eligible under the current enrollment criteria. The second part of the bill would create a grant program to fund up to four community-based demonstration projects focusing on creating more effective ways to deliver health-care services in order to reduce costs, improve the quality of medical care, and increase access to care in a community. This bill has broad bipartisan support and passed unanimously out of committee.

The other concept is a referral of the HOPE amendment to the voters in the November 2008 election. The referral, a constitutional amendment to declare that legal residents of Oregon have a right to affordable and effective health care, stirred up a great deal of debate in the committee with testimony in favor of and opposed to the referral. The debate turned out to be a very interesting philosophical discussion, that all of the parties seemed to enjoy. I was amused to read the following in the blog of Steve Buckstein of the conservative Cascade Policy Institute — *"After our prepared testimony the committee members asked us a number of questions, giving us the opportunity to expand on our position. Chairman Mitch Greenlick seemed to enjoy the back-and-forth; at one point likening it to a good college debate."* It passed on a straight party line vote.

This bill is being discussed during this session, even though it does not yet have bipartisan support, because of an agreement that was reached with the legislative leadership during the 2007 session that we would consider it in February, rather than at the end of the 2007 session. I am hoping to temper the feelings of the Republican members that this is a ploy to affect legislative races — which I certainly hope it doesn't become.

The proposals that are likely to come before us include several very critical issues, including bills to deal with the fallout of the sub-prime crisis, increases for Oregon State Police, some major capital projects, and a couple of proposals to help returning veterans. Recent events, such as the OHSU malpractice cap court case and the U.S. Dept. of Justice report on the Oregon State Hospital, will likely have an impact on the session. Fallout from both of those events seems hard to ignore. Constraining all of these considerations is the relatively modest amount of revenue available to deal with any of the very large number of requests that require increased expenditures. And hanging over all of us is the fact that we will receive a new revenue forecast on February 8. While the guesses on that forecast range between very bad and neutral, nobody expects a shower of new revenue to be falling from the sky.

I'm planning to send a mid-session *MitchMessage* reporting on our progress and am scheduling a couple of town halls after the end of the session to be held jointly by Senator Avakian and me. And as usual, please keep in touch as events unfold.

 ## The MitchMessage
February 17, 2008

The 2008 Special Session is half over. The first two weeks of the session produced many interesting moments and even some accomplishments. Opening day began with some fireworks and with a wonderful show of courtesy. The fight began over one element of the proposed House rules. In past special sessions the rules prohibited minority reports. The proposed rules for this session allowed minority reports, but only under limited conditions. The minority caucus was not happy with different alternative proposals offered by the Speaker and chose a futile floor debate instead.

The minority report process is an important tool for allowing minority opinion to be expressed on the House floor, but it also is an extraordinary tool for promoting political theatre. During a regular session a minority report may be proposed as an alternative to a bill that passed out of committee. The minority report presents an alternative to the bill that came from the committee and is debated and voted upon before consideration of the original bill. It is the closest we come to amending a bill on the floor of the House. So we began the first day with a spirited debate on the rights of the minority.

Since I remember what it was like in the minority, I would have preferred a somewhat looser version of the rule.

But the debate did offer an opportunity for the Republican caucus to act in a classy manner. Rep. Chris Edwards, a Democrat from Eugene, was ill with the flu on opening day. Dave Hunt, the majority leader asked Bruce Hanna, the Republican leader, to provide a courtesy vote on the rules so Chris didn't have to leave a sick bed to come to vote on the rules. Rep. Hanna agreed to do that and made a gentle statement about how he hated the rules, but would provide the 31st vote to pass them as a goodwill gesture to begin the session. It was a very cool gesture.

The biggest news of the first week was the presentation of the most recent revenue forecast for the remainder of the biennium. The State Economist presented a pessimistic forecast, predicting that revenues would be $183 million less that the projection used to create the biennial budget. We were pretty cautious in creating the 2007–2009 budget so that number didn't trigger any reductions in currently authorized programs. But it did put a damper on the hopes for program additions many of us brought into the session.

Life in the House Committee on Health Care was also interesting during the first week of the session. The House rules required that we act upon any House bill by Tuesday, February 12. This was not a problem because we only had two House bills before us. Both of them produced some excitement, however. HB 3614 is an important bill that proposes two things. The first section of the bill changes the way children are covered under the Oregon Health Plan, providing a 12-month period of eligibility, rather than the six-month period currently in law. Because of churning in the population that act alone would add, on the average, about 18,000 children to the health plan in addition to the 82,000 already covered.

The second part of HB 3614 would stimulate (and partially fund) four demonstration projects aimed at increasing the effectiveness of community health care by introducing concepts such as the primary care home into our health-care system. Both elements of the bill were strongly supported by all members of the committee. But several surprises entered the debate on the bill. First, the Department of Human Services strictly interpreted some language of the bill to conclude that a massive program would be required to achieve what they thought we were asking them to do. That triggered their putting a $190 million price tag on the measure. By carefully amending the measure to ensure it only proposed what we intended it to propose, the price tag was reduced to $1 million, at least for the 2007–2009 biennium. The bill passed out of the committee on a 9–0 vote, but is now in the Ways and Means Committee, both because of the price tag for this biennium and because of the potential cost of increasing the caseload of children in OHP in future biennia.

The other bill in the committee, HJR 100, triggered the most interesting debate I have observed in any legislative committee. This bill refers the HOPE amendment to the voters for the November 2008 election. It asks the voters to determine whether access to health care is a right of all Oregon citizens and further directs the legislature to create a plan to ensure that access to care is available for Oregonians. A fascinating debate followed testimony on both sides of the issue. The question of the nature and basis of rights produced an actual philosophical debate that was clearly enjoyed by all of us on the committee. The bill passed to the floor on a straight party-line vote.

The floor debate this last Wednesday was a continuation of the committee discussion. I was scheduled to lead the floor debate, which caused me to bone up on the nature of rights. The debate was so interesting that the story about it ended up on the front page of *The Oregonian* (above the fold). The bill passed to the Senate, also on a straight party-line vote. I had hoped that the Republican caucus would allow their members to vote their conscience on the bill, and I believe I could have gotten at least three Republican votes had that happened. But that isn't the way it turned out. The bill is now in the Senate Rules Committee, where it died during the 2007 session. If you have a view on the HOPE amendment, please let your senator know.

We passed several other interesting bills out of the House during the first two weeks, including SB 1080A, which requires applicants to provide proof of legal presence when applying for an Oregon driver's license. You can imagine the debate on that issue. I was one of fifteen members voting no on the bill. While I believe that Oregon licenses should be issued to actual residents of the state I also believe that bill is flawed in many ways.

We also passed HB 3630A, which regulates home mortgage loan foreclosure consultants and equity purchasers and HB 3631A, which prohibits retailers from selling children's products that were subject to a recall. It astounded me to learn that it is NOT illegal in Oregon to sell recalled products. We passed HB 3612A which increases energy conservation goals for state agencies and HB 3616 which requires health benefit plans to provide coverage for services rendered by licensed professional counselors or licensed marriage and family therapists when they cover services by other professionals providing the same or similar services.

I am looking forward to the next two weeks as we struggle with other difficult issues. I think the leadership is close to getting a budget deal, which will certainly help us move along. We could have some conflict between those whose first priority is getting out of town as quickly as possible and those who believe that we should conclude the most important business before us and not leave important issues stuck in committees in our rush to go home. It was a difficult task to get us together to explore the feasibility of annual sessions and I believe that proposition will be viewed most favorably the extent to which we provide important accomplishment. We all want to get home and we have a solid deadline of February 29. I don't think we will have proven anything if we leave a couple of days early, but avoid dealing with issues of importance to the future of the state.

I have been hearing from you on the issues of children's health care, global warming, air pollution and alternative energy, the home mortgage situation, full-day kindergartens, affordable housing, and the farm-to-school program. Keep in touch.

The MitchMessage
March 1, 2008—Post Special Session Message

The "great experimental" 2008 Special Legislative Session ground to a halt last Friday — a week early. My overall impression of the experiment is that we need a session each year, but that we need to make sure that the session is long enough to deal with the critical issues. We did some serious work in the three weeks of the session. But we also left some serious business on the table, mostly because the Senate President Peter Courtney's number one priority was ending the session early. Consequently, he shut down the Senate process prematurely.

First, let me share some of the accomplishments of the session. When we received the February revenue forecast report and the report revised the 2007–2009 forecast downward by $183 million, the value of annual sessions became immediately manifest. So the recasting of the biennial budget became the number one priority of the session. This turned out to be a manageable task because we had budgeted pretty conservatively during the 2007 regular session. (To be honest, that conservative approach made many of us very unhappy as critical programs were left underfunded.) The keystone to recasting the budget was our ability to use about $140 million that was reserved for adding to the rainy day fund as an umbrella for the current rainstorm. That still left us a little money to do a few key things, like putting more state troopers on the road and improving access to community-based long-term care for frail senior citizens.

A major problem facing the legislature was a ballot initiative proposed by Republican activist Kevin Mannix that purports to be tough on property crime and is estimated to add as much as $400 million to the biennial prison budget. (Oregon is already number one in prison spending.) A bipartisan, bicameral group of legislators, working with district attorneys from across the state, crafted a stronger alternative measure (SB 1087) to be referred to the voters in order to compete with the Mannix initiative. This measure focuses on increasing penalties for repeat property crime offenders and providing resources for substance abuse treatment for addicted first-time offenders. It will go to the ballot in November, with the requirement that if both measures pass, the one with the most votes will become law.

It is interesting to note how things come up between normal sessions that require quick fixes that can only happen during a legislative session. Full-day kindergarten is not required in Oregon. School districts are only required to offer half-day kindergarten and are only reimbursed under the state formula for the half-day. And kids are not required to attend school until they are seven years old. But many school districts, including Portland Public Schools, decided to make full-day kindergarten available. Some districts provided the funds to pay the full cost of full-day kindergarten, while others made the second half of the day available on a fee basis. Some did what Portland did, which was to use Title 1 funds (federal funds to improve the education of poor children) to pay for it in some schools, while making it available for a fee in other schools. Then an Oregon Attorney General ruling decreed that it was illegal under Oregon law for a public school district to charge tuition for a basic education service, such as kindergarten. To give the Department of Education time to solve this complicated issue we passed SB 1068, which allows districts to charge for the second half-day kindergarten for this year and the next two years. It was a small matter, but one that needed a simple fix.

The battle over the authorization of $200 million in construction bonds (SB 5555) for the University of Oregon's basketball arena lit up the House chamber for a bit. I had received a great deal of email against approving the bonds for the arena. I was troubled by many aspects of the project, but what troubled me the most was that the authorization was packaged with a total of $335 million in capital projects, most of which are worthy projects.

I began the floor debate on the capital package with a motion to refer the bill back to the Joint Committee on Ways and Means to separate the arena project from the other projects so that it could be debated on its own merit. That motion was handily defeated, as it appeared to me that many members were happy to have the cover of burying the arena within a package of projects. That led to my decision to discuss the merits of the arena project on the floor. I argued that it was unseemly to build the most expensive basketball arena on any college campus in the United States when the University of Oregon was in such poor financial shape. The University's students are complaining loudly about the condition of their dorms and the difficult financial situation they face because of high tuition. And faculty members are leaving our university system in droves because of the low salaries we pay our faculty compared to what comparable universities pay their faculty. But my arguments fell on deaf ears, and I was one of only five members who voted against the bill.

We passed some other good bills during the session. HB 3631 requires retailers to remove unsafe and recalled toys from their shelves. It amazed most of us that Oregon law did not prohibit retailers from selling recalled items. And we made some useful changes to the laws dealing with the sub-prime mortgage situation. SB 1064 placed restrictions on mortgage loan originators and HB 3630 makes changes to foreclosure laws allowing for more complete notification to homeowners facing foreclosure, ending "rescue mortgage" scams and placing restrictions on both foreclosure consultants and "equity purchasers." But the Senate refused to take the time to consider HB 3603, which passed the House, and would have placed limits on prepayment penalties and would also have required full disclosure of yield spread premium fees.

I also received a great deal of email supporting HB 3601, which creates a position in the State Department of Education to finish the establishment of the Oregon Farm-to-School Garden program to aid in getting local produce into local schools for student meals. An *Oregonian* article this week provided some evidence that this is viewed as a mixed bag from the perspective of the primary-grade students. It appears that the kids loved the cherry cobbler that came from the program, but were not quite as enthusiastic about the roasted beets that showed up with their pizza. Some reported that the beets looked like rotten potatoes, and others reported that they would not taste the beets "no matter what." But in truth it is going to be a wonderful program for the kids, the schools, and the farm community and it was broadly supported.

And finally we come to the health agenda, the subject I hold closest to my heart. First, HB 3614, the bill I described in the last *MitchMessage*, would have done two things. The first part of the bill would have extended the eligibility period for children on the Oregon Health Plan from six months to twelve months. That would have added 18,000 children to OHP when equilibrium was reached. The second part of the bill would have funded four community health-care delivery demonstrations to improve the delivery of and access to health care in Oregon. The bill ended up in the Joint Committee on Ways and Means and didn't move. But both parts of the bill got committee attention. A main Ways and Means bill included funding and authorization for two of the four demonstrations. And the main budget reconciliation bill included the following budget note: *"The Department of Human Services is directed to report to the Emergency Board by September 30, 2008 on eligibility duration and re-enrollment policies for the state's Children's*

Health Insurance Program and the Medicaid Poverty Level Medical program for children. The report should include an assessment of the impacts of re-enrollment policies on health status, program caseloads, administrative costs, and the 2009–11 biennial costs from extending the eligibility period of the Medicaid Poverty Level Medical program for children from six months to twelve months." Perhaps that will get us there and while it isn't even half-a-loaf, it is a few tasty slices.

The story on the HOPE Amendment is a much less happy one. After we passed HJR 100 out of the House, as I reported in the last message, I requested that Senate President Courtney assign the bill to the Senate Committee on Health and Human Services. But Sen. Courtney, instead, sent it to the Senate Rules Committee, with a subsequent referral to the Joint Committee on Ways and Means. The Ways and Means referral was made, even though the resolution had a fiscal analysis indicating the resolution had no fiscal impact. When I began working to get the bill out of the Rules Committee neither my advocate allies nor I were able to get any action. I then, with the backing of my caucus leadership, went to the Senate President to ask for his support for moving the bill to the floor. He refused to do anything, saying if I had the votes it would pass, and if I didn't it wouldn't pass. Well, I was pretty certain that if it got to the floor it had the votes to pass.

I then showed President Courtney the agreement he had signed in June that said passing HOPE in the February Session would be a top priority and promising to do everything possible to move it. His reply was that his top priority was finishing the session early and he would do nothing to help move the bill. As you can imagine, I was bitterly disappointed and saddened by that interaction and by realizing that once again HOPE would die in the Senate. While I don't consider myself naïve, I had to face the hard reality that for some people a signed promise means something, and for others it doesn't. And it isn't always easy to assess an individual's integrity in advance of the difficult situation. But I eventually came to know that what works best for me, even in the political world, is to continue to assume the best of people, until they prove me wrong. □

<table>
<tr><td>CHAPTER
4</td><td></td></tr>
</table>

THE VALUE OF A SUPERMAJORITY — AND THE CHALLENGE

OREGON HOUSE OF REPRESENTATIVES, 2009–2010

THE CONTEXT

The election of 2008 produced a Democratic supermajority in both the House and the Senate. The 36–24 Democratic edge in the House and the 18–12 count in the Senate obviously made it easier to move a progressive agenda, especially on bills that only required simple majorities. On the other hand, because of the heterogeneous nature of the Democratic caucuses, it was by no means a slam-dunk to get 36 and 18 votes for bills increasing revenue. There was a huge financial crisis looming over the legislature during its sesquicentennial session — the nation's sudden economic downturn and its effect on Oregon and on most other states. Consequently, the dominant theme of the messages in this chapter is the struggle to close the massive shortfall between the projected revenue and the cost of maintaining the current level of state services. This was true even though the level of services approved in the prior budgets had been reduced significantly over the past decade. Much of the session was characterized by our thrashing about exploring potential sources of new revenue, agonizing over the catastrophic impact of possible program cuts, and hoping against hope that promised stimulus aid from the federal government would arrive in time and in sufficient magnitude to save the day. The heroine was tied to the railroad tracks and the train was approaching, as we were reminded once again that our primary constitutional responsibility is to produce a balanced budget.

A second major theme that dominates the messages from this session is health-care reform. The health-care reform effort really got rolling during the 2009 session as I took the reform proposals of the Oregon Health Fund Board, chartered in the previous session, and crafted two major bills; one creating the Oregon Health Authority and one implementing a hospital tax

147

and a health insurance tax. The funds from those taxes would bring $1 billion to Oregon, funding health care for between 150,000 and 200,000 people and would provide for hundreds, if not thousands, of health-care jobs.

The messages follow the development of HB 2009, which ultimately turned into a 613-page bill that streamlined the state's management of health and health-care matters. There is even a message sent out this session that provides a history of modern health-care reform in Oregon, beginning with the formation of a commission on health care for the uninsured in 1989. This commission invented the idea of the Oregon Health Plan, which John Kitzhaber, as Senate President, guided through the legislature. This chapter also comments on the legislature's desire to begin the process of creating a health insurance exchange, before Barack Obama was elected president. However one feels about "ObamaCare," the Oregon Health Insurance Exchange proposal is certainly an Oregon proposal.

The messages in this chapter discuss why I chose to sponsor one or another bill, suggesting there is a plethora of reasons. That is especially true since I had introduced about forty bills during the session. Many of the bills were introduced because they were important to a person or to a small group of people. An example of this was the bill to name Jory soil as the state soil. And on the other end of the spectrum were bills introduced because I wanted to raise issues I considered critical to the future of the state or of the metropolitan area, such as my bills to protect Forest Park. This creative, political, and legislative tension is reflected in one way or another across the messages from most of the sessions.

The role of the legislature in the governance of the state may dominate these messages as they inevitably are legislative branch-centric, yet there is ready reference to the role of the Governor and agency staff in the dance of legislation. My reminder that everything is about 31, 16, and 1 is not to under-emphasize the importance of the "1" and his staff. When there is a good relationship between the Governor and the legislature things go much more smoothly. This session was one of those with a smooth working relationship that made a significant restructure of the executive branch possible. In fact, the creation of HB 2009 was developed cooperatively with agency leadership and the Governor's staff. So too, were the negotiations on the hospital and the health insurance tax discussed in detail in this chapter. That relationship made it possible to succeed in our reform efforts.

While there was a heavy focus on the difficulty in balancing the budget and on health-care reform, the *MitchMessage* report on several other interesting legislative activities reported during the session, ranging from the ridiculous to the sublime. Besides the naming of the state soil, there was the passage of the bill that requires state universities to interview at least one qualified minority candidate when hiring a head coach or an athletic director. This is the so-called "Rooney Rule" so named after a similar rule implemented in the National Football League. And at the other extreme we managed to craft a significant transportation package that provided resources to renew Oregon's multi-modal transportation infrastructure. There was wide agreement that the future of Oregon's business environment would be significantly enhanced by the rail, maritime, air and road projects in this package.

This session was enlivened by my proposal to reclassify tobacco products so as to require a physician's prescription for their purchase. News of this proposal went viral internationally and received press coverage from outlets as diverse as The Wall Street Journal, The Toronto Star, and Rush Limbaugh's talk show. It is safe to say that the publicity was not universally favorable. This proposal was among the top five of my career in engendering hostile email, mostly from outside my district and around the country. Other similar initiatives that occasioned impassioned, even vituperative responses include my attempts to secure fluoridation of Oregon's drinking water, a proposal to encourage stem-cell research, and an attempt to prevent members of the bicycling community from engaging in what I considered a dangerous practice. And the all-time worst, which will come in a later session, was the response to an assault-weapon ban that triggered the firing off of several thousand protesting messages over a period of several months.

Each message reports on what caused the most email traffic during the period covered. I sometimes speculate what life in the legislature was like without the advantage and the curse of email. Email comes to legislators in two different forms. First there is the message that comes when a constituent sits at the computer and composes a heartfelt message, similar to what would have been a letter in the "good old days." That message is clearly welcome and receives a quick, individual response that I compose personally.

Then there is the mass email campaign. An organization, such as the Sierra Club, pushes a button and sends a mass email to its mailing list, urging people on their list to copy the message and forward it to their legislators. Some are very sophisticated, targeting the message to the writer's own legislators. Some are not, targeting the messages to every member of the legislature. The former are still welcome and are answered, although each gets the same answer, usually sent by an aide. These messages are also useful because they help build the email address list for sending out the *MitchMessage*. The mass mail, sent to everybody, is annoying and can clog our mailbox with several hundred messages. Those messages are treated as the junk mail they are and are deleted as fast as they arrive.

This chapter reports on the 2010 Special Session, the second successful short session in a row. Its success led to a referendum measure sending a constitutional amendment to the voters. That amendment would authorize annual sessions, a long session in the odd years and a short session in the even years. The voters approved that amendment and the need for calling a special session in the even years was obviated.

On what was a sad note for me I failed once again, in the special session, to pass my proposed constitutional amendment on the right to health care. That convinced me to give up that fight and concentrate on my efforts to actually make it happen on an incremental basis. It was a somber moment when I decided to let the HOPE amendment rest in peace.

The MitchMessage
December 15, 2008 — Pre-session Report

I am eagerly awaiting the January 12 opening of Oregon's 75th legislative session, the Sesquicentennial session. We will be celebrating Oregon's 150th birthday on February 14, 2009. This session is likely to be a very challenging one because of the effect the world's financial situation is having on the Oregon economy. But I have been told that the Chinese symbol for the word *crisis* comprises the symbol for danger and the symbol for opportunity. And I tend to be a "glass-half-full" kind of person. Sometimes we are able to do things when the financial situation is dire that we could not do in good times. I will undertake a more detailed discussion about finances below.

Speaker Designate Dave Hunt announced the House of Representatives committee assignments last Thursday and I am very pleased with my assignments. I will be Chair of the House Committee on Health Care and will serve as a member of the Ways and Means Sub-committee on Human Services. Last session I was frustrated by the structural disconnect between the Committee on Health Care and the Human Services Sub-committee. This session, not only will I serve on the sub-committee, but also the sub-committee chair, Tina Kotek, will serve on the Health Care Committee.

In addition I will serve on the House Committee on Land Use. Land use is likely to be a central issue this session. The task force, whose charge was to take a "big look" at Oregon's land-use laws, will recommend significant changes to our land-use planning system. Coming to grips with those wide-reaching recommendations is likely to be a contentious, but important, task.

As usual, much of my effort will be devoted to guiding health-care bills through the House (and hopefully through the Senate and to the Governor's desk). Health-care system reform is going to be one of two big-ticket items this session, the other being transportation. In the 2007 session we passed SB 329 that created the Oregon Health Fund Board, charging it with developing a plan for moving Oregon towards universal access to health care and reforming the health-care system. The board spent more than a year crafting a plan, working with a cast of hundreds involved in many ways. The plan was released last month and I am working, with my health-care consultant Tom Burns, on a bill that is our view of what needs to be done to implement the OHFB report.

The bill, which will be five or six hundred pages long, proposes several things. First, it would create the Oregon Health Authority (OHA), bringing all of the state government health-care functions into the OHA. It proposes creating an OHA Board with several important independent functions aimed at reducing the cost of health care and improving the quality of the system. The bill proposes a Medicaid expansion, funded by provider taxes, designed to bring 100,000 children and 100,000 adults into the Oregon Health Plan. And it proposes a revitalization of Oregon's public health infrastructure, funded by a modest increase in tobacco taxes. I will keep you informed as that bill moves along (or doesn't).

The Health Care Committee, which will be meeting from 3pm to 5pm Monday, Wednesday, and Friday, will be very busy with other issues as well. During the last session the committee considered more than one hundred bills. I expect we will do the same this session. The committee worked very hard during the interim to craft a set of bills that will improve the way health professional licensing boards (such as the Medical Board) function. We did file those bills for early consideration, including one that increases the public participation on all of the boards. This naturally causes a great deal of unease among the boards and the professions they regulate. My legislative director, Tom Powers, and my health-care consultant, Tom Burns, did a great job investigating the situation and, working with our legislative counsels, drafting some very good legislation.

Of course everything this session will be affected by the financial crisis. The Governor built his budget on the basis of the most recent revenue forecast. This was a bad forecast, but the fear is that the upcoming forecasts in March and May will be even worse. The recent forecast indicates that we are about $150 million short of what is needed for the current budget period, which ends in June 2009. And the forecast also indicates that we are in the neighborhood of $1.5 billion (that is billion) short of what it would take to move the current level of services into the 2009–2011 biennium, without increasing existing services or adding new services. We have already heard from the Portland Public Schools and the Beaverton School District that the current services budget would present a significant problem for the school districts, even without reductions caused by the $1.5 billion shortfall already predicted.

And we all know that the national economy is in trouble and that trouble could easily produce new problems for Oregon. Consequently, we are all watching the situation very carefully and considering what can be done if things get worse. There are four kinds of action that would help the situation. First, we need to implement those things that would produce jobs very quickly. For example, we are considering moving forward bonding for building projects we have already approved. Construction jobs come on line very quickly. Next we need to approve new programs and projects that both provide family-wage jobs and solve pressing problems. The Governor's call for new sources of transportation funding to improve the transportation infrastructure is an example of things we will be looking at very carefully.

Next we will be looking for new sources of revenue to deal with pressing problems that will also bring large amounts of federal revenue into Oregon. The health-care reform plan we are working on is an example of that approach. We believe that if we can raise $600 million through a provider tax we will be able to use that money as a state match that will return to Oregon an additional $1 billion in federal funds to support the Medicaid expansion. That is an economic development program. And last, but not least, we will be considering how to cut obsolete services and obsolete or useless tax breaks. I expect those efforts will be easier in bad times than they are in good times.

I will share in my next message some of the legislative proposals I will be working on. And please continue to keep in contact with me as the session moves along and new issues arise. I cannot promise we will pass things you want, especially if they cost money, but we certainly will pay attention to your communications.

The MitchMessage
January 25, 2009

The opening day of session is always exciting, but the level of excitement was heightened this year because there were so many new members of the House. Seventeen of the sixty members of the House had not been at the opening session in 2007. (So much for term limits.) At 8:30 on the second Monday of January the House of Representatives gaveled in for the review of credentials and the swearing in of the House members. The Speaker, the Speaker Pro-tem, and the Clerk of the House were elected. And the rules were adopted unanimously without debate. The unanimous passage of the rules — the first time that has occurred since I have been in office, offered a positive, bipartisan start to the session. The House then adjourned and the chamber was prepared for a joint session of the House and the Senate to hear the Governor's State of the State address.

The joint session was wonderfully dramatic, with the senators, the ex-governors, and the Justices of the Supreme Court, the Appeals Court and the Tax Court each escorted into the chamber. The Justices were all in their robes. The Speaker of the House and the President of the Senate each gave short speeches before the Governor's address. Rabbi Michael Cahana, of Congregation Beth Israel in my House district, delivered the benediction. It was a great kick-off of the sesquicentennial legislative session. I remember how I was moved by the experience as a newly elected member of the House… and I was still moved as I entered my 4th term in office.

And then we got to work. There were a couple of hundred bills that had been pre-session filed by individual members, by the several interim committees and by the Governor. Each of those bills received its "first reading" in the House session that afternoon and during the regular session on Tuesday. Those bills were referred to the Speaker for assignment to the various committees so the committees could begin their work later in the week. The bill of most interest to me was HB 2009, which is the bill I designed with my health staffer Tom Burns, to begin consideration of the report from the Oregon Health Fund Board. That report proposes the first step toward healthcare reform in Oregon.

Life was a little confusing as we began the session since we were still in the middle of moving into the newly renovated wings of the Capitol. But after two weeks, it is beginning to feel like it is my office, rather than feeling as if I am temporarily sitting in some strange office. On the other hand, the lobbyists had no trouble finding me. By the end of the first day of session there was a line of lobbyists looking for an appointment to tell me about the bills that they thought I must support or the bills that it was urgent for me to oppose. And since I have a great influence on the fate of the bills in the Health Care Committee the health lobbyists presented the most compelling argument for access to my time. Harriet already has me scheduled into the second week in February with each hour that I am neither in committee nor on the floor filled with at least three 15-minute appointments. Some days I feel great empathy with that harried primary care physician running two patients behind all day long.

Of course, Oregon's financial situation dominates talk in the halls, in the caucus, and in our committees. I hesitate to quote numbers because they change as fast as I learn them. But currently the numbers look something like this: The unemployment rate in Oregon is up to 9 percent moving quickly toward 10 percent. Tax revenues for the current biennium are running significantly behind prior estimates and we are faced with an $800 million shortfall in the 2007–2009 budget period. That total budget was about $16 billion and we have only five months and less than $3 billion left in the 24-month budget period. The Governor made some adjustments, but he is only authorized to make across-the-board cuts in expenditures and that is not a very exacting tool. We have some year-end money budgeted for emergencies and we also have some rainy-day funds to help out. But frankly, we are waiting to see the scope of the federal stimulus package promised to help us through this crisis.

We also are working on a state stimulus package to help get the economy moving. The Joint Ways and Means Committee passed the first phase of the Legislature's economic stimulus plan and sent the bill to the floor of the House and Senate for a vote next week. The $176 million stimulus plan considered by the committee includes some $50 million for community colleges statewide and funding for various capital improvements to occur in all 36 counties and at all of Oregon's universities. These are all for construction and deferred maintenance projects that are already approved and are ready to go. The projects will be funded by bond sales that were scheduled to happen and that fit into the bonding budget provided to us by the Treasurer. What is different about these bills is that they are usually the last thing that comes from Ways and Means, rather than the first; because of the financial situation leadership felt that moving them now would get the jobs on the ground much more quickly.

But the real problem is the projected shortfall in the general fund budget we are considering for the 2009–2011 biennium. We heard hints that the next revenue projection will project a shortfall of at least $2.5 billion from what is needed to continue state services at their current level. And remember that 93 percent of the general fund budget is spent on three categories of services; education, public safety and prisons, and services to children, the aged, the disabled, and the sick. Unless we find other sources of revenue to supplement income tax revenues there will be some terrible cuts in services to our most vulnerable citizens. Since I am sitting on the Human Services Sub-committee of the Joint Ways and Means Committee I will have a front-row seat from which to observe and hopefully mitigate the true depth of the cuts and the impact they will have on Oregonians.

I believe we need to look at our whole approach to tax breaks and tax deductions. While we collect about $15 billion in general fund revenue from income taxes (the remainder of the budget comes from the lottery) we leave almost twice that much on the table in the form of tax deductions and tax breaks. We must begin to look at these "revenue expenditures" in the same careful way we look at fiscal expenditures. I continue to advocate periodic review of all of them so we can determine if each continues to meet the objectives they were designed to meet.

Given all of that bad news I continue to be optimistic that we will be able to do some very important things during this legislative session. As usual I have a long list of bills that I will be working. My legislative director, Tom Powers, is focusing on those bills, while Tom Burns, my health-care consultant, focuses on helping with my health-care agenda, particularly HB 2009. I continue to work on my long-term agenda, including creating the ultimate merger of PSU and OHSU and the extension to Salem of the Westside Express Service (WES) that will provide commuter service between Beaverton and Wilsonville. In addition, my agenda includes finding a way to shed more light on the relationships between drug companies and local physicians, safeguarding patient data in health-care computer systems, and improving the efficiency and effectiveness of the health-care system.

HB 2009 (which is currently 260 pages long) provides the first step for improving health care. The Oregon Health Fund Board was created by SB 329, which we passed last session. The Board was charged with creating a plan to move toward universal access to health care and with providing a blueprint for reducing the cost of health care, improving access to care, and improving the quality of care provided. HB 2009 outlines the structural first steps needed to begin movement in that direction. It proposes creating the Oregon Health Authority (OHA), which would comprise all of the state's health care and public health activities and provides that the OHA Board produce plans for the next legislative session for a variety of significant health-care system changes.

Included among these changes is the creation of a health-insurance exchange within which the state could combine its health-care purchases to make it easier for individuals and small groups to purchase affordable health insurance. The bill would also expand the Oregon Health Plan's covered population by adding 100,000 children and 100,000 adults to the plan. That expansion would be funded by provider taxes that would be used to bring $1 billion in additional federal funds into our health-care system. This would represent the largest economic stimulation package before us. We began hearing the bill in the Health Care Committee and are working closely with the other key committees in the House and the Senate to craft a bill that will be able to get the required 36 votes in the House, 18 votes in the Senate, and the Governor's signature.

However busy life gets in Salem I am always delighted to get visits from constituents or, at least, your email. If you are coming to Salem please let my office know so that I will be able to introduce you from the floor if the House is in session that day. And keep the email coming.

The MitchMessage
February 8, 2009

The economy dominates most conversations in the Capitol, as we struggle to reduce the budget by $800 million for the remainder of this fiscal year and to balance the 2009–2011 budget with an expected shortfall of $2.5 billion. As you can imagine I am getting lots of email and visits in the Capitol on this topic. Friday night I opened a very thoughtful email on the condition of education funding and asking for increased funding for K–12 education. It was late in the evening and I found myself responding much more fully than I usually do at that time of night after a difficult week. After writing that email response I decided I would share it more widely through this message. I wrote:

"I certainly agree with you. The problem is that the citizens of Oregon (including the citizens of our rich district) have refused to vote sufficient funds to keep services in our state at a reasonable level. When measure 5 passed (the 1.5 percent property tax limitation) the funding of schools was passed to the state, without providing any source of funding to pay for those schools. After that the citizens passed measure 11 (minimum sentences for crimes) which doubled our prison budget. We now spend more on prisons than we spend on higher education.

Oregon ranks 45th in the country on per capita local and state taxes, largely because most states have a property tax, an income tax, and a sales tax, shared among the local areas and the state. We have only two of those sources. And each time we vote to increase taxes, even on a temporary basis, the measure is referred to the voters and rejected. If I remember correctly the last time we proposed a modest sales tax it was rejected 80–20.

Currently we spend 92 percent of the budget on three things; education, public safety (including prisons), and services for the aged, poor, and disabled. We are now faced with a significant budget shortage. Our biennial budget (general funds and lottery funds) is about $17 billion. The severe economic downturn has caused major downward revisions in revenue estimates. (Remember when the revenue exceeds the forecast we send the money back to taxpayers in the kicker, rather than being able to save the surplus for a time like this.) We are told we need to cut about

$800 million out of the remainder of this biennium's budget. That is the five months left of the 24-month budget period. And we are told we need to reduce next biennium's budget by at least $2.5 billion. We hope the federal stimulus package will provide some relief, but that is not certain.

Assuming the budget is about $4 billion for each six-month period, we need to cut $800 million out of that last $4 billion. Imagine if education is excluded from these cuts and we can't shut down the prisons because of measure 11 and for other reasons. To balance the budget we would probably need to stop providing medical care under the Medicaid program (removing a couple of billion of federal dollars from Oregon), stop providing care for people in nursing homes, stop providing foster care, and other impossible things. And most of this we could not do even if we wanted to do so. Consequently schools are going to take their share of the hit. And we could do that same exercise for the 2009–2011 budget, which looks even bleaker.

Every day I visit with constituents who have very important messages to give me. "Don't cut funding to Headstart." "Don't reduce services to frail elderly." "Fully fund mental health services." "Increase mandatory sentences for sex offenders." "Provide free tuition at our universities for returning veterans." "Provide more support for poor college students." "Increase requirements for high school graduation." And on and on and on. And then over and over, "don't increase our tax burden during a recession" or "you can't tax your way out of a recession."

We are going to balance our budget, as our constitution requires us to do. And we are going to do it in a way that doesn't destroy the state. And perhaps we will even look for a way to increase revenue. But we are going to need to have our constituents behind us. And we are all going to have to find ways to mitigate the destruction to our families during this most difficult time."

I hope my constituent took this message the way it was intended, to be supportive. But as the Senate President said in today's *Oregonian*, it isn't clear that Oregonians realize just how difficult the situation really is. In fact, I am not sure I really realize how difficult it is going to be.

We have put a plan in place to address the problem. On February 4 the House passed HB 2157, which disconnected Oregon's tax code from the federal tax code for any recent and future federal actions. It particularly referenced the changes in the definition of taxable income made after December

31, 2008. We want to make sure that Oregon isn't whipsawed by congressional changes to the tax code taken in as a part of the federal stimulus package that would worsen Oregon's budget crisis.

The next day we passed SB 5562 and SB 338, the first phase of Oregon's own stimulus package. These bills authorized the bond sale to finance about $170 million of construction projects throughout Oregon. The project list included both new construction and deferred maintenance projects. The deferred maintenance projects were included to ensure that jobs were created in all 36 Oregon counties, at all seven universities and all 17 community colleges. These projects were approved first because they are shovel ready and just waiting for funding.

I was discouraged by the tone of the debate. As I have mentioned before, most of the real work of the legislature is done in committees. This bill came from the Joint Ways and Means Committee, which includes twelve members of the House — seven Democrats and five Republicans. The committee vote to move the bill to the floor with a "do pass" recommendation included a majority of both the Ds and the Rs. Yet the floor debate raged on about how the Republicans were not consulted and consequently how it was a terrible idea. It was discouraging, although I was pleased to note that all of the Republicans who had voted in favor of the bill in committee also voted for the bill in the final vote. There has been some criticism that we don't really know if the bill will stimulate the economy. And that is partly true — we do not have certainty. But the cost of the projects keep the state well within its recommended bonding authority and most would have likely been passed later in the session. It makes much more sense to get those projects moving through process to see if we can keep Oregonians working.

As Speaker Hunt has said on several occasions, "we choose action over inaction; jobs over unemployment."

Much of my attention has been spent working on our health-care reform package, especially HB 2009, the bill that would take the first steps toward reforming the health-care system as suggested in the Oregon Health Fund Board Report. I have been holding hearings on the bill in the House Health Care Committee. We are beginning to propose amendments to the bill as written and will have a significant amendment to consider as soon as the Legislative Counsel can draft it. The hospital association has generated most of the heat against our proposal to tax hospitals and health insurance plans to bring $1 billion of federal funds into Oregon to help save our health-care system. There is a $1 billion check sitting in Washington, DC with Oregon's name on it, waiting for us to put up our share ($600 million) and to ask for it.

Hospitals make a convincing case about how much they are suffering now, but they stretch reality with their whining that we should do something, but should not tax them. "Don't tax me, don't tax thee. Tax the man behind the tree." The reality is that the hospitals' financial woes, for those that have financial woes, are caused by the fact that we don't provide sufficient reimbursement for caring for Oregon Health Plan patients and the fact that as the economy worsens there is an increasing number of patients without health insurance flooding the hospitals. The provider tax, plus the extra $1 billion that would come into the system, would allow us to increase the reimbursement for OHP patients and would provide resources to add 100,000 children and 100,000 adults into the OHP. Those things should offset most or all of the tax paid by the hospitals, at least those hospitals that care for OHP patients and/or provide uncompensated care for people without health insurance. And it would reduce the number of uninsured from 600,000 to 400,000. We are doing everything possible to bring that money into Oregon as an important part of our economic recovery plan.

I have begun to receive emails, with the most active topics being support of paid family leave, commenting on cap and trade proposals, about global warming generally, about salmon fishing, and many suggesting we don't raise taxes. I also expect email to pick up as we continue hearings in the Land Use Committee on HB 2229, the bill to change land-use laws as proposed by the "big look" commission on land-use law reform. Please keep in touch and if you have specific suggestions on specific bills you might also contact my legislative director, Tom Powers.

The MitchMessage
February 22, 2009

I decided not to begin this message with what is the most pressing matter before the legislature. Rather, I want to note what are a couple of things on my personal agenda that mean the most to me. Tom Powers informed me that there are now more than 40 bills of which I am either the chief sponsor or one of the chief co-sponsors. Of course, they are not all likely to pass, or even to have a serious hearing. And most of my attention right now is on passing HB 2009, sponsored by my House Health Care Committee, rather than on any of my individual bills. When the caucus asked me to identify which of my bills were my priorities for this session, I was forced to think about the question and about my personal agenda.

There are a variety of reasons to sponsor a bill. Many of the bills I sponsor are modest solutions to simple problems suggested to me by constituents or by others. Those solutions are important to them, even though they are not of critical importance to others. The bills I have successfully sponsored on annexation are critical to my district and to a few other districts, but are irrelevant to many. My quest to name a state soil is relevant to a friend and to the soil scientists in the state. But some things I propose are critical to the long-term health of the state and to its citizens. And those are the bills that are closest to my heart — and are the hardest to accomplish. The first of those is HJR 18, a measure that would refer to a vote of the people in the November, 2010 election a constitutional amendment to declare that every citizen of Oregon has a right to affordable, effective, medically necessary health care. You will remember that I tried to put that on the 2008 ballot as an initiative, but fell short of the required signatures to achieve that. I will stay with that until it is accomplished.

The second critical bill is my proposal to create the ultimate merger of PSU and OHSU. I firmly believe that the two universities will inevitably merge to create a major research university in the Portland metropolitan area. I hope to hasten that day and to create a rational pathway for it to occur. The future viability of the Portland metropolitan area needs it and the two universities need it. I propose moving PSU out of the state system of higher education, expanding the public corporation board that currently oversees OHSU, putting PSU under that expanded board, and giving the board ten years to create incrementally a single university out of the two. If it is inevitable, let's do it in an orderly way.

And the third bill is HB 2408, which creates a task force to explore the continuation of the Westside Express Service (WES) from the terminus of its Beaverton to Wilsonville service down to Salem (and perhaps ultimately to Eugene and Corvallis). This is important to me both on its own merit and because it continues my campaign to make light rail, commuter rail, and intercity passenger rail service a significant part of the 21st century transportation system. The WES commuter rail service took 14 years to bring to fruition, as will its expansion. Therefore we need to start it on its way immediately. If you have not taken a ride on WES I recommend you do so. It is really cool. Take MAX or a bus to the Beaverton Transit Center and pick it up any weekday morning or afternoon.

As I said above, much of my time and energy are occupied shepherding HB 2009 that will begin the process of reforming Oregon's health-care system by creating an Oregon Health Authority (OHA) that consolidates the state government's health and health-care activities into a single agency. This should create some significant efficiency as state government addresses health-care issues and should move us toward consolidating the state's health-care purchasing power. The OHA board is charged with continuing the work of the Oregon Health Fund Board, including defining a new health insurance exchange, creating a quality institute, and finding ways to control the cost of health care for Oregonians. And it is charged with creating a clear, bright path to including 90 percent of Oregon's uninsured in the health-care system by 2015.

The bill will also expand the Oregon Health Plan coverage by 100,000 kids and 100,000 adults financed by a tax on large hospitals and health insurance plans. This is a very complicated process, including the negotiations on the very nature of the tax system. But the important thing is if we can find a reasonable and equitable way to implement that tax (and I believe we can) it will produce $600 million in matching funds that will bring *$1 billion* in federal Medicaid money into the state to put directly into the health-care system. We need that money, which is currently sitting in Washington, D.C. set aside for us, and will support 30,000 jobs in the health-care system.

Bringing this *$1 billion* into Oregon is increasingly important as the state of our economy deteriorates. The economic forecast delivered Friday increased the gloom around the Capitol. We thought we needed to cut $800 million out of the budget for the period ending June 30. It turned into more than $850 million. And we thought that the 2009–2011 budget was between $2 billion and $2.5 billion short. That turned into $2.9 billion. It is stunning. The potential consequences are unimaginable. While the federal stimulus money will help some in both periods, we clearly need to find some new source of revenue for the next four years, but that won't be easy. Further, new revenue won't be available for the current budget period. We are working seriously on this problem and we are getting a great deal of advice, including from my constituents.

The email flow has greatly increased the last two weeks. There have been three main topics stimulated by different advocacy groups. The children's groups, such as Stand for Children, have stimulated a great deal of mail suggesting we use reserve funds to temporarily save the local school systems from closing the school year early. That discussion is complicated because the Governor just said he would veto any budget that tapped the reserve funds for use in the current school year.

The second set of emails is stimulated by environmental groups, such as the Sierra Club, and encourages me to support the green legislative agenda, and most especially a cap and trade system to reduce carbon emissions and, therefore, to reduce global warming. This is a very complex issue and one I am watching closely. Since it is not my specific area of expertise, I am relying on my friends who are working the issue, including Representatives Ben Cannon, Jules Bailey, and Tobias Read. They are getting plenty of coaching from the sidelines.

And finally, I am getting a great deal of mail from my beer-loving constituents, who are outraged by a proposal that will raise the tax on beer produced in Oregon by an amount they characterize as a 1900 percent increase. The beer tax in Oregon has not been raised since 1982 and is currently at less than one cent per pint. The proposal will increase the tax to about 15 cents per pint, consequently the 1900 percent increase. I am not sure that bill will actually get to the floor for a vote.

Please keep the email coming and forgive me if I don't get a response back to you for a couple of days. Starting Monday there will be daily floor sessions at 10:15, frequently followed by a caucus meeting through the lunch hour. Then I have committee meetings from 1pm to 5pm. Since I answer most of my email myself, it is easy to fall behind.

The MitchMessage
March 8, 2009

We came home from Salem Friday and found a phone message on the district phone that began something like "I am a citizen of Oregon and I think you should stop wasting your time with stupid things and just focus on important things like jobs and the economy." (I am a citizen of Oregon is code for I am not one of your constituents, but listen to me anyway.) The message had an impact on me as it got me thinking about the nature of a legislative session.

Each of us has a list of the most important issues facing the state right now. I would nominate Oregon's economy, the health-care system mess, and providing sufficient revenue to fund properly the services required of state government. President Obama would probably name those three as key problems facing the nation and would likely add national security as a fourth. And if life was simple the legislature would meet for a week or so every couple of years, pass a few bills solving these problems and go home.

But the truth is we have a state to run and there are nearly 4,000,000 people who are affected in many ways by things that go on in Oregon. We passed four bills during Friday's meeting of the House Health Care Committee. The Senate, without a dissenting vote, had passed them all previously. It took us 30 minutes to deal with all four bills. They all could have seemed trivial but, in fact, each was important to some group of people and at least one seemingly trivial bill was potentially important to many people.

One of the bills we passed changed a statute requiring the Board of Nursing to issue wallet-sized licenses to nurses when their licenses are renewed every two years. How trivial is that? (I didn't receive a single email urging action on the bill.) Well, it turns out not trivial at all. It is required that an employer ascertains that a nurse is currently licensed as a part of hiring that nurse. The current practice is that the nurse shows the potential employer that card as proof of being licensed.

But the Board could restrict or revoke that license at any time during the two-year period and wants a potential employer to check the Board's website to determine if a nurse is in good standing. Consequently, the Board wanted the ability to stop issuing any hard copy certification of licensure. All of a sudden, the bill did not seem so trivial. Passing it did not improve Oregon's economy, it did not reform the health-care system, it did not restore the $1.8 million taken out of the Cultural Trust's balance of $11.8 million to help deal with the 2007–09 shortfall — but it was not trivial.

This week we did pass legislation necessary for balancing the budget for the remainder of the 2007–09 budget. It was not easy and required doing some unpopular things. For example, we swept up 12 percent of the reserves of the cultural trust and removed some funds from the 911 system intended to begin enhancements that will now be delayed by four months. None of these so-called fund sweeps affected any operating expenses. And our choice was to capture those unspent funds or face the real threat that most schools in Oregon would close early. We made that tough call to take those funds to offset even more disastrous cuts. But with judicious use of federal stimulus funds and a modest use of some reserves we mitigated several potential disasters. Still many of these cuts were really painful.

We continue to move forward on health-care reform, on a transportation package to deal with our ailing transportation system, and on seeking a way to improve the revenue picture for the 2009–11 biennium's budget.

We are moving toward perfecting HB 2009 in the Health Care Committee, spending hours of committee time reviewing the 260-page bill that will create the Oregon Health Authority and add 100,000 adults and 100,000 children to the Oregon Health Plan. We hope to have the bill to the Governor by mid-April, including a plan to pay for the OHP expansion in a way that will bring $1 billion of federal funds into Oregon to support the health-care system.

While dealing with these important matters I have managed to create enough fuss with less important things (remember — important to some people) to get into the national media. I introduced a bill that would require Oregon's state universities to interview at least one qualified minority candidate when hiring a head coach. A constituent, Sam Sachs, who was a football player at Western Oregon University and is a minority rights activist, suggested this bill. The bill is patterned after the "Rooney Rule" in the National Football League, which has resulted in the hiring of many more minority head coaches in the NFL than have been hired by Division I university programs. You may have noticed that both of the coaches in the Super Bowl were African-American. This story was covered in the *USA Today* sport section last week and is the subject of a raging debate triggered by Ken Goe's favorable post in oregonlive.com. Of the about 40 bills I introduced this session, this one seems to be getting the most attention.

The email box has been quite active these last two weeks, including a blast supporting a bill that would outlaw puppy mills in Oregon, outrage at the raid on the Cultural Trust, and emails supporting ACLU's position on three bills. There were many emails suggesting that we find new ways to increase revenue to help the financial situation and about the same number of hysterical messages about the possibility of increasing the price of a bottle of beer by 15 cents to increase revenue to help the financial situation. There were also several from the environmental community supporting a Senate bill on developing "a cap and trade" system and a House bill limiting the placement of LNG facilities. Keep the email coming, and if you have the opportunity come and visit the peoples' building.

The MitchMessage
March 22, 2009

I warn you that this message is going to be a boring message, because I want to talk about Oregon's financial situation. Money talk is always boring — right? My sense that this is an appropriate time to talk about money was triggered by an *Oregonian* editorial this morning, urging the legislators to be bold and move forward changes in revenue during this critical period. Well, rest assured that I am willing to be as bold as is necessary to deal with the current shortfall and to improve the situation when we face the next recession.

This is only my fourth term in the legislature, yet it is the second time I have had to deal with a major recession. My first session was in 2003 and we sent two short-term income tax surcharge measures to the voters because we were still dealing with revenue shortfalls left over from the five-special session 2001–2003 legislature. Of course, both of those failed at the polls and we were required to further decimate important state government functions.

But that was nowhere near as bad as the situation we face in this session. The Legislative Fiscal Office has warned us to prepare for a revenue forecast in May that will leave us at least $4.4 billion short of the $17 billion revenue (general funds and lottery funds) needed to keep state-funded programs at their current level. The steady-state budget includes about $8.7 billion for education, $4.4 billion for human services, and $2.9 billion for public safety and the judicial department, leaving about $1 billion for the remainder of state government.

Consequently, the Revenue Committee is working on a number of ways to raise revenue, seeking ones that will pass muster with the voters and will raise sufficient funds to help the situation. That seems necessary to most of us, because the alternatives seem unimaginable. If we decide to deal with the situation without raising revenue we can use about $1 billion in federal stimulus money and use every penny of our meager reserve funds, about $800 million. That would still require us to cut the budget by $2.5 billion or 15.7 percent. You can do the math, but nobody thinks cutting education by $1.4 billion is an acceptable option. Nor could we stand the cuts to human services of about $700 million when child protective services and care for the elderly are so drastically short now.

Those boring numbers are the background within which this session is progressing. Advocates for various causes still come into my office every day to instruct me to increase or maintain funding for their favorite program. However meritorious the program, that is not likely to happen. And we have hundreds of new bills we are considering, many of which require significant funding to make them happen. Any of those that do not come with additional revenue, are unlikely to see the light of day.

This brings me to the bill that continues to occupy most of my time and energy. That is HB 2009, the bill to begin the process of reforming Oregon's health-care system. This is not the first time I have reported on this bill, nor will it be the last. The bill does four things. The first is to create the Oregon Health Authority (OHA), a department reporting to the Governor that will gather together all of the health and health-care activities currently housed in other departments, most notably the Department of Human Services. It is clear to me (and others) that DHS is too big and too complex to be manageable, even by as extraordinary a manager as its current director, Bruce Goldberg. Secondly, the bill creates the OHA Board and charges it with continuing the planning for reforming the health-care system begun by the Oregon Health Fund Board over the last 18 months. It will report the plans they develop back to the legislature for the 2011 session. Principal among their topics is the development of a new health insurance exchange in Oregon that will allow a way to combine public purchases of health insurance to reduce the overall costs of health care and to improve its quality.

Next the bill extends health insurance coverage to about 80,000 kids and 100,000 adults. Finally, the bill will finance that expansion by a provider tax that will bring to Oregon $1 billion in federal Medicaid matching money to support the health-care system. This approach, which will return more money to the provider community than it contributes, promises to be one of the major economic development projects we have going, creating 6000 new jobs in health care and financing countless thousands of existing jobs in the health-care industry.

Working this bill, which is already 260 pages long, is very complex. I am holding two to three sessions of the Health Care Committee each week, focusing now on dozens of potential amendments. At the same time countless meetings are taking place discussing alternative proposals for the provider tax. It turns out that everybody supports the idea of the provider tax, especially if it turns out to be a tax on somebody else. We are quite committed to finding a way to work out the situation so as to bring that federal money back to Oregon. Oregon is a federal tax donor state, sending more money to Washington, D.C. than is returned. This can help redress that balance, returning money that will otherwise go to some other state.

In the meantime, we continue to work the hundreds of bills before us. We are beginning to move bills out of the House over to the Senate, as they move their bills over to the House. We only have until the end of April to move House bills out of the policy committees, after which only the Revenue, Rules, and Ways and Means committees may consider House bills. That time limit seems to be crashing down on us as we still have dozens of bills, some of them very complex, to consider in the Health Care Committee and we only are scheduled to meet six hours a week. The leadership is absolutely committed to adjourn by the end of June.

The email load continues to increase as several mass mailings, stimulated by one interest group or another, have flooded us. In one case I have no one to blame but myself, as I introduced another fluoride bill this year producing a stream of protest from both the left and the right. An anti-puppy mill bill keeps the email coming, as did a bill we passed out of the House encouraging age-appropriate sex education in the schools. But by far the most email has been stimulated by what appears to be three different organizations encouraging me to continue to move forward with what we are trying to do in HB 2009. I try very hard to answer the email within a day or two at most, but I only answer email from my constituents. There just isn't time to answer them from all over Oregon. On the other hand we love to hear from our constituents.

The MitchMessage
April 5, 2009

I am writing this message as I contemplate a town hall I had this weekend in the far rural end of my district. Constituents from rural Washington County (and a piece of Multnomah County as well) packed the Helvetia Tavern at 9am on a sunny Saturday to talk about land-use issues with me and with Rep. Mary Nolan, the House Majority Leader and the chair of the House Land Use Committee. I always enjoy talking to folks from the western part of my district because we can talk about land-use planning in a very concrete way, rather than the abstract way my city constituents discuss it.

To illustrate that point we hear statements like "my family has been farming on my farm for 100 years and is *the government* going to allow somebody to build a housing development so nearby that I will not be able to continue farming the land." Or on the other hand "why won't *the government* let me build a house for my mother-in-law on my (exclusive farm use) land?" Or I heard "my kids don't want to farm and I need to sell my farm so I can retire. I can secure my retirement if I can sell the land to a developer, but I can't get the zoning change I need to get the best price for the land."

The land these folks are talking about is as fertile and beautiful as any farmland anywhere. And as I drove home I came to the boundary of the battlefield. As I looked over some absolutely beautiful farmland toward NW 185th, I saw block after block of multi-story apartment buildings. The residents of these apartments are people who work nearby at Intel, Nike, Portland Community College and other institutions in the area. I imagine how the local farmers feel looking over their pastoral land to ugly suburban sprawl, threatened about their ability to live their lives as their parents and grandparents lived theirs.

Revisiting this experience brought me a renewed purpose to bring to my deliberations on the Land Use Committee. As I sit with Rep. Nolan and hear testimony about the future of the "exclusive farm use" designation and the protection of our extremely valuable farmland, I do so with refreshed vigor and determination.

As I have been doing with any meeting I have with my constituents I could not pass up the opportunity to discuss the dire financial situation facing Oregon. The Ways and Means co-chairs, the people who guide the legislature's budget process, asked state agencies to prepare reports on what they would do if their budget was cut 30 percent and this list has been posted on the legislative website. While we currently estimate we are now $4 billion short of the revenue needed to meet the $16 billion budget for the next two years, we will not know until May if the situation is actually worse than that. Consequently, the co-chairs requested the 30 percent cut list. As you might expect, the items on the list are horrendous. The list includes such things as the need to close ten prisons and release prisoners early. I didn't even know we had ten prisons. And the education cuts could require the schools to close 35 days early for the next two years. And so on and so on.

We don't expect to make such drastic cuts, partly because there are federal stimulus funds available to supplement our budget and partly because we expect to look for increased revenue to offset some of the income tax shortfalls. But the situation has definitely moved into threat-level-red territory. The situation has affected all of the legislature's deliberations. We have heard some very good bills in my committee that will not have a chance to be brought to the floor of the House if they require any funds to implement or to continue. Since we know that extremely important existing programs are being threatened, it is unlikely that new programs that cost money will be seriously considered unless there are proposed new sources of revenue to support the programs. The two most important such programs that are likely to be brought forward are the transportation and the health-care reform packages, each of which will bring revenue.

Our transportation system is near collapse. We remain about $1 billion a year behind in the maintenance of our highways, roads, and streets. And we have a great need for new transportation infrastructure. I expect a package to emerge that will include revenue increases in some form or another. I am not close to those negotiations, so I do not have any inside information about the nature of those revenue increases, but they should be coming clear soon.

On the other hand, I continue to be in intimate contact with the health-care reform situation. The legislative calendar requires that all of the House policy committees complete work on bills that originate in the House by the end of April. Consequently, I am working to perfect HB 2009.

I have been getting several questions about this bill, which is the logical next step in a process that began in 1989 with the creation of the Oregon Health Plan and reached its penultimate step in the work of the Oregon Health Fund Board, which worked on the problem during this last interim. The bill creates the structure for step one of the OHFB report. A common question is "doesn't this bill create a giant new government bureaucracy?" The answer is that it does not do that, but rather gathers the health and health policy components currently included in three agencies, most notably in the Department of Human Services, and brings them into an agency that can concentrate on health policy issues and programs. There is not any new government bureaucracy created by this bill. It streamlines government, rather than increasing it. But it does create an agency that can be agile enough to get some control over health-care costs and quality. We charge the OHA to create reform plans to bring to the legislature in the 2011 session.

The other question I am asked is "how can you tax health-care institutions like hospitals when they are facing difficult financial times?" And the answer is that we are taxing health-care institutions to gather $600 million to earn $1 billion in federal funds to spend in the health-care system. Our plan returns each dollar to the hospital community for each dollar taxed and uses the federal $1 billion to expand the Oregon Health Plan by 180,000 currently uninsured people. It is definitely a win-win situation that will cover more people and will fund the addition of several thousand health-care jobs.

We are working hard to get this bill perfected. It is hard to imagine, but we have just received a rewrite of the bill that is 1000 pages long, 40 pages of substance and 960 pages of boilerplate. We have several more amendments to consider, but I hope to have the bill passed out of the committee by about April 15.

A few days ago my Health Care Committee was considering a bill to raise the cigarette tax. I was arguing that a central purpose of an increase in tobacco tax was to reduce smoking among teenagers. I was challenged by Rep. Jim Thompson, a member of the committee, with the question "why don't you simply propose banning the sale of cigarettes altogether?" I began to ponder that question and got an idea when I was reminded that there was action in Congress to give the Federal Drug Administration oversight of the tobacco industry.

I decided to introduce an amendment to a bill I was co-sponsoring that would raise the legal age for purchasing cigarettes from 18 to 21. The amendment, which I introduced in a press conference last Tuesday, would require a prescription for purchase of any product containing nicotine. I modeled that plan after a bill passed last session that moved pseudoephedrine products from over-the-counter sales to sale by prescription only. That simple step worked to effectively stop the local production of methamphetamine. You might imagine the messages I am getting about that proposal, mostly containing very angry suggestions about my sanity and about the final fall of western civilization. But I consider it a very sensible way to control an extremely addictive and very dangerous drug. There were about 500 deaths in Oregon last year from an overdose of the legal and illegal narcotic drugs. Tobacco is more addictive than most of those drugs and kills thousands each year. Is it so weird to think we should take serious steps to control that dangerous drug?

As is usual for this time of the session messages are flooding in, especially the messages stimulated by special interest groups, such as the American Humane Society or the Sierra Club. These messages come in bunches and I respond to any that are from one of my constituents. This last two weeks the mail was dominated by email concerning outlawing puppy mills, regulating commercial salmon fishing on the Columbia, encouraging transparency in government, protecting the Metolius River, and expanding the bottle bill. I also received a great deal of email recommending I support two of my own bills, HB 2009 and a bill to require nutritional information on the posted menus of chain restaurants. Keep the mail coming, although it is probably unnecessary to remind me to support a bill of which I am a sponsor.

The MitchMessage
April 19, 2009

The *MitchMessage* serves as the chronicle of my experiences as a member of the House of Representatives, as I do not keep any other log or diary of events. So I hope those of you who read the messages have some patience with me as I reflect on my experiences. My attention during the last couple of weeks has been dominated by the health-care reform question, including negotiations with representatives of the hospital community and the health insurers about provider taxes to help support the Oregon Health Plan. Those negotiations continue against tight time constraints.

Friday, the House Health Care Committee passed HB 2116 out on to the next stop for the bill, the House Committee on Revenue. That bill will carry the provider taxes. Monday, the committee will pass HB 2009 on to the Joint Committee on Ways and Means. That bill contains the remainder of step one of the health-care reforms proposed by the Oregon Health Fund Board that was charged with crafting Oregon's health-care reform package. More about the specifics of those bills follow, but first I want to take a bit of a detour to reflect on the legislative process. It has come home to me just how conservative is Oregon's legislative process. By that I mean conservative in a classic rather than in a political sense. The word conserve comes from the Latin *conservare*, meaning to keep or guard. Everything in the legislative process serves to protect and guard the status quo.

Before these bills (or any other bills) pass into law they must negotiate a complicated and torturous path. We have been working on HB 2009 in committee for weeks and before we finish the bill we will be considering the amendment numbered -65. That means at this point the legislative counsel has prepared 65 amendments to the bill. And there will be many more to come before this bill leaves the legislature. We have actually considered many of the 65 and adopted several into the bill on its way to being perfected. Two of those amendments removed two critical sections, the Oregon Health Plan expansion and the tax to pay for that expansion. Those elements were placed, by the -10 amendments, into HB 2116. All of this work was critical because bills may not be amended on either the House or the Senate floor. And at any time I, as chair of the committee, can kill any bill simply by refusing to open a hearing or a work session on it. Most bills that are proposed die simply because the chair of the committee to which the bill was assigned refuses to hear it or refuses to open a work session on the bill after a hearing.

After a bill is perfected, it must gather a majority of votes on the committee. Sometimes a bill does not even get that far because a careful vote count of members of the House or the Senate indicates it will fail on the floor if passed out of committee. The water fluoridation bill is an example of that. I decided not to work the bill because I knew it would not pass the House and the Senate. But if a bill does pass out of the policy committee it may have more hurdles to jump or obstacles to overcome before it gets to the House floor. HB 2009 will go to the Committee on Ways and Means and HB 2116 will go to both the Committees on Revenue and Ways and Means. And the bills go through a similar process in each committee. Each must get a hearing, get a work session, perhaps add several amendments, and get enough votes in each committee before it moves out to the floor. If they pass on the House floor they begin the process all over again in the Senate.

Contemplating the complexity of actually getting these two important bills into law today is what has me thinking about the conservative nature of the system. When there is something I like in place I take comfort in the nature of the system. When I try to change something I chafe at the system's conservative nature.

I am pretty proud of where we have come in the crafting of these two bills. HB 2116 moved to the Revenue Committee with a structure for adding tens of thousands of kids and adults into the Oregon Health Plan and a structure for the provider taxes to pay for those additions. But it does not include specific tax rates. Those rates will be decided by the outcome of the negotiations or independently by the Revenue Committee. Then the bill will be passed (I hope) to the Ways and Means Committee, where HB 2009 will be waiting for it. It is then my hope, and the hope of other members of my committee, that they will move in tandem to the House floor.

HB 2009 is the product of intense negotiations with dozens of interested parties. It creates the Oregon Health Authority (OHA) by moving all of the health and health-care activities of state government into a single agency that will be able to focus on creating a rational health-care approach for Oregon. That process will streamline government by breaking Oregon's mega-agency, DHS, into a health agency and a social welfare agency giving each an enhanced potential for meeting its mission.

In addition, the bill charges the OHA board, among its duties, to continue the planning necessary to create a health insurance exchange within which state purchases of health care can be pooled along with individual and small-group health insurance purchases in a coherent way. It is also charged with considering the creation of a public entity to compete in the health insurance exchange with private insurance companies, in a similar manner to which SAIF competes in the workers comp market. And it puts more health input into the process of approving health insurance rate increases. All of these plans are to be ready for consideration by the 2011 legislature. (This is another example of the conservative nature of the process for changing the world.)

While all of this was going on, the Health Care Committee was moving on the rest of the agenda assigned to it. The legislature adopted a rigid time schedule to ensure that we finish our work before July 1. That schedule requires that the policy committees finish work on same-chamber bills by April 28. That means our committee needs to act on House bills (bills that begin with HB) before that date or they die. My committee has only four meetings left before the deadline and I still have 40 bills on the agenda for possible action in those four meetings. I have an active interest in moving at least half of them. We certainly have our work cut out for us. Since all of the other policy committees face that same deadline, I am also trying to keep track of my bills that are still alive in other committees. That keeps my legislative director, Tom Powers, on his toes.

During the last two weeks the House managed to keep moving things, large and small. Among those notable bills was SB 30B, a modest rewrite of the state ethics law passed during the 2007 session. The original bill caused members of state and local commissions and boards to file an annual and quarterly report that includes information these volunteer members thought was inappropriate, including naming members of their families. Dozens resigned rather than fill out the form. SB 30B reduced the filing requirements.

The Health Care Committee's agenda for strengthening the regulation of health professional licensing began moving through the House, including HB 2059A. And of course, we passed HB 2470, prohibiting puppy mills, a bill that created a flood of email from my district. We passed HB 2095A, to improve the system for doing hand recounts of ballots to check the computerized counting system. I had sponsored the original bill. We passed a bill (HB 2794) requiring insurance companies to cover the cost of HPV vaccine for female beneficiaries 11 years old or older. And many, many more, each of which was very important to somebody.

I am still getting lots of email. The most mass mail from my constituents suggested I support HB 2009, which I obviously support. I think that mail was triggered by a prompt from the Archimedes Movement. I continue to get a great deal of mail about the proposed insurance mandate to cover applied behavior analysis therapy for autism and about proposed destination resorts near the Metolius River. Most, but not all, of these messages come from outside the district. I think the mail will increase as we begin getting more Senate bills during the upcoming month.

The MitchMessage

May 3, 2009

We are two-thirds of the way through the 2009 session of the legislature. Last Tuesday was the final day that House policy committees could work on House bills. You can imagine how swamped we were both getting bills out of the House Health Care Committee and getting our bills out of the other policy committees. The only committees that may continue to work on House-originated bills are the Revenue, the Rules and the Ways and Means Committees.

Consequently this seems like a good time to check the scoreboard and see how we are doing on moving bills for which I was either the chief sponsor or a co-chief sponsor. There were about 40 bills introduced that met that criterion. It looks like we are doing pretty well. Twelve of those bills have already passed out of the House and are in the Senate for consideration. And there are five more that have passed a House committee and are awaiting action on the House floor. Most will be on the schedule this week. There are also three bills alive in House Rules, two in the House Revenue committee, and four in the Joint Ways and Means Committee. I am also tracking two bills that I introduced as committee bills, but for which I am managing their process — HB 2009 and HB 2116. Those are the two health-care reform bills.

Friday was an exciting day for me because I carried two of my bills onto the House floor — HB 3118 and HB 3367. And both passed with only two or four no votes. HB 3118 is the bill that requires Oregon universities to interview at least one qualified minority candidate when hiring a head coach or an athletic director. And HB 3367 is my dark sky bill that encourages the use of unidirectional light fixtures of the proper power when designing the lighting for a new public building. Not only does that approach make sense, but also well-designed lighting can produce the proper amount of light and save 50 percent of the power costs. Those bills are on to the Senate for action.

Ten other of my bills already passed out of the House, including one to solve a problem in the Portland part of my district caused by shared sewer lines, one to further the possibility of extending the west side commuter service (WES) all the way down to Salem, one that makes it easier for physicians to get licensed when they move to rural Oregon, and one fixing a problem with Metro boundary lines caused by future expansion of the urban growth boundary.

In addition, we passed three bills out of the House Land Use Committee on the last possible day. We moved a bill implementing suggestions from the final report of the "Big Look" committee streamlining land-use planning in

Oregon. The bill making the Metolius Basin an area of special state concern moved out of committee and we passed a bill intending to speed up Measure 40 land-use claims. Each of those took a great deal of negotiation.

It feels like all of my time during the last few weeks was spent negotiating one thing or another. As a committee chair I find myself urging competing factions on a bill to get together and negotiate a compromise. I tell them if you get a compromise your bill will pass. However, if you don't, I will pick one version or the other and just pass it. I am involved in negotiating with my caucus on crafting a majority for important bills. I have been actively involved in intensive negotiations with the hospital industry and the health insurance industry over provider taxes needed to fund expansion of the Oregon Health Plan as suggested in the final report of the Oregon Health Fund Board. And there is a great deal of negotiation required to pass a set of House bills out of the Senate and vice-versa.

Each of these forms of negotiations can be difficult and sometimes they succeed and sometimes they don't. For more than two years I have been trying to negotiate an agreement between psychologists and psychiatrists. The psychologists want to create a way that a few specially trained psychologists can get permission to prescribe psychotropic drugs for their patients. The physicians believe the only way that should happen is if the psychologists go to medical school. I opposed the bill last session, but the inability to get psychiatrists to seriously address the question of a proper training program finally frustrated me. I finally decided to introduce the bill this session with what seems to me are the proper sideboards around the process (HB 2702). It became clear that the situation had become "if you win — I lose." That makes negotiation impossible.

The negotiation concerning the provider tax is burning up hours of several legislators and legislative staff time and that of several highly paid hospital and health insurance representatives. Some days it seems as if we are within minutes of crafting an acceptable deal and other times it doesn't feel that close. But the clock is running on that set of negotiations and I am optimistic that the deal will be reached this week. But I am not holding my breath.

Sometimes I yearn for a unicameral legislature when I consider the effort some of the negotiations take in trying to move our bills through the Senate. Dealing with one chamber is hard enough. It seems like cruel and unusual punishment to require moving things through two chambers. But that is the great American way. I am sure there are Senators who feel the same way and don't understand why we in the "lower chamber" don't simply roll over and follow orders.

The email traffic the past two weeks has featured many messages from physicians objecting to the psychologist prescribing bill, several supporting a proposal to tax workers to create a program for paid family leave (SB 966), and many about a bill taking first steps to create a feed-in-tariff allowing consumers to sell power they generate back to power companies (HB 3039). In addition I have received many messages demanding we protect our children and save the schools. That message usually ends *"I am calling on you to protect Oregon's kids and schools by enacting reasonable increases in taxes on profitable corporations and the wealthiest Oregonians and reducing tax loopholes."* I don't generally get messages urging me to raise taxes.

The MitchMessage
May 25, 2009

The 2009 session of the legislature is rapidly drawing toward *sine die*, the end of session. The co-chairs' budget is now public and the three major packages that are expected to emerge are scheduled in the next week or so. Those packages include health-care reform, transportation and revenue, which will include a change in the corporate minimum tax.

I have been spending much of my time during the session dealing with the health-care reform package, which will comprise two bills — HB 2009 and HB 2116. HB 2009 creates the Oregon Health Authority, moving all state health and health-care functions out of other state agencies. It also creates the Oregon Health Policy Board, replacing the Oregon Health Fund Board and the Oregon Health Policy Commission. The board will guide the design of the future health-care reform agenda and will provide oversight of the Authority. HB 2116 continues the hospital tax, implements a tax on health insurers, and leverages over $1 billion in federal dollars we can use for health insurance coverage expansion. It aims at insuring all children in Oregon and covering a great many more adults in the Oregon Health Plan. It is likely that the negotiated version of these bills will be unveiled in the Ways and Means Committee and the Revenue Committee this week.

The transportation package emerged Friday from a joint House-Senate Transportation Committee and will be coming to the floor soon with broad bipartisan support. The deal meets the practical criterion of not satisfying any interest group completely. A bipartisan-bicameral group that also included representatives of various transportation interest groups crafted the package. Some of the members of our caucus and many of my constituents are unhappy that the package does not do more for the reduction of greenhouse gases. I will be supporting the package even though I do not think it raises enough money to deal with the very difficult problems we now have.

Further, it is too road focused and only targets the Portland metropolitan area with its greenhouse gas reduction efforts.

On the positive side, we'll put people back to work (about 4,500 a year for ten years), fix traffic bottlenecks around the state, reduce commuter times and improve freight mobility. The package does contain a new Urban Trails Fund, sends 50 percent of the money we raise to cities and counties, and authorizes $100 million for projects involving rail, air, marine and other non-automobile improvements.

And finally, the revenue package is still being crafted, but at the moment it includes a significant increase in the corporate minimum tax and an increase in personal income tax for households with net incomes over $250,000. I think the current corporate minimum gets more angry comments in my town halls than any other single topic, except perhaps Oregon's lack of a sales tax. Perhaps my district is an unusual district, but taxes seem a bit more popular in House District 33, which is about the wealthiest district in Oregon.

I do not believe we can balance the budget without raising some new revenue. If we do not raise revenue, we will be harming critical programs, like education, caring for the very needy and public safety, as 94 percent of the budget is consumed by those three areas. The total 2009–2011 state budget (general funds and lottery funds) proposed is $14.6 billion, down from the 2007–2009 approved budget. This is nearly $4 billion less than what is needed to do what is currently being done by state government. To balance the budget about $2 billion is cut from the current service level of the various functions of state government. But projected revenues are only about $13 billion for the 2009–2011 budget period. The budget proposes meeting that shortfall by raising revenue by about $800 million and taking about that same amount out of reserve funds. As I review the proposed cuts across the various functions of state government most are taking about an 11 percent cut. If we can actually raise $800 million and if the revenue forecast does not get worse, I believe critical state services will not be destroyed.

I am getting two types of email messages from my constituents about the budget situation. The first type says, "Do not raise taxes, just cut wasteful spending." The second type of message says, "Do not cut funds for (blank) service. I know we are having hard times, but (blank) is critical to the future of Oregon (or to my family)." That (blank) could be K–12 education, state troopers, child protective services, home care for the elderly (especially OPI), state universities, DEQ, or one of several others. Both kinds of message are triggered by one advocacy group or another. But sometimes they simply come from the heart of a constituent.

I try to answer both of them simply and in a straightforward way. (Although if Harriet doesn't stop me from answering email after 11pm, I sometimes get a bit cranky as I get tired.). In truth the answer to each is simple. To the second set of emails, the answer is that everything is on the chopping block, but the co-chairs have tried very hard to be fair in the formulation of the budget and have tried not to kill needed programs that are doing a good job. To the first set of messages the answer is about the same, everything is on the chopping block, the Ways and Means process looks very carefully at each budget, and if you have any suggestions about specific "wasteful spending" to cut I would welcome hearing about them.

And, of course, as specific bills come to my committee or to the floor of the House I get a bunch of mail about those bills. I do listen to my constituents, although usually I get email on both sides of the issue. But the email traffic does help to frame the issues for me. So keep the emails coming.

Several of my critical bills are moving along. My legislative director, Tom Powers keeps a close eye on those bills to help them get over hurdles when the hurdles unexpectedly pop up. The next week is a critical week for our legislative agenda, since all bills need to be out of the policy committees by Wednesday or they die. We still have hope for several that are in a Senate committee at this time. And we also have a few in the Ways and Means Committee and in the Rules Committee, which are still working.

The MitchMessage

June 14, 2009 — Health Reform Edition

Thursday, the Senate passed and sent to the Governor the two bills that comprise our 2009 health reform package. HB 2009, creating the Oregon Health Authority and filled with strong cost containment measures, passed 23-6. HB 2116 passed 20-9. HB 2116 provides coverage for 80,000 uninsured children and 60,000 low-income adults by imposing a tax on hospitals and health insurers to help us to get an additional $2 billion in federal funds over the next four years. These two bills traveled a long and arduous journey from their conception to the Governor's desk. This message is totally dedicated to documenting that journey and to discussing the specifics of the bills.

In my floor speech during the House debate on HB 2009 I reviewed the journey, which actually began during the inaugural ball celebrating the inauguration of Governor Neil Goldschmidt in January 1987. Neil took me aside during that ball and told me that he intended to name a commission to address the problem of health care for uninsured Oregonians. I was on that commission, which created the Oregon Health Plan. That plan included a high-risk pool, a Medicaid reform plan, and a proposal for mandating employers to provide health insurance coverage for their employees.

Under the leadership of Senator John Kitzhaber, then President of the Senate, those proposals passed into law in 1989, including HB 935 — the employer mandate. The employer mandate was repealed after the Republicans took control of the House in 1991, but the other elements of the plan remained in place. The high-risk pool, allowing people to purchase health insurance after being refused insurance because of a health condition, now covers more than 15,000 people. And, of course, the Oregon Health Plan (OHP) now covers more than 400,000 low-income Oregonians.

While OHP prospered during the 1990s our economic problems at the turn of the century created a flood of uninsured not covered by the OHP. The promise of covering all Oregonians below the poverty line was unfulfilled, creating great pressure and costs on the health-care system. During my first session in the legislature (in 2003) Ben Westlund and Alan Bates, then members of the House, led a special House committee on the OHP. They crafted a plan to implement a tax on hospitals to create a fund to support expanding the OHP. Since every $1 of local funds could be matched by $1.66 of federal funds, the hospitals were willing to be taxed as long as the tax and the federal match were spent providing hospital coverage for the uninsured. A special OHP plan, called OHP Standard, was developed to give limited health insurance coverage to those adults with incomes below the poverty line. That plan provided coverage to 100,000 adults.

But by the end of 2005 it was clear that Oregon's financial problems were not disappearing and that our total Oregon Health Plan was in danger. There were still 600,000 uninsured, health insurance premiums were rising well above inflation, the quality of care was in question, and primary care physicians were becoming increasingly difficult to locate. So between the 2005 and 2007 session, I joined Senators Bates and Westlund in an interim mission to design a way to solve the health-care problems. That effort led to a set of principles to guide a major effort to reform health care. During the 2007 session we passed SB 329, which created the Oregon Health Fund Board (OHFB). The board was charged with designing a clear, bright path to the future. That future was to include universal access for all Oregonians to affordable, effective, medically appropriate health care.

The board went to work, bringing more than 100 Oregonians together to draft that plan, then taking it to scores of community meetings to allow Oregonians across the state to have input to the plan. The plan was released late in 2008, including proposals for the first step in the process to be undertaken during the 2009 session of the legislature and guidelines for moving in future sessions toward the vision that illuminated the plan.

I hired a staff advisor, Tom Burns, to facilitate the legislative journey to implement the OHFB report. Tom had worked 20 years in the California legislature and is an expert on the legislative process. Tom, with some modest help from me, took the report and turned it into a 10-page request for a bill that we sent to legislative counsel. And we asked the Speaker of the House to assign the number 2009 to the bill. The OHFB report suggested four things for step one on the way to total reform of the health-care system. The plan we crafted was designed to implement the first phase of their proposal.

First it established the Oregon Health Authority (OHA), consolidating all of the health and health-care activities of the state government into a single agency. The creation of the OHA effectively cut the Department of Human Services in half, but also included functions gathered from other parts of state government. Secondly, it created the Oregon Health Policy Board, providing oversight to the OHA.

The board was also given a set of responsibilities and the tools needed to accomplish these responsibilities. Among their critical responsibilities is the continuation of the planning process to provide proposals to future legislatures to move us to the health-care system we need. Specifically, the board is charged with developing a plan for a health insurance exchange that would bring all of the purchasing power of the state into the market with individual and small group purchasers to reform the health insurance market.

The OHA was also given a set of tools, such as the power to create an all-claims, all-payers data system that would allow us to examine the nature of the current health-care system and to guide system changes. The OHA was also charged with developing methods to change the way health-care providers are reimbursed to provide more focus on prevention, primary care services, and chronic disease management. And it was provided resources to stimulate the spread of electronic patient records using funds available in the federal stimulus package intended for that purpose. The bill also created a POLST registry that would assure people that their end-of-life preferences were honored. The OHA staffers have a big job ahead of them.

The process for considering HB 2009 was extremely complex and difficult. The bill ended up being 613 pages long. The size alone frightened many, although the heart of the bill was covered in about 30 pages. The remainder was boilerplate, amending statutes to change DHS references to OHA. I held more than 20 hearings on the bill in my House Committee on Health Care. Those hearings took more than 70 hours. Tom and I worked with all of the interested parties and considered amendment after amendment. We worked closely with all members of the committee in perfecting the bill. While we were considering the main bill the Health Policy Committee of the Senate was working on a set of seven specific bills providing the tools for the Authority. We then amended all of the Senate bills into HB 2009. We ultimately considered 86 amendments.

We worked very closely with our Senate colleagues, especially Senator Bates and Senator Monnes-Anderson in crafting the final bill. Key staffers from the House and Senate caucuses spent hours bringing us together to create a single bill that could be owned by all of the key members of both Houses. The House co-chair of the Ways and Means Human Services Sub-committee, Rep. Tina Kotek and Rep. Chris Harker, the Health Care Com-mittee vice-chair, were active participants in the negotiations with the Senate members. The bill passed out of the House on a bipartisan vote, out of the Sub-committee of the Ways and Means Committee and the full committee on a bipartisan vote and out of the Senate with a strongly bipartisan vote.

HB 2116, which began as a part of HB 2009, also had a complex journey, although we always viewed the two bills as a package. This bill also does two things. First it implements a tax on health insurers and on hospitals. Sec-ondly, it authorizes a plan to offer health insurance to every uninsured child in Oregon and expands OHP Standard coverage to about 60,000 uninsured, low-income adults. The negotiations leading to this final bill were exhaustive and exhausting. Two members of the House and two members of the Senate, along with the chiefs of staff to the Speaker and the Senate President made up our negotiating team. The House Majority Leader, Mary Nolan and I rep-resented the House. Senators Betsy Johnson and Alan Bates represented the Senate. Chiefs of staff Jeanne Atkins and Connie Seeley were the glue that held things together. Dr. Bruce Goldberg, the DHS director, and John Britton of the Legislative Fiscal Office provided the technical expertise needed to deal with these complicated questions and were extraordinary assets.

The negotiations were complicated, but the hospitals and the health in-surers wanted the taxes. The hospitals because they would get all the money collected, dollar for dollar, back through improved reimbursement for all of their Medicaid patients, and would benefit from a reduction of uncompen-sated care from adding adults to the OHP. The health insurers know they will benefit from the reduction of the cost shift from the uninsured to the insured. They know that currently 10 percent of health insurance premiums pay for this cost shift.

We ended up with a health insurance tax of 1 percent of premiums and a hospital tax of about 3 percent of revenue. That will raise nearly $600 mil-lion per biennium and will bring nearly $1 billion in federal matching funds to finance the expansion of health insurance coverage of 140,000 people. The Kids Connect part of the package will offer OHP coverage to children in families under 200 percent of the federal poverty line, subsidized health insurance coverage (on a sliding scale) to children in families between 200 percent and 300 percent of the FPL, and will offer the same coverage with no subsidy to children in families above 300 percent of the FPL. The goal is to get 95 percent of children covered, and DHS/OHA are provided resources to recruit and enroll all uninsured children. The funds will also be sufficient to increase the enrollment in OHP Standard to 60,000 adults by the end of the upcoming biennium. I think we reached a place where everybody benefits.

I am feeling very good about where we got after five months of effort and there are so many people who contributed. It really serves as an example of where we can go if we all work together. In a speech I gave a couple of weeks ago I mentioned "the enemy" and the first question out of the box was "who is the enemy?" I responded by saying the first enemy was "the perfect" — because the perfect is always the enemy of the good. And the second enemy is anybody with a fear of the future and, therefore, an interest in keeping things the way they are. Fear of an unknown future frequently trumps a desire to try to make things better. We managed to subdue both of these "enemies", even though they were out in force in the debate over these two bills. In addition, the debate was confounded by the possibility of federal action on health-care reform. But in the end almost everybody agreed that we had made a giant step forward, one that could easily place Oregon in an excellent position to benefit from any federal action.

The leadership and staff of DHS have a tremendous job ahead of them to create the new agency. But I have total confidence in the DHS Director Dr. Bruce Goldberg. He was a true hero in the negotiations, providing a quiet confidence that the task was possible. And the Governor's staff, particularly Tim Nesbitt, played a critical role in establishing the Oregon Health Policy Board, which will replace the Oregon Health Fund Board and the Oregon Health Policy Commission.

Finally, the Oregon Legislature will have a significant task in the 2011 and the 2013 sessions dealing with the plans that will emerge from the OHPB, the plans that will move us forward in reforming Oregon's health-care system. It is my intention to be there to help meet those legislative challenges.

The MitchMessage
August 6, 2009 — 2009 Legislative Session in Review

The regular readers of The *MitchMessage* have noticed that these messages serve as my personal journal of the legislative sessions. Consequently, they are different, in form and in tone, than many of the legislative reports sent out by my colleagues. In this message I invite you to join with me as I reflect on the events of the recently ended session.

This was my fourth full session in the Oregon House of Representatives, serving the first two in the minority and the last two in the majority. The Democratic caucus increased steadily from 25 members in 2003 and 27 in 2005 to 31 members in 2007 and 36 members in 2009. I mention that because the Republican-Democratic distribution obviously defines the context within which the session emerges. In addition to moving to the larger caucus room, taking the majority means naming the Speaker and each of the committee chairs.

The 36-member caucus is a very different group than was the 25-member caucus in 2003. The Democratic caucus has become more politically diverse, while the Republican caucus has become more homogeneous and more conservative. Members from the heart of Portland and Eugene are less dominant than we once were as the caucus now includes members from Bend, the Oregon Coast, east Multnomah County, The Dalles, Hillsboro and Woodburn. These members represent a more conservative voter mix.

But a significant advantage of having 36 Democratic members is that it truly helped bring Republican support to key Legislative proposals. Here's one example. Early in the session we passed a bill to build and renovate affordable housing all over Oregon. It required 36 votes because it established a $15 recording fee on real estate transaction documents. Though supported by the homebuilding industry, affordable housing advocates and the building trade unions, it failed in 2007 because we could never get enough Republicans to vote yes. This year, because we had all 36 Democratic members voting in support, eight Republicans joined our efforts — including some who had voted against the very same bill two years ago. That's the power of 36.

I obviously like being in the majority, but the critical issue was that I was able to become chair of the House Health Care Committee when we took the majority. That gave me the ability to guide health policy development in the House and to work with Democratic colleagues in the Senate and on the Governor's staff to craft health policy bills and move them through the process into law. Given that position, my reflections on the 2009 session are dominated by the health policy bills, although I did pass more than a dozen bills outside of my specific health policy agenda. Tom Burns, my health-care advisor, staffed the health-care reform agenda, while much of the credit for the success of my general legislative package goes to my Legislative Director, Tom Powers. I will list some of those bills at the end of this message.

From opening day, the state of Oregon's economy made the session extremely challenging. Because of the extraordinarily difficult economic climate, the shadow of a $4 billion budgetary shortfall loomed over the delicate political interaction that characterizes any legislative session. The kabuki theatre that defines the relationships between the majority and the minority was calmer and more civil than during any of my three previous sessions. I think this reflected the relationships among three key actors, House Speaker Dave Hunt, Majority Leader Mary Nolan, and Minority Leader Bruce Hanna. They worked together to create a set of streamlined House rules that made the process much smoother and less contentious. And they modeled courtesy and respect in their day-to-day interactions in the management of the House process. That is not to say, however, that we did not have our moments of drama.

In the end we passed a balanced budget that protects vital services, such as education, care for our vulnerable citizens, and public safety. We ensured significant advances caring for the needs of children and families. We created a large number of family wage jobs. We improved government accountability and we took major steps forward in reforming Oregon's health-care system.

The House Health Care Committee had a very active workload, but the cornerstone of that agenda comprised the two health-care reform bills — HB 2009 and HB 2116 discussed in the last *MitchMessage*. These bills improve the quality and consistency of health care, provide greater accountability to the public for resources spent in the health-care system, and begin the process of transforming Oregon's health-care system.

In addition to crafting and guiding those two bills through the legislature to the Governor's desk, the House Health Care Committee moved a set of bills that reformed the way Oregon's health-care professional licensing boards operated. During the 2007 session we began investigating scandals in a couple of health professional licensing boards, especially the Nursing Board. We focused on the boards during interim hearings and found out that there was very little oversight to the action of the boards and the situation was out of control in some of the boards. Many were doing fine, but it was clear that general improvement could be obtained. We developed what became a four-bill package overhauling how the boards were structured and how they operate. These bills include improvements in the way impaired professionals are treated, clarification about how health professionals report misconduct on the part of other health professionals, and methods to improve board oversight by the Governor.

The legislature passed some landmark legislation in addition to health reform, including the most significant transportation package in a decade. We finally moved some resources into maintenance and modernization of our roads and of our multi-modal transportation system. And we passed a package of bills that created and saved jobs.

We passed an important bill that will put a sunset on all tax breaks and deductions currently on the books. We scrutinize budget expenditures, but we have not, until now, systematically examined tax breaks already on the books. This bill will ensure that we formally reconsider once every ten years whether we want to continue each tax break and deduction.

And we passed a balanced budget, something that eluded California for several months. We protected K–12 education and public safety. We cut human services programs by an average of about 15 percent, but we did it in a way that did not kill needed services. We did a much less satisfactory job supporting higher education and for the fourth session in a row I voted against the higher education budget.

But in the end we reduced the $4 billion projected deficit in our $15 billion budget by using $2 billion of federal stimulus funds and reserves, reducing budgets by $1.2 billion and passing a revenue package intended to produce $800,000 million in new revenue. The revenue package has two parts. The first component raises the corporate minimum tax from the current minimum of $10 per year. About 60 percent of corporations doing business in Oregon pay that minimum tax. The second component of the revenue package includes an increase of income tax on couples making more than $250,000 per year (individuals making more than $125,000). The new tax bracket increases the effective tax rate on the component of income above $250,000 by about 1 percent. There is an effort to refer this tax package and it will likely go to the voters in a special election the last week in January. If it fails in that election it is clear we will be focusing on drastic budget cuts during the special session that is scheduled for the month of February 2010. I urge you all to vote to support this fair and equitable tax package.

All in all, this was a very interesting and productive session. It was tightly scheduled, ending one day ahead of schedule. We passed important legislation, although we left important work on the table, including an increase in the cigarette tax designed to reduce teenage smoking. I had my own share of bills left to die in a House committee or over in the Senate. But I did pass a significant number of important bills of which I was either the chief sponsor or the chief co-sponsor, in addition to the Health Care Committee bills. Among those bills are:

- SB 735 — Expands the Oregon Prescription Drug Program to cover many more Oregonians
- HB 2408 — Establishes a task force to study the viability of expanding the Beaverton to Wilsonville commuter rail line to Salem
- HB 2610 — Clarifies health professionals' credentials and expertise

- HB 3043 — Clarifies Metro Urban Growth Boundary
- HB 2755 — Studies ways to improve health-care reinsurance
- HB 2435 — Speeds licensing of doctors moving to Oregon
- HB 3022 — Improves treatment for sexually transmitted diseases
- HB 2822 — Improves homeowners' access to sewer lines
- HB 2726 — Requires fast food franchises to provide nutrition information on menus
- HB 3367 — Provides common sense outdoor lighting standards to reduce energy usage and to reduce light pollution
- HB 2702 — Begins the process to determine the safety and effectiveness of allowing psychologists to prescribe medication
- HB 2600 — Requires improved hotel access for individuals with disabilities
- HB 3118 — Requires state universities to interview at least one qualified minority applicant for open head coaching or athletic director positions, following the "Rooney Rule" of professional football

During the session I communicated with thousands of my constituents via email, over the telephone, at town halls, or during personal visits at the Capitol. And those communications helped us produce better legislation. This message reviewed some of the achievements of this legislative session, including several to which I was a major contributor. The members of the Democratic House Caucus are proud of the legislative achievements we accomplished. I expect to be back in the House next session and I invite you all to keep in touch with me, sharing your concerns about Oregon and ideas for improving our state.

The MitchMessage
Oregon House of Representatives — 2010 Session
January 28, 2010 — Pre-session edition

As I prepare for the brief legislative session beginning on February 1st I do so with a sense of relief. Because the voters of the state approved Measures 66 and 67 we will not be spending the next month trying to cut $1 billion out of a $14 billion budget with nearly a third of the biennium already gone. We will have a chance to deal with several important housekeeping measures and will also be teeing up bills on several critical issues that might not be resolved until the 2011 regular session. But beginning the discussion is very useful.

Among these issues is kicker reform, banning oil drilling off the Oregon coast, reform of the ban on teachers wearing religious garb, bringing mortgage banks and insurance companies under the Oregon Unlawful Trade Practices Act, and several other critical issues. The very tight time frame of the February session reduces the possibility of passing the more controversial bills. The Speaker and the Senate President set extremely tight time limits to ensure that we will adjourn no later than February 28. For example each of the House policy committees will need to be finished working bills originating in the House by February 11.

That means my House Committee on Health Care will only have five two-hour meetings to deal with our whole agenda. The Speaker has already assigned eight bills sponsored by House members to us and has approved for consideration five concepts that we will introduce as committee bills on the first day of the session. That means we have thirteen bills to hear and possibly debate and vote on in ten hours of hearings. We will have an equally tight time schedule for dealing with bills that come over from the Senate.

Included among the bills that have been assigned to the Health Care Committee is my HJR 100. This Joint House Resolution would refer to the voters the question of whether to amend the Oregon Constitution to include the statement: *it is the obligation of the state to ensure that every legal resident of Oregon has access to effective, medically appropriate, and affordable health care as a fundamental right.* You might remember that Harriet and I led an effort to get an initiative on the ballot in 2006 to amend the constitution to include health care as a right. We gathered, with a lot of help from our friends, more than 120,000 signatures. But we fell several thousand short of the required number. I then tried to pass a joint resolution doing that during the 2007 session and again during the 2008 special session, passing it in the House both times. But the resolution failed to get a hearing in the Senate both times.

The current resolution has Senator Bates and Senator Morrisette as chief-co sponsors and has fourteen Representatives and four Senators as co-sponsors. I remain ever hopeful, because it seems critical to get voters' views on the question of health care as a right as we move into the next round of health-care reform debates in the 2011 session. It is clear to me that we can do much better in the continuing debate on health-care reform than they are doing in Washington, D.C.

I have been asked why I am so willing to tilt at windmills. My usual answer is that sometimes when you tilt at a windmill it turns into a dragon, which can be slain. The real answer is that I believe the best way to predict the future is to invent it. And that takes me to my continuing proposal to merge PSU and OHSU over the next ten years. The proposal is gathering advocates and will be seriously considered during the 2011 session. The presidents of the two universities have established a task force to consider that proposal, among other proposals, and to report recommendations to them by June. I hope a committee of the State Board of Higher Education will also consider the task force report so we can have a more substantive discussion in the legislature. We are beyond the question of what would be the mascot of the new university. (Answer — a Viking in a white coat.)

My office keeps busy during the interim dealing with constituent problems with state agencies. We have received requests recently for help from several constituents, many coming jointly to our office and that of Sen. Suzanne Bonamici. Sometimes there is nothing we can do except to get clarifying information from the agency. But frequently, when we get into the situation with an agency we can facilitate the resolution of the matter. My new legislative aide, Justin Freeman, is quite effective at coordinating with Sen. Bonamici's office and in helping resolve difficult problems for constituents. Don't hesitate to contact us if you think we might be able to help. Sometimes we actually can help.

I have been getting a lot of email in advance of the February session. ACLU stimulated a brief flurry of email on two issues; the religious dress question and concerns with the implementation of a prescription-monitoring database. But offshore drilling has brought some traffic, as have a set of other matters. The volume winner of the last month was messages on both sides of Measure 66 and 67. Constituent messages are important to me and I take them seriously. Please keep them coming.

 ## The MitchMessage
February 28, 2010 — Post-session edition

It was the best of times; it was the worst of times. Well, not exactly. The 2010 February special session turned out to be a pretty straightforward type of session, finishing ahead of schedule and under budget. We accomplished a great deal, mostly things that had been tied up in the last session or in the interim, but we also took time along the way to engage in a fair bit of rhetoric aimed at influencing the voters in the May and November elections. More about that later.

The first order of business in the session was balancing the budget. Even with the passage of Measures 66 and 67, we faced the need to fill a budget hole of nearly $200 million because of declining revenues projected in February. We had established some reserves in the original budget to help with this. We added about $30 million in new budget cuts and released funds from education reserves to provide the final $200 million we had targeted for K–12 education.

More than 200 bills were introduced during the session. Each House member was allowed to introduce one bill; each Senate member was allowed two bills. In addition, committees were allowed to introduce committee-sponsored bills. More than 100 bills made it through the House and the Senate and went to the Governor's desk. The Health Care Committee considered more than 15 bills, with several of them being enacted. My favorite one of those was HB 3664, a bill I carried on the House floor that extends Oregon Health Plan coverage to kids 18–21 who age out of the foster care system. These kids have so many special needs and excluding them from health coverage creates one more obstacle they need to overcome in their quest for a successful life.

The most controversial health-care bill to emerge was SB 1046, which allows certain specially trained psychologists to prescribe psychotropic drugs. The House and Senate Health Care Committees have been working on the bill for about four years, including a major consensus process carried on during the recent interim. In the end it came down to a political zero-sum game between the psychologists and the psychiatrists, the worst kind of outcome. The psychologists finally won one. The final outcome is still in doubt, however, because the battle has shifted to the Governor's office. The psychiatrists are massing forces to urge the Governor to veto the bill. (Editor's note: The Governor vetoed the bill.)

A very difficult vote for me was on HB 3686, a bill to repeal an Oregon statute from the 1920s that banned public school teachers from wearing religious dress. It was originally a Ku Klux Klan-sponsored statute intended to keep Catholic priests and nuns from teaching in the public schools. I viewed the decision as one that needed to balance the establishment clause in the Constitution with the constitutional freedom of religious expression. And I had a great deal of strident email on both sides of the issue, partly because of strong ACLU opposition to the bill. Finally, a set of amendments satisfied me there were sufficient safeguards in the bill to ensure that children would be protected from inappropriate religious expression in the classroom.

My most dramatic moment in the session was the defeat of the HOPE amendment in a House vote 30–29, lacking a single vote needed to pass it out of the House. The measure was HJR 100, with which I tried, one more time, to refer to the voters a constitutional amendment to establish health care as a fundamental right for the citizens of Oregon. Harriet and I ran an initiative campaign during 2006, in which we gathered more than 120,000 signatures, but fell several thousand short of what was required to get the measure on the ballot. I then tried to pass a referral (HJR 18) during the 2007 session and tried HJR 100 during the 2008 special session. In both cases I was able to pass the referral out of the House 31–29 with all the Democrats in the House voting yes. But in both cases it failed to make it out of a Senate committee, killed by the Senate leadership.

With 36 Democrats in the House Caucus this time I thought I had a good chance of passing it out of the House and an improved chance of having the measure heard in the Senate. But when the chips were down I failed to get six key Democratic votes. I thought I had 31 votes right up to the last moment, when a Democratic colleague left the House floor rather than vote. I have decided that is the end of the road for the constitutional amendment approach to ensuring health care for all Oregonians. But that won't stop me from moving ahead on reform of the health-care system on the way to providing health care for all Oregonians. The 2011 session is going to be one more critical session as we receive a set of proposals from the Oregon Health Policy Board to improve health care in Oregon and to move us toward the goal of insuring 95 percent of all Oregonians by the year 2015.

I mentioned above that there was a great deal of rhetoric aimed at the 2010 elections. And at the end of almost every day's session at least one Republican member stood up and announced that the Democratic majority had pounded one more nail into the coffin of business in Oregon (or on one occasion pointed out that Democrats had once more "kicked sand into the face of Oregon business"). It got me wondering what triggered that response, other than the recent vote on Measures 66 and 67 and the upcoming elections. During the session we were passing one business-friendly, jobs-creating bill after another. We passed bills that streamlined the process for obtaining business loans from Oregon's Business Development fund and created a new fund to give loans and grants to small businesses that create jobs for Oregonians. We funded employment-related day care, supported the development of biomass energy, reformed the business energy tax credit program, and created the Economic Gardening program giving small businesses the tools they need to succeed.

It finally came to me that the minority became most vocal, and locked up their caucus votes, when we did consumer protection things. For example, we added lending institutions to the statutes covering almost all businesses defining unlawful trade practices. This action protects victims of misleading and fraudulent lending practices by giving consumers the chance to hold lenders accountable. And we added some protections to homeowners who lost their homes to foreclosure. Somehow those things were seen as anti-business. When we increased the ability of credit unions to hold state funds, the banking lobby came unglued, and the Republicans argued that we were trying to kill community banks. (It turned out that most of the state funds under consideration were being held in large interstate banks.)

It got so annoying that I took to asking the carrier of bills, especially when the carrier was a minority member, if the bill being carried was a "business friendly" bill, because I wanted to make sure I was voting for business friendly bills. It is true that I want very badly to vote for bills that help businesses in our state and bills that create jobs. And I think we did an extraordinary job of doing that during this session, despite a difficult budget situation.

In truth, the relationship between the Ds and the Rs is extremely cordial in day-to-day interactions during the session. On a personal basis we all have very close relationships across the aisle. I have relied on Rep. Ron Maurer, my committee vice chair, for a great deal of committee work and we like and respect each other, even though we sometimes disagree on difficult policy issues. I have worked very closely with and like and respect several other minority members. Remember I spent my first four years in the minority, but passed nearly 15 bills out of the House during that period because of my close relationship with Republican members. And the day-to-day business of the House went very smoothly, because of the respectful relationship between the Majority Leader Mary Nolan and Representative Hanna. We did not have a single motion to cut off debate during the 2009 and the 2010 session and we mostly respected each other in debate and off the floor.

However, that broke down a little bit in closing the session. The issue surrounded the process of passing a referral to the voters to change the constitution to allow annual sessions of the Legislature. The Constitution calls for a biennial session held during odd years and for special sessions called either by the Governor or by the legislature itself. In 2008 and in 2010 we called ourselves into special session in February to test whether it makes sense to change the constitution to allow annual sessions. Basically most of us agree we should have a short session in the even-numbered years.

A proposal (SJR 41) was worked out with participation of leaders of both caucuses in both Houses. That resolution included time limits for both sessions — 135 days for the odd-numbered years and 45 days for the even numbered years. I objected to that approach in meetings with the four leadership members, as did some other House members. We did not believe there should be limits in the Constitution, but should be done by statute. Rep. Hanna said in that meeting that the Republicans could not support a bill without limits, leading all to assume they would support a bill with limits. Some members of our caucus, including me, told our leadership we would not vote for that measure because of the limits. That did not seem to matter, since the assumption was there would be plenty of Republican votes to pass the measure. Then the fun began during the last week of the session.

The Senate passed SJR 41, on a broad bipartisan vote, and sent it to the House. The Minority Leader informed the Speaker that his members would not support the measure in its current form, asking for limits on what could be discussed during the short session. This topic had not been broached before. That was not acceptable to any Democrats, leaving the caucus with the necessity of changing the bill so it would get 31 votes from Democrats. A compromise was worked out to change the time limits by adding 30 days to the odd-numbered years. That made it marginally acceptable to me and to others. Enough of us agreed to vote for that version, but said we would not vote for a number of days smaller than 165 and 45.

The measure was amended, passed and moved back to the Senate, where all hell broke loose. The Republicans refused to vote for that version of the bill and it was reported that the Democrats did not want to vote for the measure strictly along party lines. This was all happening last Wednesday, the day we thought we were going home. The House waited for the Senate to act, expecting to adjourn *sine die* before dinner. At 7:30 the Senate adjourned until 10am on Thursday, with all other business completed. Later that night I received a call asking if I would be willing to vote for a resolution that included 160 and 35 days. I agreed to that, as did others, and the compromise was sealed. The compromise measure went to the Senate floor the following morning and the Senators, especially the Republican Senators, stormed that they had been held hostage by partisan politics on the House side. Senators do not mind stuffing House bills, but they don't handle it very well when the House behaves independently. However, the compromise measure passed, mostly along party lines, which is a very sad way to end the session. On the other hand, most of us feel any way to end the session is a good way. □

WHERE DID EVERYBODY GO? LIVING WITH CO-GOVERNANCE

OREGON HOUSE OF REPRESENTATIVES, 2011–2012

THE CONTEXT

This session was unique in the history of the Oregon House of Representatives in that the House comprised thirty Democratic and thirty Republican members. The Democratic caucus was shocked by the loss of six seats in an election that moved many legislatures and many governorships around the country into Republican control. In fact, the Democrats in Oregon fared better than the party did in most other states.

The messages of this chapter chronicle the odyssey as we navigated the potentially dangerous waters created by the realities of shared power. And despite several glitches, the journey was a relatively calm and successful one.

As in past sessions, balancing the budget was a central activity. We entered the session with a budgetary shortfall estimated to be more than $3.2 billion. One of the causes of the shortfall was that the prior legislature dealt with its budget shortfall, in part, by using one-time federal stimulus funds. Another budgetary problem was the continuing threat of rising medical care costs in the Medicaid program. The story, however, had a happy ending with the production of a balanced budget.

Another major story of this session was the final chapter of the health-care reform activities in Oregon, with the passages of bills that put the finishing touches on the Oregon Health Plan transformation and the Oregon health insurance exchange. In addition, we celebrated the enrollment of nearly 100,000 children into health insurance as a result of the Healthy Kids program passed in the prior session. Reaching these significant mileposts turned out not to be straightforward, but was nonetheless achieved with forbearance and determination. One of the factors that helped this process along was the recognition, by the legislative leadership, that nearly $800 million of federal funds was available with the completion of the Oregon Health Plan transformation, money that was desperately needed to balance the budget.

Another budgetary issue discussed in this chapter is the impact of what is formally known as revenue expenditures, for example, tax deductions, tax credits and other tax breaks. The tax code includes so many deductions that our effective tax rate is about a third of our gross tax rate. This provides a tempting target for increasing revenue during times of financial stress. This complex topic is addressed during this session.

The session's messages follow several other significant achievements, including among them the completion of the next step in the Governor's plan for reorganizing Oregon's K–20 education system. This reorganization included changing the Superintendent of Public Instruction from an elective to an appointed position. In that process the Governor becomes the formal director of the Oregon Department of Education and the appointed associate director becomes the de facto head of the department. A whole new set of boards and commissions was established, including the Higher Education Coordinating Council and the Oregon Education Investment Board. And the position of chief education officer was created. While the Governor was pleased that the legislature moved these bills, it was clear that a great deal of future clarification was going to be needed to specify how this whole new paradigm was to actually work on the ground. But there was sufficient agreement that the existing situation was not facilitating the development of a functional system of education for the state.

Included in the messages of this session is the story of how Jory soil finally got to be named Oregon's official soil. The story is relevant because it illustrates how ideas frequently travel a long and bumpy road on their way to becoming law. This story has been told over three sessions, finally coming to fruition, but not without some drama, including the telling of the tale of the most unfortunate email I ever sent to one of my colleagues. But patience and perseverance, and a little help from my friends, finally won the day.

The rumination on the role of email in the life of a 21st century legislator continues in this chapter with ongoing discussion about which messages were flooding my inbox, including further discussion about the ability of organizations to produce mass email with the push of a button. In one way it is the digital version of junk mail, but in another way it is the modern expression of direct democracy. I frequently feel very close to what my constituents are thinking and feeling. At other times I feel I am only hearing from a small minority of my constituents, with a few "frequent fliers" constantly pinging my consciousness. I have even told some of the "frequent fliers" that I wouldn't bother to answer them if I agree with them, which I usually do.

I was featured in a news article during this session on "nanny bills" — bills where the state requires citizens to act in a way to protect themselves. The motorcycle helmet law, which incidentally I strongly favor, is an example of a nanny law. (I have fought the motorcycle caucus on this bill since I have been in the legislature.) Anti-smoking laws are another example of nanny bills. I absolutely favor nanny laws that relate to health and safety because to a certain extent I see my service in the legislature as a continuation of my public health practice. And I will continue to work to improve the health of Oregonians in whatever way I can. (I have commented that people who don't like nanny bills must not have liked their nanny.)

This session produced another major accomplishment — a redistricting bill. The legislature had not produced the decennial redistricting map in decades; the job defaulting to the Secretary of State or to the courts. The fact that the legislature produced a bipartisan and bicameral plan, in a time of co-governance in the House, is a tribute to great statesmanship and great staffing.

And finally, the messages cover the work of the short session in 2012, Oregon's first regular short session. It turned out that the short session was a very useful enterprise, as it provided the opportunity to complete some complex work begun in 2011. This work particularly included putting the final touches on the health-care reform process and moving the Governor's education reform package down the track. And, it gave us the opportunity to refine the budget in the light of current revenue forecasts.

The MitchMessage

January 3, 2011 — Pre-session Edition

As you probably know by now the results of the 2010 General Election left the Oregon House of Representatives in a 30–30 split between the Democrats and the Republicans. That put the Democratic Caucus into a state of shock for a few days, but we soon rallied and named a team to negotiate with the Republicans on the rules for operating the House during these unusual circumstances. There is no precedent for this, since there has not been a tie in the House in the history of Oregon. We also soon named a co-speaker nominee, Rep. Arnie Roblan of Coos Bay. That of course assumed that the ultimate decision would be to operate the House using a co-speaker model. While negotiations continue, it currently seems the decision will be to organize the House, using co-speakers and probably co-chairs for each of the committees. But there have been no final decisions and the negotiations continue.

In some ways this is an awkward time to have so much uncertainty so close to the opening of the 2011 Legislative Session on January 10. We are facing a $3.2 billion budget deficit in the 2011–2013 budget and need to create a plan for redistricting the House and Senate using the results of the census of 2010. And we have all the other legislative issues we usually face. But on the other hand, there are some advantages in facing the terrible budget situation with both parties needing to take responsibility for the outcome.

The passage of the annual meeting referral voted on in the November election caused us to begin the session in a way that differs from our past approach. Because we have a limited number of days available for the longer-year session the decision was made to come in to organize the House on January 10, stay in Salem for two more days doing preliminary work, and then adjourn until February 1. We have been urged to pre-session file most of our proposed bills, which will allow the first reading of more than 1000 bills on January 10 and will provide time during the adjournment to assign the bills to committees. That will allow the committees to get right to work considering assigned bills as soon as we return in February.

A part of the ongoing negotiations includes the decision on how the committee co-chairs will be named, assuming there will be co-chairs. But there was an announcement today that there will be a House Health Care Committee and I hope I will be named one of the co-chairs of that committee. But I wait on that decision, with all the other members of the House. I have served two terms in the minority and two in the majority. Now I look forward to what will certainly be an interesting session, given the 30–30 split in the House.

As usual, I welcome your email messages. I will get another *MitchMessage* out as soon as there is anything to communicate. In the meantime come to the Town Hall this Saturday and talk to your legislative team about whatever is on your mind.

The MitchMessage
February 20, 2011

The first month of session has been fascinating, from so many different perspectives. We have had the preliminary opportunity to test drive a shared leadership model of legislative governance, given the 30–30 Democrat-Republican split in the House. Adding to the inherent complexity of that situation is the need to integrate ten new members into the House Republican caucus and into the culture of the Oregon Legislature. At the same time, we are exploring moving committee business along, each committee having co-chairs with shared power. This has created challenging problems and unique opportunities, dealing with the dynamics of personality differences in the co-chairs, as well as with different political agendas.

And to add to the structural complexities we face, I have had some personal health challenges to begin the session. I was diagnosed with pneumonia the week before the session began followed in two weeks with a case of shingles. But I just kept putting one foot in front of the other and I have begun to get my energy and my good humor back toward normal.

The challenges that face the legislature remain daunting. We need to rebalance the budget for the current biennium, create a balanced budget for the next biennium, and develop a redistricting plan using the 2010 U.S. Census data. There are many other challenges we face as we help get Oregon's economy back on track, and to restructure state services to match the projected revenue available over the next ten years.

Governor Kitzhaber has been very helpful, offering a budget model which appeals to members in both the Democratic and the Republican caucus. His approach begins with the current spending level and asks what needs to change from that level. The more traditional approach begins with a budget proposal that assumes changes for caseload, inflation, and many other factors. That model is what creates the budget shortfall of $3.5 billion to begin the process. The Governor's balanced budget proposal has a much smaller shortfall, but leaves services, such as K–12 education, state police, and health services with extreme shortfalls. The Governor proposes to mitigate some of those shortfalls by restructuring the way we do business in Oregon, particularly in education, health care, and social services.

As an example of that effort the Governor has organized a 42-member work group meeting three hours every Wednesday night to create a new way to deliver Oregon Health Plan services. Because the Health Plan was supported during the current biennium by an extra $800 million of one-time federal funds, the program begins the 2011–2013 biennium nearly $2 billion short. And that is without taking caseload increase or medical inflation into account. The task of the work group, of which I am a member, is to find ways to restructure the health-care delivery system to create sufficient efficiencies to buffer providers and patients from the impact of severely reduced resources.

The first test of the bipartisan budget process will come in the next week or two as the bills that rebalance the 2009–2011 budget come to the House floor. A budget proposal that has been developed and agreed upon by Democratic and Republican House co-chairs of the Joint Ways and Means Committee and the Senate co-chair passed its first test Friday. I look forward to seeing if the Republican leadership can deliver their share of the votes needed to pass budget bills. This is very important because there is a hope that it will be possible to keep votes on difficult 2011–2013 budget decisions out of the 2012 election fights by keeping them truly bipartisan. I am hoping we can actually do that, as we face the extreme difficulty of balancing that budget.

One of the most difficult tasks for each of the members of the House is to keep our expectations under control. It is always difficult to move a bill from the idea stage to the Governor's desk. I have talked in past *MitchMessages* about getting a bill drafted, receiving a hearing in a House committee, being approved in that committee and going to the House floor for a vote. If it passes off the House floor it goes through the same process in the Senate. The process is infinitely more difficult this session, because no bill will receive a hearing or a vote in a committee unless both co-chairs agree to schedule the hearing and the vote. The going is more difficult in some committees than others. One of my bills received a public hearing in a committee recently, but I was later told that one of the co-chairs has not yet agreed to schedule votes on any bills.

I have found the process working pretty well in the House Health Care Committee where Rep. Jim Thompson (my co-chair) and I have developed a smooth working relationship. We have already moved several non-controversial, technical bills to the floor. But we both recognize we will have to deal with the influence of our two caucuses as the agenda gets to the more controversial bills, such as health-care reform. The most critical of these bills will be those that deal with the creation of the health insurance exchange. The Senate created a special sub-committee of its Health Policy Committee to deal with health reform. They invited our House committee to send representatives to meet with that committee as they deal with critical bills.

Rep. Thompson and I named two Democrat and two Republican members of our committee to serve that function and we began meeting with them two weeks ago. They are currently hearing SB 99, which deals with the Oregon Health Authority's proposal for an independent state agency to create and manage a new health insurance exchange. This is a time-critical issue, because if we do not have an exchange in place by 2014 we will be swept into a federal exchange. While there is plenty of controversy in this process it is somewhat bipartisan and has become a high priority of the business community. They hope that the exchange will be a vehicle to reduce the cost of health insurance for small business. We had several small business owners testify in support of the exchange bill, as did the lobbyist for Associated Oregon Industries, the most conservative of the three largest Oregon business organizations.

As usual I have been getting a great deal of email on many topics. But nothing in my experience matches the reaction to my proposal (HB 2228) to ban very young children from seats on the back of bicycles and from trailers hauled behind bikes. I have been excoriated in hundreds of emails and phone calls from all over the country. The story ran in bike blogs around the country, in newspapers around the state and even ended up in an *Oregonian* editorial suggesting people cool their rhetoric. My position is that we have not established the safety of this mode of transportation for small children and that we should examine the situation. The email ran from rational, thoughtful arguments against the proposal to one that simply said "**** you, your [sic] a fascist" (My response to that one was "Very cogent argument.") Early in the process I announced the bill would be amended by Rep. Bailey to suggest a study of the problem if it gets a hearing in the House. Since then Senator Floyd Prozanski and I have introduced SB 846, which would look to establish safety standards for bike trailers. Sen. Prozanski is one of the leading bike proponents in the legislature. Now it's time to set aside the inflammatory rhetoric and have a reasonable discussion about bike trailer safety.

As many of you know I have been working to find a way to protect Forest Park as urbanization increases around the park. This park is a jewel and its development in the 20th century was guided by a plan created by the Olmsted brothers in 1905. These brothers were the men who created the plan for New York's Central Park. This year I introduced a simple bill. The bill asked the State Parks Department to make a good faith effort to negotiate a plan for the state to acquire Forest Park to ultimately become a state park. This proposal has stimulated a plan for Portland City Commissioner Nick Fish and State Park Director Tim Wood to begin talks to explore how the city and the state (and perhaps others) can work together to assure the future of the park. If such talks do take place, without regard to the outcome of the talks, I have agreed to withdraw the bill.

I have been receiving my usual number of mass emails. These emails have been on such topics as removing bisphenol A (BPA) from children's products, banning plastic grocery bags, creating a state bank, labeling food created using GMOs, developing a birth anomaly registry, and banning unlicensed midwives. When organizations such as the Sierra Club, 1000 Friends of Oregon, the Natural Solutions Foundation, or Consumers Union press a button, I hear from the same list of constituents, each sending the same or a similar message. I love to hear from my constituents, but as you might expect when I get a mass mailing my response is pretty standard. And in most, but not all, cases I have already committed to vote the way they want.

The MitchMessage
March 13, 2011

The session has begun to pick up steam as committees have begun to work bills and pass them to the floor of the House. There continues to be good cooperation across the aisle. Since the last *MitchMessage* we had the first major test of this cooperation. Our first budget task of the year was rebalancing the current biennium's budget. A solution to that budget problem was worked out by the Joint Committee on Ways and Means and came out of committee with a unanimous vote. We were holding our breath on the floor to see if a significant number of Republicans would vote for the budget, but it passed on a 60–0 vote and you could almost hear the collective sigh of relief.

However, the first major break in that cooperation came about early last week with a set of parliamentary squabbles that shook up the House. The Revenue Committee was working on a bill that would reconnect the Oregon tax code to the federal code for the 2010 tax year. The set of issues, which almost everyone supported, would provide tax breaks to families for tuition and health-care expenses, costing the state approximately $10–$15 million and benefiting over 50,000 Oregon families. It was about to be passed in a bipartisan manner when two Republican members moved to consider a 2011 reconnect item at the same time. That item was reconnecting to the federal treatment of accelerated "bonus" depreciation for purchases of business equipment. The motion was defeated on a bipartisan vote and the 2010 tax breaks for families were sent to the floor for consideration.

But the minority report, combining the 2010 and 2011 items, would cost more than $100 million in revenue for the next biennium. This caused some consternation in the Democratic caucus because some members, myself included, wanted to vote yes on one component and no on the other. There was much communication over the weekend before the scheduled Monday morning vote. A deal was proposed that would have put things off until Wednesday and would have guaranteed a vote on the two items separately. But a motion to put off consideration until later in the week was rejected by the Republican caucus. They were confident they had at least one Democratic vote to replace the committee report with the minority report. The bonus depreciation section was added to the bill on a 32–28 vote. Then they insisted on a vote on the combined bill, which passed with about 15 Democrats voting no. It was the first event of that kind this session.

I have been getting hearings on several of my bills including the bill to make Jory soil the state soil, one to require a prescription for tobacco products, and a bill to allow videotaping of the conduct of police officers in their official duties. I think the Jory soil bill will pass the House as it has before and move on to the tender mercies of the Senate. (I was delighted when Earl Blumenauer characterized the U.S. Senate as the hospice where good bills go to die.). Of course the tobacco bill, which was introduced to make a point about the dangers of tobacco, will die in my committee. And we are working on a compromise on the video bill with the police associations.

A bill that I co-sponsored with Rep. Carolyn Tomei passed on the floor of the House last week. That bill, HB 2721, takes away the religious defense from parents who are tried for murder when they willfully and recklessly refuse to seek medical care for a seriously ill child, insisting that faith-healing is the only proper way to deal with the problem. The bill passed unanimously on the House floor.

In the last edition of the *MitchMessage* I reported a hearing was scheduled for a bill I submitted to require the State Parks Department to undertake a good faith effort to acquire Forest Park from the City of Portland. At the hearing Tim Wood, the department director, testified he would be delighted to begin talking with Portland City Commissioner Nick Fish (and perhaps others) about finding resources to ensure the survival of the park. I said that if serious discussions would begin I would withdraw the bill. Since then I have been assured that serious talks will begin, including the city, the state, Metro and perhaps others. And I have told the committee that no further action was needed on the bill this session. We will see.

Much of my time and attention has been taken up by my committee activities. I now serve on the Human Services Committee, the Human Services Sub-committee of Ways and Means, the Health Reform Sub-committee of the Senate Committee on Health Policy, and am co-chairing the House Committee on Health Care. In addition, I have been serving on the Governor's group on Health Care Transformation and will soon likely be named to a joint House-Senate committee on Health Care Transformation. The days generally begin at 8am and can go to 8 or 9pm two to three nights a week. Since I have very little time when I am not in a meeting, my legislative aide, Justin Freeman, has taken most of the burden of meeting with the various groups that need to check in. That has been very helpful.

The House Health Care Committee has been working very well, with my co-chair Rep. Jim Thompson, the committee administrator Sandy Thiele-Cirka and me forming a great team. We are passing out a number of technical bills, including some we have been working on for as long as four years. For example, I carried a bill on the floor (HB 2381) that will streamline operations in three health-licensing boards. We began working this bill several years ago with the total opposition of the boards and ended up with total support of the boards and a unanimous vote on the floor of the House.

Two issues have taken up a great deal of time — the development of Oregon's health insurance exchange and the Governor's work to transform the Oregon Health Plan's delivery system. More than 100 suggestions came in response to the first amendment to the health exchange bill (SB 99) that needed to be considered by the group working on the bill. The next set of amendments are due next week, dealing with many controversial elements including the role of insurance agents, the nature of the governance of the exchange, the regulation of insurance products to be sold inside and outside the exchange, and many, many more issues. We need to deal with these issues in order to have an exchange in operation by 2014. The transformation project seems to be even more complicated than the exchange deliberations. The next couple of weeks should be critical for the future of the health-care system in Oregon.

The email continues to arrive in a steady stream. As I have said before, we pay attention to email from our constituents, but do not have the time to answer the hundreds of messages we receive from outside of the district. For example, we had so many messages from around the state reacting to our hearing on a single-payer health-care bill that it almost crashed the email system. There were hundreds of messages supporting the bill and hundreds against it from a group called something like "Americans for Prosperity." They were all deleted without comment. But again, we are delighted to receive email from our constituents.

The emails that are the hardest to deal with are those urging us not to cut very important human service programs. We get messages daily from supporters of programs scheduled for a twenty percent cut in the Governor's budget, or even eliminated in that budget. As I sit on the Ways and Means Human Services subcommittee I see these budgets close up. I leave many of these hearings in tears, because I know important programs are going to be cut and I know that there are faces behind these budget cuts — people that will not receive vital services. My answer to these messages is pretty simple. It is "I agree the program you support is vital, but it is very likely its budget will be cut."

Sometimes this job is harder than other times.

The MitchMessage
April 3, 2011

We have completed the first two months of our five-month session and things are heating up. We have a proposed legislative budget on the table, reacting to the Governor's balanced budget. The health-care reform issues of most interest to me are moving into the critical stage of development. Many other important bills have begun to move out of committees and are coming to the floor of the chambers.

The Ways and Means co-chairs have proposed a general fund and lottery fund budget of $14.65 billion. This number is about $200 million less than the budget for the current biennium, which we adjusted earlier in this session. However, it is supported by about $1.3 billion more in general and lottery funds, partially offsetting a loss in about $1.5 billion in federal stimulus funds that are no longer available. The K–12 budget is proposed at $5.7

billion, with another $55 million to become available depending on future revenue forecasts. That would keep the schools at about the same revenue as in this biennium. But many school districts are reporting they will still be forced to cut days or increase class sizes.

To offset cuts to schools and the disastrous proposed cuts to health care and other critical programs that help seniors and vulnerable Oregonians, I support using at least a portion of the state's $440 million in rainy day funds this session. As our economy continues to recover it makes no sense to eliminate vital services while stashing hundreds of millions of dollars away. We've managed our way through the worst of the recession without the kind of devastating cuts to middle-class families proposed in this budget. If we can avoid the worst of the cuts now, I believe our economy will continue to improve and our budget will stabilize. House Democratic Co-Chair Buckley has proposed using $200 million of the reserve funds; I support the proposal.

The assumptions built into the budget also have strict restrictions in state employee expenses that will result in no COLA or step increases in pay, shrinking in PEBB and PERS expenditures, and cuts in vacant positions in the budget. The proposed budget calls for very harsh cuts in human services and very little increase in support for higher education or community colleges.

When the co-chairs reported on the budget they announced that a proposed transformation of the health-care system must happen or the budget collapses. Work on this transformation is well underway, focusing first on the Oregon Health Plan. It is intended to redesign the system so it can absorb a drastic cut in revenues supporting care for the Medicaid population. Governor Kitzhaber's staff has guided a process over the last two months that included a committee of 45 people, including 11 legislators, meeting for several hours every Wednesday night. The product of the process has now been handed to the legislature to implement. Last week a joint House/Senate committee was named to consider the proposals, with three co-chairs leading the process. I was named as one of the two House co-chairs. We were given only six weeks to complete the process, so that gets us back to the Wednesday night meetings.

In addition to the transformation project and the consideration of many bills in the House Health Care Committee, which I co-chair, I have been working on the development of a health insurance exchange, which is mandated as a part of the federal health reform plan. I have been working with the Senate committee, which has been perfecting their bill, SB 99. In addition I have begun focusing on the House version, HB 3137, to attempt to get broad support for the exchange in both the Democratic and the Republican caucus. This seems possible since the approach has strong support from business groups hoping to reduce the cost of health care for small business and from community health-care advocates hoping to reduce the cost to individual purchasers. The exchange will put in place the mechanism by which individuals and small group purchasers can receive federal income tax credits for purchasing health insurance.

There have been some fun things happening as well. Last week I was proud to carry my bill to name Jory soil as the official Oregon soil as it passed out of the House with an overwhelming positive vote. This bill is very important to Oregon's soil scientists because they have been working with the Smithsonian Institution on the creation of a traveling exhibition of the various states' soils. As a part of this process Jory was named as the unofficial soil of Oregon. It is the red clay that makes up the wonderful red hills you see in many counties around the state, including Marion and Yamhill counties. I hope to pass it out of the Senate this year.

Harry Esteve of *The Oregonian* wrote a story about what he called nanny bills introduced into the legislature. Those are bills in which the legislature attempts to protect citizens from themselves, such as legislation requiring kids to wear bike helmets. In the article he commented on a couple of my bills, such as the now-famous bill to prohibit young kids from riding in bike trailers and a bill to make cigarettes a prescription-only product. He named me "the Mary Poppins" of the Oregon Legislature. This is a title I will wear proudly as it recognizes this phase of my life's work in public health. This also stimulated me to agree to be the co-carrier of a resolution in the House to recognize the HUGS program, which encourages person-to-person helping, especially in senior care complexes.

Speaking of the cigarettes, I had a chance to testify on my proposal to raise the cigarette tax by $1 per pack in the Revenue Committee as they held a hearing on various proposals to increase tobacco taxes. I continue to argue that raising revenue is not the most important point of a cigarette tax, although it will do that. But the most important point is to discourage teenage smoking. Tobacco is the most addictive product teenagers will face and their demand for cigarettes has been proven to be especially price-sensitive. The higher the price of cigarettes the fewer teenagers smoke them. And the data also indicate that if individuals do not get addicted to tobacco as teenagers they do not become smokers. Tobacco companies clearly understand this and therefore direct multi-million dollar promotion campaigns in order to entice their future loyal customers. I doubt however, that any cigarette tax increase will happen given the political distribution of the House.

I also had an opportunity to testify on a resolution favoring the Columbia River Crossing project. I have a bill proposing that the Oregon Department of Transportation cease spending any more planning money on the CRC until the legislature has a chance to fully debate this project and there is more certainty that federal money will really be available. I believe there are less expensive alternatives available to do the job and do it better than any of the three existing plans. However, I am not optimistic that I can slow the process, which I believe has a very high chance of failure anyway. The force pushing hard to keep the project moving is a powerful business and labor coalition.

We continue to get lots of email. In addition to the messages sharing the constituent's position on specific bills before one or another of our committees we continue to get mass mail on a variety of topics. The flavors of the months this month include pleas to close debtors' prisons (we can't figure out what this one means), encouraging us to support the national popular vote movement (I am signed on to the bill), messages supporting labeling of genetically modified foods, and ones on both sides of a bill to allow in-state tuition for children of undocumented parents. These children have lived here for years and have completed school in Oregon. I favor that bill. The most difficult emails are the ones that urge me to oppose budget cuts in critical areas. One set of emails support the farm-to-school program, which is a great program. But it is very vulnerable. And then there are a whole set of emails opposing cuts in the human services and health-care budgets.

I sit on the Ways and Means Human Services Sub-committee and have a front-row seat from which to watch the bloodshed of the terrible budget cuts in health care and other human services. We have begun evening hearings where we take testimony from the people and families whose lives may be destroyed by these cuts. During the day we listen to the state agencies talk about their budgets and how they expect to deal with them. It can be very dry stuff. Then in the evening we get to put faces on those dry numbers. And it is not possible to hold back tears as we listen to the stories of their fragile lives, their valiant efforts to deal with adversity, and the realization that the only thing that allows them to survive is the aid provided by the state. This is extraordinarily difficult, but I firmly believe we are ultimately judged by the way we treat the most vulnerable among us.

 ## The MitchMessage
April 24, 2011

I was talking to a lobbyist the other day and it came to me just how whacked-out is Oregon's fiscal and revenue system. If I went out into the Capitol Rotunda and asked 100 visitors to name Oregon's single largest class of expenditures, I would be astounded if even a single one produced the correct answer. (STOP — what is your answer?) I would hear education, those awful state employees, prisons, bureaucratic waste, roads etc. All wrong. The single largest class of expenditures is what we call "revenue expenditures." We collect about $15 billion a biennium in personal and corporate income taxes and we do not collect nearly $30 billion because of tax deductions and credits. Those $30 billion comprise our revenue expenditures. Some people call them tax breaks, tax loopholes or tax shelters.

The lobbyist I was talking to was urging me to vote for a multi-million-dollar revenue expenditure and I was explaining that I generally vote no on all revenue expenditures, even ones I might like. And here is why I take that stance. I sit on the Human Services Sub-committee of the Joint Committee on Ways and Means. That sub-committee goes painstakingly, line by line, over every budget of the Department of Human Services and the Oregon Health Authority. And it does this task each biennium. But we rarely examine revenue expenditures. Usually if they are put into the federal tax code we generally simply take them without any formal examination. Revenue expenditures generally do not help the aged, the poor, the frail, the disabled, because they are much less likely to pay income tax and consequently benefit less from tax deductions or tax credits.

People complain about Oregon's high tax rate. The 9 percent rate on taxable income could be reduced to 3.3 percent on total income and produce the same revenue, because that is our effective tax rate. But that is not the main problem. Citizens expect us to be prudent in budgeting. We are prudent as we develop our general fund budget, but we do not pay proper attention to the much larger class of revenue expenditures, mostly because we simply tie to the federal tax code. We then give special Oregon tax breaks to industries like the film industry and the energy industry. Many of them benefit out-of-state, multi-national corporations.

This has become much more relevant to me because we have now passed a K–12 education budget which is inadequate. We will follow this with an inadequate higher education budget and a human services budget, which is horribly inadequate. And despite the great and often poignant emails I receive everyday explaining why we must not cut funds for such valuable things as employment-related day care, services for the developmentally disabled, commissions for children and families, and other wonderful programs, many will be killed or severely cut if some more money to fund them doesn't show up soon. It feels like the social programs serving our most vulnerable feed on the budget crumbs. Eliminating just a handful of tax expenditures would provide that much-needed assistance.

Having vented on the budget, I can tell you there are many other important things going on. The bill to create a health insurance exchange (SB 99) will be voted on in the Senate and will move to the House for consideration. Pending debate on one or two significant issues, we should be able to move it quickly out of the House Health Care Committee and on its way. The Special Joint Committee on Health Care Transformation (of which I am a Co-Chair) has begun working on the Governor's proposal for transforming the delivery of Oregon Health Plan services. He argues this transformation is intended to create the efficiencies needed to mitigate the budget shortfall we face in this area. We expect to have a bill crafted for consideration within the next four weeks. As always, the bill won't satisfy everyone, but it should offer significant potential to improve the present situation.

A few of my bills moved a bit forward during the last couple of weeks. One important bill (HB 2107) expanded the health-care, advanced-directive process to include admission to a mental hospital. We discovered during the 2009 session that, when somebody signed a health-care power of attorney, it did not grant that power. A case arose that required a spouse to go to court to gain guardianship over her spouse to facilitate admission to a hospital for behavior effects of cognitive impairment. The bill to correct that oversight in our system has moved to the Senate.

I had a bill drafted: HJM 6, which in its original form would have referred a constitutional amendment to the voters allowing the merger of Washington, Multnomah, and Clackamas Counties. The measure was designed to raise the issue of the nature of metropolitan government. I found that a constitutional amendment was needed to merge counties. While there was no interest in the General Government Committee of moving the original form of the bill, there was interest in the idea that counties might need to be merged in the future, mostly for financial reasons. My bill was the vehicle for that discussion. The committee decided to work with me to create a new measure for consideration in the 2012 session to achieve that goal.

We passed several useful bills in the House Health Care Committee, but we ran into a couple of hiccups along the way. One of my key bills, HB 2224, would have required that CEOs of health-care organizations certify each year that they had personally reviewed the data security systems protecting personal health information and had notified their own boards of any shortcoming of the system or breaches to the system. I felt that was a strong consumer protection bill. But the Oregon hospital association lobbied hard against the bill, arguing that it might put CEOs at risk of being sued if there was a security breach. The bill failed four to four in my own committee because I underestimated the power of the lobbying and miscounted the vote. (It should not be that hard to count up to five, should it?)

Then on the last day we could pass House bills in the committee, the Republican Co-Chair, Rep. Jim Thompson, and I ran into a very unusual situation. A Republican member of the committee came to me with a demand that I move a bill, including providing two Democratic votes, or face the

Republican caucus locking up against all eight bills on the agenda for the day. I responded that I do not like blackmail and that they were free to do what they wanted to do. Rep. Thompson told his caucus that he had made promises on two of the bills and was not going to vote against those important bills. But all Republicans voted no on the other six bills as I brought each one up and they all failed, including two bills that were very important to Republican members. The sad thing about this episode is that I had worked out a way to save that member's bill, but the response was "do it my way or face the consequences." OK!! It is hard to understand not being able to take yes for an answer.

All this is to say that the legislature is a complex social system that generally works remarkably well. And this session could have been particularly stressful because of the 30–30 Republican-Democratic split. But it has worked nonetheless. The cooperation between the two Co-Speakers was the topic of a *New York Times* article this week and most of the committees have worked extremely well under equal co-chairs. Until this nonsense, the Health Care Committee has just done its work with no fuss, and my co-chair and I expect to resume that mode as we address Senate bills.

To close I want to acknowledge a milestone we celebrated on April 11. When we passed HB 2116, the Healthy Kids Bill, we hoped to use the 1 percent health insurance tax to finance health insurance for 80,000 uninsured children in Oregon. The Oregon Health Authority announced that they had enrolled that number, during a ceremony that featured many happy faces. It was great to get some good news during times that have been so difficult.

The MitchMessage

July 28, 2011— 2011 Legislative Session in Review

This was my fifth full session in the Oregon House of Representatives, serving the first two in the minority and the second two in the majority, and this session in a House tied 30–30. The Democratic caucus had increased steadily from 25 members in 2003 and 27 in 2005 to 31 members in 2007 and 36 members in 2009. The Democrats lost six seats in the red wave of the 2010 election. I mention that because the Republican-Democratic distribution obviously defines the context within which the session emerges. Since a 30–30 tie had not happened in Oregon's history, the lead-up to the session was without precedent and was certainly interesting.

There were at least two options open for organizing the House. First, either party could try to get one member of the opposition to vote with them in organizing the House. Or the two parties could agree, in advance of opening day, to a power-sharing arrangement. When the Senate had a 15–15 split in 2003 they picked a sort of hybrid arrangement with the Republicans agreeing to a Democratic Senate President in return for other power concessions.

Both parties made modest attempts to get a vote for their Speaker choice before we settled down to create a reasonable power-sharing agreement, which was certainly my choice from the beginning. After significant negotiations the decision was made to name co-speakers, each with a great deal of power and co-chairs and co-vice chairs of each committee. I was named co-chair of the House Committee on Health Care, as well as a member of the House Committee on Human Services and of the Human Services Sub-Committee of the Joint Committee on Ways and Means.

Generally speaking the shared-power process seemed to work, with the Republican Co-Speaker Bruce Hanna and the Democratic Co-Speaker Arnie Roblan working to create a cooperative spirit throughout the body. Some committees worked very well with co-chairs, others not so much. The Health Care Committee worked very well, achieving a high-level of productivity. Representative Jim Thompson was named Republican co-chair. Jim and I have been working together for several years on health-care issues and we respect and like each other. That, combined with the addition to the mix of an extremely competent and experienced committee administrator in Sandy Thiele-Cirka, helped smooth the process. We found we could assist and protect each other. That level of trust got us through some complicated situations.

In other committees that was not always the case, since the rules allowed either co-chair to prevent any measure from being brought before the committee. That model paralyzed some committees. For example, the House Committee on Education was unable to do any work for most of the session, due to the intransigence of Rep. Matt Wingard, the Republican co-chair of the committee. The Co-Speakers eventually assigned many education bills to the Committee on Rules because of the impasse in the Education Committee. The result of this problem led to the situation that the whole education package was held up until the last week of the session. There was a very complicated and stormy debate on elements of the package. Other committees had more or less success moving an agenda.

Because of the 30–30 split in the House I began the session with relatively modest expectations. I knew we had to pass a balanced budget before we could go home. I also expected we would deal with redistricting, which was required after the census of 2010. The legislature had not achieved a redistricting plan for decades, the job being left to the Secretary of State or the courts. But it seemed to me that the Republicans in the legislature would have a preference for creating a compromise legislative plan, rather than leaving the job to the Secretary of State, Democrat Kate Brown. That turned out to be the case and the legislature passed plans for both the legislative districts and the five congressional districts that were signed by the Governor.

But it turned out that the legislature produced some important legislation. More than 3,000 bills were introduced, slightly more than usual. We passed 807 bills, about 100 fewer than during the past several sessions. I will talk about some of the more consequential bills below. But this observation reminds me that most of the work we do in the legislature is pretty technical and non-controversial. Generally speaking bills are worked out in a bipartisan way in committee and come to the floor without controversy. I have estimated that about 60 percent of the bills that come to the floor pass with less than five no votes. Another 25 percent or so pass by a much closer margin, but the split is not along party lines. It is the remaining 15 percent that are split closely along party lines, and these are the bills that get the most attention.

The dynamics within the Democratic caucus were very different this session, with the evenly split House. The Republican caucus seemed quite able to maintain discipline and was able to hold 30 votes and block any measure from being considered in the House. On the other hand, it seemed more difficult to maintain this same kind of discipline in the Democratic caucus. I believe it was Will Rogers who said, "I am not a member of any organized political party — I am a Democrat."

From opening day, the state of Oregon's economy made the session extremely challenging. Because of the extraordinarily difficult economic climate, the shadow of a $3.5 billion budgetary shortfall loomed over the delicate political interaction that characterizes any legislative session. That shortfall was caused by the loss of a significant amount of federal stimulus funds that were poured into all the states during the 2009–2011 biennium and the continuing slow pace of economic recovery nationally and in Oregon. We lost about $1 billion in federal funds for the Oregon Health Plan and some social services alone. The education system also lost a large chunk of federal stimulus funds, as did cities and counties.

The Governor proposed a new way to look at the budget, beginning with how much money we had, rather than with how much money we needed. The Ways and Means co-chairs agreed to that approach, although the first cut of the budget they produced was significantly different than the Governor's proposed budget. Finally, we did pass a balanced budget with no tax increase and an honest attempt to balance the pain across the budget lines. As I mentioned in an earlier *MitchMessage*, I found sitting on the Human Services Sub-committee of the Ways and Means Committee to be a very painful exercise. And I ended up voting against the Human Services budget because I think the total amount of money allocated to those critical services was completely inadequate. I also voted against the higher education budget for the fifth straight time because I think the way we starve the state university system is completely dysfunctional. We need a strong university system to compete with other states and with other countries in the global economy.

Much of my time and energy this session was devoted to the work of the Health Care Committee and particularly to the two major health-care reform bills we passed during this session — HB 3650 and SB 99. I discussed these bills in detail in the last *MitchMessage*. SB 99 creates the Oregon Health Insurance Exchange. The exchange will provide a uniquely Oregon opportunity for individuals and small businesses to purchase more reasonably priced health insurance and to receive a federal subsidy for that purchase. The exchange board, when named, has to begin developing a business plan to present to the legislature in February. I have been appointed to the Legislative Advisory and Oversight Committee for the Oregon Health Insurance Exchange Corporation, which will monitor the progress toward achieving that task.

HB 3650, the Health Care Transformation Bill, created a process to move toward transforming the way we deliver health-care services to the Oregon Health Plan population, with an eye toward creating new models for care that will be both more efficient and more effective. The plan is to create Coordinated Care Organizations (CCOs), each with a global budget for all health care and with a focus on moving the locus of care into integrated primary care systems. Both of these bills, which were priority bills for Governor Kitzhaber, gathered a great deal of attention, with advocates on all sides having very strong opinions about the only possible way to achieve the widely agreed upon objectives and savings. While both bills passed with very strong bipartisan support, the path to the Governor's desk was arduous, steep and treacherous. And the process was very time and energy consuming.

But even with the spotlight focusing on those two bills, the Health Care Committee had a very busy agenda. For example, we continued to reform the way Oregon's health-care professional licensing boards operate. After extensive hearings in the interim and during the session reviewing the impact of legislation we passed during the past three sessions, we passed several important bills, including HB 2380 and HB 2381, to continue the reform work.

We also passed a series of bills, including HB 2397 and HB 2401, to help increase the supply of primary care providers in Oregon. The supply of primary care is a growing problem. In addition, the committee monitored the progress of two bills passed in the 2009 session, HB 2009 and HB 2116, the Healthy Kids Act. HB 2009 created the Oregon Health Authority, which became fully operational on July 1. This agency has the responsibility for coordinating all of the state's health-care decision making within a single agency and has already made significant progress improving our health-care system. HB 2116 provided the opportunity for all of Oregon's children to obtain health insurance. Since the bill passed, nearly 100,000 children have received health insurance through the program, either fully-paid if their family was below 200 percent of poverty or aided by a premium subsidy if their family income was between 200 percent and 300 percent of poverty. This reduced the percentage of uninsured kids in Oregon from more than 10 percent to about 5 percent.

All in all, the legislature made progress in several areas. In my last message I reviewed the situation that led us to pass a sweeping, eleven-bill, education reform package, some elements of which I favored and some of which I opposed. Among the bills I supported in that package were SB 909 creating a board to coordinate education policy from pre–K to graduate education, SB 552 replacing an elected Superintendent of Public Instruction with an appointed one, and SB 248 requiring full-day kindergarten in Oregon.

We passed significant economic development legislation. Included in that legislation were:

- HB 3000, the Buy Oregon First legislation,
- HB 2960, which provides jobs for retrofitting schools to make them more energy-efficient, and
- HB 3507, which expands the scope of Oregon InC (Oregon's economic development agency) to provide more incentives for creating new technological breakthroughs available for commercialization.

We also passed HB 3596, reviving the Coos Bay rail line, which is crucial for the economic health of the south coast. We extended unemployment compensation benefits. And we passed HB 3145, revamping Oregon's bottle bill to make the bottle recycling process more efficient and to extend its scope.

Among the most important public safety bills we passed was HB 3110, which restructured the way we deal with alcohol and drug policy at the state level. We all recognize how substance-abuse problems fuel public safety and other social problems in Oregon. But the authority for dealing with substance abuse treatment and prevention is very defused and is found scattered across several state agencies. Attorney General John Kroger, Oregon Health Authority Director Bruce Goldberg and Corrections Director Max Williams spearheaded an effort to create a method for coordinating their agencies' responsibilities and the responsibilities of other agencies. The new Alcohol and Drug Policy Commission, created by this bill, is one of the mechanisms for achieving that goal.

During the 2009 session we passed an important bill that put a sunset on many tax breaks currently on the books. We scrutinize budget expenditures, but we have not, until now, systematically examined tax breaks already on the books. We had the first test of the measure during this session. The Joint Committee on Tax Credits was charged with considering the tax credits due to sunset this year and determine which would be the most useful to continue. There were 20 tax credits at the center of the tax credit review process. If they simply had been extended, without any other policy modifications, the revenue reductions would have been $40 million in 2011–13, $170 million in 2013–15, and $294 million in 2015–17. In the committee's bill, HB 3672, the revenue impacts of the tax credits they chose to renew were reduced to $10 million in 2011–13, $53 million in 2013–15, and $73 million in 2015–17.

During this session, in addition to my focus on SB 99 and HB 3650, my legislative director Justin Freeman and I also paid attention to the rest of my personal legislative agenda. While I was pretty certain that none of the more controversial issues would have a chance in the split legislature, we were able to pass bills that were important to one of my constituencies or another.

For example we passed HB 2314 the final legislation needed to bring to fruition a program to prepare specially trained social workers to work in the public school system. I believe this is particularly important as the schools are facing an autism tsunami. The Teacher Standards and Practices Commission last week approved Portland State University's curriculum for training school social workers. The school social workers will be certified by TSPC.

In addition, I was delighted to see HB 2375, which I introduced as a committee bill, pass the legislature. Prior to passing this bill the Health Care Power of Attorney excluded the ability to admit the patient to a mental hospital. This bill ensured that when an individual signs a Health Care Power of Attorney the designee had the authority to allow that individual to be admitted to any hospital, without regard to the nature of the diagnosis.

I was also pleased to see HB 2721 pass the legislature. I sponsored this bill with Rep. Carolyn Tomei and Rep. Dave Hunt. It eliminates reliance on belief of spiritual treatment as a defense to certain crimes in which the victim was a child for whom medical care services had been withheld.

I was also extremely pleased to pass HCR 3 that named Jory soil as Oregon's state soil. Prior *MitchMessages* documented the journey this bill took over the last few sessions. While some people scoff at this bill, I can tell you I continue to hear how thrilled Oregon's soil science community is over the passage of this measure. In addition, I have discovered that a restaurant named "Jory" has opened for business at the Allison Inn in Newberg. Professor Jay Noller, an OSU soil scientist and artist, has produced a set of paintings using Jory soil in the paint and several of them hang in the Allison Inn.

But several of my most important issues await a Democratic majority for serious consideration. Among those issues include my proposals for merging

OHSU and PSU, making Forest Park a state park, stopping the Columbia River Crossing in its current form, easing the ability to consolidate counties, and providing further restrictions on the use of nicotine products. Because of the size and scope of my unfinished agenda I have been telling people, only partly in jest, that I want to be the first member of the Oregon Legislature to be 100 years old. But we shall see what the coming years bring.

The MitchMessage
Oregon House of Representatives, January 25, 2012

I am looking forward to the opening of the 2012 short session of the legislature, the first short session since the voters approved annual sessions in 2010. I believe the issues we face validate the importance of our getting together each year to deal with the emerging issues of the day. I see three sets of critical issues with which to deal; at least there will be three taking up most of my time and attention. These issues are health-care reform, education reform, and balancing the budget in times of declining revenues.

As co-chair of the House Committee on Health Care, I am at the center of the continuing discussions on the next steps of health-care reform; legislative approval of the Oregon Health Authority's health-care transformation plan and of the business plan of the Oregon Health Insurance Exchange (ORHIX). The transformation bill is SB 1580 and the Health Insurance Exchange bill is HB 4164. Exchange will begin in the House Committee, while transformation will begin by working its way through the Senate. Staffs of both OHA and ORHIX have done an excellent job of crafting plans, all the while staying in touch with the relevant constituencies along the way. HB 4164 should pass easily out of the committee and out of the House, with only modest modification.

SB 1580, the Health Plan Transformation bill, should pass as well, but it faces a more tangled passage. However, it is central to balancing Oregon's budget over the next several biennia. Savings estimates are somewhat modest for the current biennium, perhaps as much as $100 million of state funds. But the downstream estimates call for multi-billion dollar savings in the state general fund over the next three biennia. In addition, every billion saved in state funds means more than a billion saved in federal funds. Consequently, the Feds are considering our request that they help fund the costs of innovations required for successful transformation. The Feds want and need the savings as much as we do.

There is a slight hitch in SB 1580. HB 3650, which began the transformation process, contained a requirement that there be a plan for dealing with medical malpractice reform in the transformation business plan. The OHA folks did a great job in my mind creating a report on defensive medicine and on potential solutions to the malpractice problem. The report, using two very different methods, produced a relatively low estimate of the cost of defensive medicine of three to four percent of health-care costs, while indicating malpractice reform would produce only a modest reduction in these costs. However, some members of the body continue to report that they will block the bill if it does not include the reforms. Others, myself included, believe the bill should not be held up because it doesn't include a policy issue we have been unable to resolve during my five sessions in the legislature.

Education reform also has some thorny issues, with Gov. Kitzhaber's education reform package likely to show up in my two other committees. Work during the last session created two new bodies as the centerpiece of the Governor's education reform. The first is the Oregon Education Investment Board, designed to coordinate education in Oregon for people from 0–20 years of age. The other is the Early Learning Council, designed to focus on both education and social welfare issues in young children. The House Committee on Higher Education, of which I am co-vice chair, is already dealing with issues surrounding the Investment Board, whose bill will begin in the Senate as SB 1581. (I switched off of the Human Services Sub-Committee of the Joint Ways and Means Committee to take the vice-chair of the Higher Education Committee.)

HB 4165, the Early Learning Council bill, will begin its 2012 journey in the House Committee on Human Services, of which I am also a member. This bill comes to Human Services because it not only includes things like Head Start and other pre–K education programs, but also includes such issues as managing programs of the county commissions on families and children. The proposed changes bring some knotty problems, but have great potential for improving readiness of kids to succeed in school.

Higher Ed will also be facing emerging issues in the organization of higher education services in Oregon as we move toward the decentralization of Oregon University System authority and the continuing cry from the Eugene delegation in the legislature to "free the University of Oregon." (To say nothing of my continuing cry to "free Portland State University" and get it its own board, in coordination with OHSU.)

The most difficult problem we face, as usual, is balancing the budget. We do not expect the revenue situation to get a great deal worse than is currently forecast, but that still leaves some very difficult budget problems. I am assured by the Ways and Means Co-Chair Peter Buckley that we are close to closing the gap with agreed upon cuts, freezes and fund sweeps. But even then we are about $100 million short. That will leave some room for

Democrats and Republicans to fight. But we dealt with the problem during the 2011 session in a rational way, without totally dismantling state government, and I fully expect we will do so in this session.

I have one personal priority bill, HB 4110, the Iranian divestment bill. This bill would reduce investments supervised by the Oregon Investment Council in "Scrutinized Companies." That means companies that have currently made an investment in the energy sector of Iran in violation of current United States policy. The bill has among its 18 co-sponsors members from both Houses, both political parties, and across the political spectrum. And it does not have any identified opposition. I agreed to be the main sponsor of the bill because I believe it has serious symbolic importance in a world increasingly threatened by Iran's nuclear ambitions.

The MitchMessage
2012 Session in Review

The first voter-approved, annual short session was an extremely successful event, with the legislature finishing all its required business, including successfully rebalancing the 2011–2013 biennial budget. We were able to balance the budget without decimating critical services or cutting education funding. While there are many things to be unhappy about in the budget, the co-chairs did a great job balancing things and even finished with an ending fund balance and money set aside in the Emergency Board to deal with any unexpected financial disasters.

As I said in my pre-session report, my main focus during the session, as co-chair of the House Health Care Committee, was guiding the passage in the House of the final two pieces of the health-care reform legislation. We successfully passed the two bills, the Oregon Health Insurance Exchange Bill (HB 4164) and the Oregon Health Plan Transformation Bill (SB 1580), although not without a fair portion of political drama.

We managed the Exchange bill in the House. The transformation bill began in the Senate. Since every business, labor, and consumer group in Oregon supported the Exchange bill, I expected no problem passing the bill. For example, here is the Associated Oregon Industry's take on the bill. "Passage of the Oregon Health Insurance Exchange's business plan, (will allow) it to meet federal deadlines and continue working toward implementation. The Exchange would create a marketplace for health insurance policies for individuals as well as the small group market and would allow employers to allocate defined contributions to employee coverage and let employees shop for coverage that best meets their needs."

We easily got the bill out of committee and to the floor of the House. Then the Republican leadership decided to play political hide and go seek with it, hoping to hold it hostage as a bargaining chip in the session-ending negotiations. So the bill was sent to the Ways and Means Committee on some phony pretext that there were a couple of details that needed working out. Last week the bill came out of committee after we added some face-saving language that might allow school boards to join the exchange (which everybody supported). The bill passed the House 55–5. The Senate passed the bill 26–4 on the last morning of the session.

The Transformation bill had a slightly rockier road in the Senate. While the primary focus of this bill is on the 600,000 people receiving care in the Oregon Health Plan, it provides a powerful mechanism to change the nature of health-care delivery generally in Oregon. It creates a new health-care delivery model, the Coordinated Care Organization, designed to integrate physical, mental, and oral health care, focusing on primary care, disease prevention, early diagnosis, and chronic disease management. The bill got hung up in the Senate over Republican Senators' demand that it be used as a vehicle for solving the medical malpractice problem in Oregon. Eventually some compromise language was inserted, promising action on the malpractice system for the 2013 session and the bill moved easily out of both Houses to the Governor's desk for signature.

Even the short session held plenty of political theatre. It all began for me on the first day of session when I objected to the House rules and offered an amendment to the rules as a part of the organizing activities. I have become quite concerned over the House conflict of interest procedures. The rules not only allow members with an announced conflict of interest to vote on a measure, but *actually require them to vote*. This problem came to a head for me during the last session when a member declared a blatant conflict of interest on a bill I opposed and I got into trouble with the Speaker for declaring in the debate that I had no financial conflict of interest. It was ruled that I was impugning my colleague. My response was "if the shoe fits…" To deal with this problem, I proposed an amendment that would differentiate actual conflict from potential conflict and would require that a member with an actual conflict ask the body for permission not to vote on the measure. The proposed rule change was referred to the Rules Committee, where it got a public hearing and a promise that the committee would work on the issue for the design of the 2013 session rules. The situation got a supporting *Oregonian* editorial and my promise to keep up the fight for 2013.

Among the other important issues resolved by the session were two bills that were the cornerstone of Governor Kitzhaber's education reform package. The first was the Early Learning Improvement bill (HB 4165) designed to streamline and improve early childhood services to help more kids at risk. This approach recognizes that education services, such as Head Start, and social services for kids aged 0–6 need to be coordinated. Children need to be ready to learn when they get to kindergarten. That means they will likely fail in school if they come hungry, homeless, or from a shattered family.

The second education bill was one featuring the development of achievement compacts between school districts and the Oregon Education Investment Board (SB 1581). These achievement compacts are a piece of what is needed to achieve Oregon waivers to the No Child Left Behind federal law and to focus all Oregon school districts, universities and community colleges on moving toward the 40–40–20 goal (By 2025, 40 percent of Oregonians will have at least a bachelor's degree or higher, 40 percent at least an associate's or technical degree and 20 percent at least a high school diploma). The bill also included some interesting language about giving each district their budget numbers and at the same time providing them with an estimate of how much money it would actually take to achieve the goals, using estimates from the Quality Education Model.

It appears that our economy is slowly on the mend. We have added jobs over the past year. Our most recent unemployment rate was down to 8.8 percent, a far cry from last February's 10 percent rate. And while new jobless claims continue to fall, too many Oregonians are still unemployed and under-employed. Consequently, we passed several bills to speed along recovery and to reduce the severity of future recessions in Oregon.

HB 4040, one of my priorities, brings together all of the funds for economic development and small business assistance under one umbrella to ensure more of those dollars reach the workforce. HB 4150 opens up some of these dollars to new business, providing federally backed grants and loans for businesses looking to expand and add new workers. And we passed legislation to better coordinate our workforce development activities, ensuring that our community colleges, universities, and technical training programs are all working together to provide Oregon businesses with skilled Oregon workers. While we were able to provide nearly $10 million for community college construction projects, I was disappointed we did not fund the Portland Sustainability Center and other critical infrastructure projects that would have provided us the best opportunity for state government to get private sector workers back on the job.

The one bill that I personally introduced this session was HB 4110, the Iran Divestment Bill. This bill requires the Treasurer to remove Oregon investments in companies that are on the U.S. State Department's Surveillance List, a list of companies that are invested in Iran's energy sector. The energy sector investments are what finances Iran's nuclear development. The bill had wide bipartisan and bicameral support. I believe this is important both practically and symbolically. We currently have about $200 million invested in these companies. And this approach allows us to support a peaceful attempt to convince the Iranian government that developing nuclear weapons is unacceptable to most of the world community. The bill, which had the enthusiastic support of Treasurer Ted Wheeler, passed the House 57–0 and the Senate 26–2.

I was reminded in this session that sometimes a legislator can play an important role in improving legislation that is being championed by other members. We heard testimony, in the House Human Services Committee, on HB 4084. This bill came from an interim task force focusing on reducing elder abuse, a very important goal. But as I studied the bill I came to believe that it was a terrible bill, however worthy its goals. Among its problems it defined everybody in Oregon over 65 years of age as "vulnerable." It authorized any DHS employee or any police officer to gain total and free access to any senior citizen's bank records or medical records without any court supervision. All that was necessary was for the requester to assert that they were doing an elder abuse investigation and they could copy and carry away all of the records. It did several other bad things, including creating a new and totally unnecessary felony.

After complaining bitterly in the hearing I went to work to improve the bill, because I did feel the goal was very valuable. I worked with the ACLU and the criminal defense lawyers' lobbyists and with the advocates of the bill to create amendments that would improve the bill and make it acceptable. The final amendments removed DHS access to the critical records and required public safety officers to get a subpoena for access to financial records. Those changes allowed me to vote yes on the amended bill as it passed the House easily.

One of the last acts of the session was to pass foreclosure legislation. This bill will require banks to enter into mediation with homeowners and stop the practice of dual track foreclosures. Protecting homeowners and home values is a significant step in our economic recovery.

In summary, I think we had a productive session. But so very much remains to be done to improve our schools, to renew our economy, and to support health-care reform. I will be working hard in the coming months to lay the groundwork for a successful 2013 session. And I am always delighted to hear your ideas. □

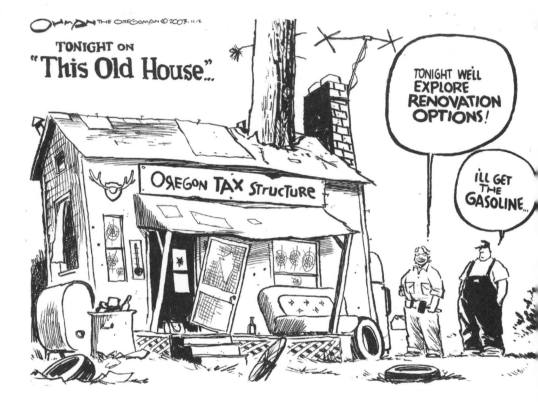

6 BACK IN CHARGE

OREGON HOUSE OF REPRESENTATIVES, 2013

THE CONTEXT

The elections of 2012 returned the House to a Democratic majority, with thirty-four Democrats and twenty-six Republicans. The movement of the Republican caucus back into the minority was a bitter pill for the caucus, whose leaders had hoped to regain the majority. And it caused some reported bitter fights within the caucus. But the messages in this session reflect a very interesting session, with many important legislative actions, including a great deal of bipartisan support for issues such as continuation of health-care reform. Since I have been in the legislature it has been my impression that when the chips are down we can usually find a way to work together for the good of the state.

Messages from this, my sixth session, focused on several critical long-term issues. We made progress on some of those issues; on others, not so much. On the progress side, we moved forward on the Governor's reorganization plan for higher education. Several of the messages discuss changes in higher education governance as we passed significant bills; including one creating new governing boards for some of the state universities.

These changes came about after years of negotiation among the Oregon University System (OUS), representatives of the universities, statewide student and faculty organizations, and leading members of the House and Senate committees responsible for higher education. The process was very contentious because of the need to resolve many knotty issues, both at the micro and the macro levels.

One very contentious issue at the micro level was whether faculty representatives should be on the governing boards and if so, with what powers. At the macro level we grappled with such questions as the role of the legislature in regulating tuition levels at the universities and the extent to which the OUS had a continuing role in Oregon's higher education system. As I reflect on the session I fear the changes we put in place, including moving forward on an independent governing board for Portland State University, have set back the ultimate merger of PSU and OHSU by several years.

In an even more contentious long-term fight we finally, after a decade of debate, passed a tuition-equity bill providing in-state tuition for the children of undocumented parents at Oregon's state universities and colleges. This provides access to higher education for kids who have lived in Oregon for most of their lives and attended and graduated from an Oregon high school. That measure was introduced for the first time during my first term in 2003 and failed.

A long-term policy issue that did not fare well was my effort to move a referral to the voters to abolish the death penalty. I had decided that it was time, in my sixth legislative session, to begin a legislative discussion on abolishing the death penalty focusing on moral, fiscal, and practical elements of the situation. It seemed like a propitious moment to introduce such a measure because Governor Kitzhaber, while inviting Oregonians to begin a serious discussion about the death penalty, announced that there would no executions during his term as governor. As the messages report the measure gathered a strong group of supporters, had an exciting hearing in the House Committee on the Judiciary, and died, without a vote, in that committee.

My tendency to introduce tough long-term issues is characterized by my effort to deal with abolition of the death penalty. As discussed in one of the messages in this chapter I am sometimes criticized for wasting time by forcing discussion of matters that are unlikely to be passed in a given session of the legislature. I believe introducing long-term and difficult issues into the legislative process is one of a legislator's most critical responsibilities. It is, of course, not the only responsibility, and I would not consider it productive to spend all of my time tilting such windmills. But occasionally, a windmill turns into a dragon and becomes slayable.

Efforts to restrict access to assault weapons and assault level ammunition triggered a series of events that occupied parts of several messages during this session. My introduction of an assault weapon restriction bill, in response to mass murders in Oregon and in other states, unleashed a firestorm of opposition. This opposition was expressed in the form of several thousand emails and phone calls to my office from all over Oregon and across the country. Many were just straightforward "don't mess with our second-amendment rights" messages composed by the NRA and other pro-gun groups. But many were abusive, obscene, and even threatening. The more threatening ones were turned over to the state police.

There was at least one positive outcome in this struggle reported in one of the messages of this session. That began when a rally was scheduled that promised to bring several hundred armed demonstrators to the Capitol to protest threats to their unfettered access to weapons. In recognition of the fact that our state Capitol is wide open and that people with carry permits are allowed to bring weapons into the Capitol, the state police crafted a security plan. The plan included a beefed-up uniformed presence in the building and some training of building staff on emergency procedures. However, the demonstration was completely peaceful, held on the steps to the Capitol, as are most demonstrations, and led to no aggressive show of force inside the building.

That event led me to contemplate the wonder of our open state Capitol. It is truly the "peoples' building" with citizens wandering, unrestricted, all over the building. It is a very different feeling from other capitol buildings I have visited, characterized by weapon scanners at the entrances and offices tucked into locked corridors. I hope we never change that by restricting the public's access to the legislators and to the legislative process.

There were other important issues addressed during this legislative session, including an important step in the development of a new I-5 bridge across the Columbia River. As the message reports I have been opposed to continuing to spend money on the bridge design without legislative approval. So I introduced a bill that would have restricted continuing expenditures until a set of four criteria had been met. My bill did not get a hearing, but my proposed triggers were amended into the bill authorizing the Treasurer to sell the bonds for the bridge project. And I asked questions during the floor debate that made it clear that the Treasurer was not authorized to sell those bonds until and unless those conditions were met. As the project has moved forward since the bill passed, it turns out those triggers are very important, as the Washington Legislature has refused to authorize the sale of Washington bonds to fund their share of the cost of the project.

The question of the viability of PERS, the Public Employee Retirement System, dominated much of this session. During the 2003 session we modified the system to change the conditions for all public employees hired after 2003, but that still left a potential problem for the tier-one employees, those eligible for PERS at the time we made the changes in 2003. The fund at that time had a very large potential unfunded liability. The legislature attempted to deal with that by reducing the promised cost-of-living increase across the board. That however, was overturned by the Oregon Supreme Court. Then the financial crash of the mid-decade dramatically increased the unfunded liability, triggering huge increases in employee payroll expenses for school districts, local governments and the state budget.

Governor Kitzhaber proposed a "grand bargain" restricting PERS expenses (by reducing the COLA in a different way) and increasing revenue for schools, higher education, mental health services and care of the elderly. The Senate and the House passed a bill to reduce PERS expenses, but could not get the Senate Republicans to agree to revenue increases and further action on the matter was delayed to a special session called by the Governor in September. It definitely reminds me of the saying attributed to Winston Churchill "You can always count on Americans to do the right thing — after they've tried everything else."

The MitchMessage

January 9, 2013 — Pre-session Report

I am eagerly awaiting my sixth session in the Oregon House of Representatives. This 77th session of the Oregon Legislature will begin with a one-day organizing meeting on January 14 and will adjourn until we get down to work in earnest on February 4. Three things will happen on the 14th — we will elect the Speaker, we will adopt the rules, and we will have the first reading for about 800 bills that have been pre-session filed. The first reading is an actual reading of the bill number and the "relating to" clause of each of the bills by the reading clerk. This wonderfully archaic ritual is fun to watch, as the clerk buzzes through the bill reading in about an hour. The importance of doing the first reading in advance of February 4 is that the Speaker's staff will then be able to assign the bills to committees so we can get right down to work on the first day we come back into session. This is all programmed to have us finish by June 30.

During the last session the House was split 30–30 between the Democrats and the Republicans. As a result of the last election the House now has 34 Democrats and 26 Republicans. Rep. Tina Kotek will almost certainly be elected Speaker, since she is the unanimous choice of the Democratic Caucus. I think she has all of the characteristics necessary to become a great Speaker — she is smart, hardworking, universally courteous, and very tough. Tina will become the first openly lesbian Speaker of any house of representatives in the United States. She was, during last session, the leader of the Democratic Caucus. Rep. Val Hoyle, of the Eugene area, is now Majority Leader in the House. It is worth noting that with Senator Diane Rosenbaum, the Majority Leader of the Senate, three of the four leadership positions of the legislature are held by women. Only the President of the Senate is a man. That is another important first for Oregon.

CAPITOL LETTERS

I have been named to chair the House Committee on Health Care once again, with two able vice-chairs, Republican Rep. Jim Thompson and Democratic Rep. Alissa Keny-Guyer. I expect that a great deal of my time and energy will be occupied with duties of the chair this session, as we continue the work we began in past sessions transforming the Oregon Health Plan and implementing the Oregon Health Insurance Exchange, now called "Cover Oregon." I will keep you informed on these topics as the session progresses. I can say that the health-care system in Oregon is going to change in some very dramatic ways, and I continue to believe that these changes will improve the access, effectiveness, and efficiency of health care in Oregon.

In addition to my work as Health Care Chair I have my usual ambitious legislative agenda. Fortunately, I have an able legislative aide this session to share the burden. Autumn Shreve, a recent graduate of the University of Oregon Law School, joined the staff in August and has already begun to focus on that agenda. She will be a primary resource if you need help with any issue and will probably be easier to connect with than me. As usual Harriet is always readily available to deal with scheduling problems and to be generally there to help.

Among the new things I will be focusing on this session is a measure (HJR 1) to refer to the voters a constitutional amendment to abolish the death penalty in Oregon. I have consistently spoken against the death penalty since my very first campaign in 2000, but I have done nothing to act on my beliefs. I decided my conscience did not allow me to ignore the issue any longer. Stimulated by Governor Kitzhaber's call for the citizens of Oregon to have a serious conversation about the death penalty I had the measure drafted. I am now in active conversations with groups interested in helping get the measure passed if we can get the referral out of the legislature.

Legislators are frequently invited to do "ride-alongs" with various professionals, such as state troopers, school principals, and teachers. Legislative concepts frequently come out of these experiences. About a year ago I did a "teacher for a day" stint in a grade school in northeast Portland. I was appalled by the alarming lack of security at that school. I was teaching in a third grade classroom right next to an unlocked door, one of several unmonitored and unlocked doors at that school. I checked in with the security department of Portland Public Schools and found out they were as concerned as I was, but because of budget limitations they were not able to implement limited access systems, security TV systems or other security infrastructure improvements. That got me to work on a bill (HB 2337) that would create a matching fund to which school districts could apply for help in improving the safety of their schools. Ironically, I introduced the bill the day of the tragic school massacre in the East.

I will be back with some of my old chestnuts this year. I have noted that it frequently takes several sessions to pass complicated legislation. I have a couple of anti-smoking bills, including a $1 per-pack cigarette tax and a proposal to move cigarettes behind the prescription counter. The later proposal is in recognition that tobacco is more addictive than heroin and its use needs to be controlled. I also have a gas tax proposal to provide resources for our failing highway system.

I have a bill to slow spending money on developing the Columbia River Crossing proposal until we have some indication that it really is possible to fund and carry out. The Governor, the Speaker of the House, the entire business community, and most labor unions, oppose this bill. But it is clear to me there are better alternatives to do the job and that the current plan cannot possibly happen, despite the fact that we have already spent nearly $200 million planning the project.

I am very worried about Oregon's public health system. Currently we lodge the responsibility for local public health in our counties. But counties are currently under terrible fiscal stress and some are facing bankruptcy. Few counties put general funds into the local public health system. Consequently most of the local health agencies are fully funded by funds coming from the state, most of which come to the state through the Centers for Disease Control. I have a proposal to create a regional public health system to relieve the counties by moving local public health to a system of eight regional public health agencies which could combine the resources to allow much more effective organizations. This would modernize Oregon's public health system.

My other committee assignment is the House Committee on Higher Education and Workforce Development. This session will provide special focus on our system of higher education as a part of the recognition that we have failed to support higher education in Oregon. At the same time we have created goals for educational attainment in our population that will only be achieved by a new focus on the organization and delivery of higher education services. We will particularly be dealing with the governance of our major universities and the questions of creating independent boards for Portland State and the University of Oregon. I will continue to advocate for the idea that Portland State should become independent of the Oregon University System and should be governed by the same board that governs the Oregon Health & Science University. An augmented board with responsibility for both major metropolitan universities would be in a stronger position to create a world-class system of higher education in the metropolitan area and therefore for Oregon.

We continue to welcome your emails urging certain policies. We receive a great deal of mass emails from folks on all sides of issues. But I can tell you that two or three original emails about heartfelt positions communicate much more effectively than 100 of the robot messages sent in response to a mass communication from the Sierra Club, the National Rifle Association, or change.org. But, whichever, keep the messages coming.

The MitchMessage
February 17, 2013

The first two weeks of the session flashed by as we got organized and got back to work with a running start. Because of the way the session was organized, meeting one day in January to introduce bills, we had a full committee agenda when we got back on Feb. 4. I am pleased to return as chair of the House Health Care Committee with two terrific vice-chairs, Republican Jim Thompson and Democrat Alissa Keny-Guyer. Jim and I were co-chairs last session and we have a great working relationship. I have a new committee administrator this year, which was a bit of a shock after working with one for several sessions. But she was moved to the Senate Health Committee this year. However, Tyler Larson, the new administrator, and my two co-chairs are quickly becoming the nucleus of a great team.

We have already had more than 80 bills assigned to our committee and we passed the first two bills out of any committee this session. I carried one of them on the floor and Rep. John Lively, a freshman, carried the other one. Since he was the first freshman to carry a bill to the floor he was the victim of a friendly hazing ritual, in which he was bombarded with questions from members of both parties. Rep. Lively, an experienced politician from Springfield, handled himself admirably and upheld the honor of the rather large freshman class. In addition to hearing and working bills for the first month of the session I have scheduled a series of informational hearings to help new members of the committee catch up with what has been happening in health care and health reform during the last couple of years. We have reviewed the health-care transformation process and the development of the health insurance exchange (Cover Oregon) and several other critical health policy issues.

I am a member of the House Committee on Higher Education and Workforce Development. Rep. Michael Dembrow, the chair, has scheduled a similar informational process to which he refers as "Higher Ed 101". The committee got into a real issue this week by working HB 2787, a bill to provide in-state tuition to undocumented students who have attended high school in Oregon for three years, graduated from an Oregon high school, and had applied to get on a path to permanent residence or citizenship. You cannot imagine what a fuss such a modest bill caused. This bill is projected to serve less than 40 students in the first year and perhaps 80 during the second year. And it would bring in an additional $400,000 a year to the university budgets. But the hearing was filled with xenophobic testimony warning that passing the bill would signal the end of modern civilization, as we know it. But this testimony was balanced by some powerful supporting testimony pointing out the inherent fairness of the proposal and enumerating the potential benefits to Oregon of encouraging these students to get a higher education in Oregon. I expect the bill will pass out of the committee this coming week and pass a floor vote.

The tuition equity bill was one of several that caused large crowds to pack the halls of the Capitol. We were particularly worried when we were made aware that a very large rally was planned in opposition to proposed legislation restricting firearms, such as a bill restricting the sale of assault weapons that I am planning on introducing. We were told by our security team that as many as two thousand people, each with a concealed carry permit and carrying weapons, would descend on the Capitol. We were also told that with a concealed carry permit they would be permitted to enter the Capitol. I, for one, am very proud that "the peoples' building" is wide open, with no security lines to go through and nothing that restricts citizens from wandering the halls. And I love that. But the possible scenarios that we all could imagine were pretty daunting.

The building is usually guarded by a small state police contingent and by a few retired state troopers who monitor the hearing rooms. We were briefed on the security procedures, and most carried on with business as usual, with extra troopers in the building and in full sight. And what happened was nothing at all out of the ordinary. Two to three hundred peaceful demonstrators were out on the mall making their political statement. I am sure several visited the building without incident and mixed with several other demonstrations going on in the building, including a large contingent of Oregon Public Health Association members, whom I assume were armed only with the justice of their causes.

I have been getting a bunch of static because of a few of my bills. The one that caused the most noise is a bill I introduced last session and nobody noticed, even though it had a hearing. The bill is HB 2077, a bill to make tobacco products a class III drug, for sale only on a physician's prescription and is intended to point out that nicotine is more addictive than heroin. The opposition to this bill went viral, with a long rant by Rush Limbaugh and lots of coverage on conservative blogs. I was interviewed by the *Toronto Star* on the bill, on drive-time radio in Los Angeles and Seattle, and on several programs in Portland. I was invited on *Fox and Friends*, but Harriet put her foot down. The bill is one of a series of three anti-smoking bills I have introduced, including one that would raise the tax on cigarettes by $1 per pack. I have received hundreds of emails on the topic, most providing a coherent argument, such as "You suck, you liberal moron." Other bills that are causing a great deal of commotion include a bill to require a paid permit for the use of studded snow tires, and my proposal to refer a constitutional amendment to the voters to abolish the death penalty.

Interviewers asked me whether I expect the cigarette bill to pass. I answered no, but the bill was a part of a package, and was designed to change the conversation on smoking, and perhaps to pave the way for the passage of the tax bill. I was asked, in several interviews, whether I thought that was a legitimate function for a legislator. My answer was that I did not think a legislator is doing the job without raising, for discussion, important public policy questions. And I certainly view that function as central to my job as a legislator.

We are beginning to settle into a routine in Salem. We have taken a room in a suites motel and will have the same room for the next five months. It is a home away from home. We tend to stay in Salem on Sunday, Tuesday, and Thursday nights. That allows us to drive only one way per day. We have our scoreboard up in our office and have begun to follow which committee has which of our bills. And I have begun to testify on behalf of the bills I sponsor. We have received notice that a hearing has been scheduled on Feb.26 for HJR 1, the death penalty abolition referral. My legislative assistant, Autumn Shreve, has been as busy as I have become, but she remains available if you need help from our office. Stop by if you are in the building and keep the email coming.

The MitchMessage
February 24, 2013

Events of the last couple of days led me to use this edition of the *MitchMessage* to reflect on the role bullying plays in the public policy debate. The first event was the passage of HB 2787, the Tuition Equity Bill. The second event was my introducing HB 3200, the bill to limit access to assault weapons.

I was first involved in a debate on tuition equity during my first session in the House ten years ago. The reaction to that bill was fast and harsh, with the anti-immigrant group out for blood. The sponsor of that bill was Republican Representative Billy Dalto, a Latino political conservative. But he was severely punished by his caucus for sponsoring the bill and causing the rabid opposition to it. Even though he thought he had enough votes in the House to pass the bill if it came to a vote, he was forced by his caucus to move it back to committee to die. The bullies won that battle.

We move forward a decade to this session. I mentioned in my last message the nature of the debate on HB 2787. I have been reflecting on the calm, orderly, polite, and reasoned testimony by a group of Latino students in support of that bill. And reflecting on the emails supporting the bill, that were uniformly of that same nature. The emails opposing the bill, on the other hand, tended to be wild, abusive and somewhat threatening. I believe it was the nature of that debate that caused us to take ten years to pass a modest and totally reasonable bill.

But what has really triggered this message is the abusive and threatening responses I have received as a result of my sponsorship of HB 3200. This bill was drafted by CeaseFire Oregon, who was encouraged by several of us to work on an assault weapon bill. It was not clear who was going to be the chief sponsor of the bill, but they knew I was willing to do so. By the time of the deadline to introduce the bill last week, opposition to the idea of limiting access to assault weapons had already caused President Obama to drop plans for a federal bill renewing the assault weapon ban and had caused members of the Oregon Senate to drop their plans for bills to limit access to some forms of ammunition.

I believed that because of recent deadly events in Oregon and in other places in the United States we needed to have an option in Oregon to try to limit the availability of extremely lethal weapons. So when nobody else was willing to sponsor the bill, I introduced it. The reaction was almost instantaneous. The office phone began to ring and the emails began pouring in. The calls were so abusive and threatening that Harriet stopped answering the phone and we began deleting emails. Almost none of the calls or emails were from my constituents, whom I believe overwhelmingly support an assault weapon ban.

So far, we have deleted about 1000 messages, most of them accusing me of treason for willful violation of the U.S. Constitution. I have answered a few of the semi-rational ones explaining my view of the Second Amendment. I point out that the Second Amendment does not allow citizens to have nuclear weapons, fighter aircraft, tanks, and other war weapons. We are not deciding whether or not the Second Amendment authorizes unlimited access to all weapons. It obviously does not. Our public policy responsibility is to decide where to draw a line on a continuum — in this case whether to include or exclude assault weapon availability.

The few messages that explain why they need assault weapons vary from saying I am trying to take away their means of protecting their children to explaining they need the weapons to protect themselves when the totalitarian government comes for them. Many of the messages seem rational in their outrage and in their arguments. But an unfortunately large number sound simply paranoid. And a large number report they are beginning to mobilize a campaign against me in case I don't notice that I have destroyed my political career by this anti-American proposal. To show the pace of the emails, about a dozen new ones arrived while I was writing this message. But I also received word that a SignOn.org petition entitled "Gun Control Now: Oregon Must Act" has received nearly 4000 signers, including more than 100 of my constituents.

I have to say that I don't feel very threatened by this spiteful outpouring, but I am really saddened by it. It is clear to me that some people who feel strongly that we must do something about gun deaths in the United States are unwilling to take the issue on because they don't want to subject themselves to this kind of abuse. I seem to be having a banner year for getting attacked from near and far, because I believe it is the responsibility of a legislator to raise the difficult issues and to endeavor to have a rational debate on those issues. This year the issues include tobacco use reduction, tuition equity, studded tire use, the death penalty, and certainly gun deaths. The lesson we learn from HB 2787 is that it sometimes takes a decade for the stars to line up for something good to happen. I hope it does not take another multiple-gun victim tragedy in Oregon for that to happen on the gun control issue.

The MitchMessage
March 10, 2013

The pace of activity continues to grow as we move into the second full month of the 2013 session. We passed a major piece of legislation out of the legislature, saw the introduction of the co-chairs' budget, had hearings on several of my legislative proposals. And the electronic fusillade aimed at me by the gun lobby continues unabated.

The process of moving the Columbia River Crossing (CRC) bill (HB 2800), provided a clear example of the power of special-interest politics. And of the ability of individual members to influence the outcome while the process grinds on. I have believed for some years now that the CRC is extremely unlikely to succeed in its current form. During the last session I had a bill to stop spending money on the process until the legislature voted on it. The legislature named a special joint committee to study the project and to propose a bill to move it forward. While they were working I introduced HB 2690, to stop spending money on the project until a set of four conditions had been met, including an analysis of its funding by the State Treasurer indicated there was really going to be enough money to do the project without subjecting Oregon to extra liability.

When the special committee introduced its bill I was delighted to find that they had adopted all four of my conditions into the bill, as required triggers before the Treasurer could sell the $480 million worth of bonds to fund Oregon's share of the CRC. Since the Governor, the Speaker of the House, the President of the Senate, and most labor unions and business groups in Oregon backed the bill, the steamroller was moving. I decided that because my conditions were included in the bill I would vote yes, but I took the opportunity of the floor debate to get assurances from the bill's sponsors that my conditions were firm and absolute. That helped to record legislative intent, in case there was any dispute about our intent. I continue to doubt, as I stated in my floor speech, that this project could succeed in its present form. It easily passed in the House (45–11) and the Senate (18–11) and was sent on its way to the Governor.

The co-chairs' budget was released this week and provided an interesting contrast to the Governor's proposed budget. This is the budget that will serve as the base of the final budget to be developed over the next couple of months. The big news was the strong support for the K–12 education budget. Most of us were concerned at the level of support in the Governor's budget, which proposed a funding level of $6.1 billion in direct funding and some support in the form of PERS reforms. The co-chairs' budget proposes support of $6.75 billion, including direct funding of $6.55 billion and $200 million in PERS reforms. And they recommend that we pass the K–12 budget as early in the session as is possible. That level will provide stability for most school districts, although it is far short of the support needed to bring schools back where they need to be.

There are several assumptions in the budget proposal that are needed to balance it and to keep funding for other services at a reasonable level. First the legislature will need to pass some significant PERS reform, as will the PERS governing board. We will have to take on serious discussions of the value of several tax breaks. And we will need to pass several of the prison sentencing reforms suggested by the bipartisan commission on sentencing. Balancing the budget will require some tough votes by both Democrats and Republicans, but we have no choice but to balance the budget.

As I said in the opening paragraph, the relentless barrage of email and phone calls attacking me for supporting restrictions on assault weapons continues. While most of them are canned messages triggered by NRA or other organizations, several are obscene, anti-semitic, or mildly threatening. In the last message I pointed out my disgust at politics by intimidation, but it is clear to me that it is successful. The introduction of HB 3200 triggered a barrage on my email junk file of a couple of thousand emails and on the junk file of many of my colleagues in the legislature.

February 26 was a day featuring another controversial topic, abolishing the death penalty. I introduced, with Senator Chip Shields, HJR 1, a bill to refer to the voters a constitutional amendment that would abolish the death penalty in Oregon. And the House Judiciary Committee agreed to hear the measure on the 26th. We had a stimulating day working with several groups that support abolishing the death penalty. Among those groups are Oregonians for Alternatives to the Death Penalty, Ecumenical Ministries of Oregon, ACLU Oregon and others. Prior to the hearing we had a press conference where several legislators spoke, as did several representatives of the groups. And we had a wonderful hearing with extraordinary testimony.

The hearing began with me submitting a letter from the Governor strongly supporting the measure to give the citizens of Oregon a chance to vote on the death penalty. The Catholic Church representative supported the measure, as did other clergy. And others talked about the moral, legal, and fiscal reasons for abolishing the death penalty. A former superintendent of the Oregon State Prison spoke about his experience overseeing the only two executions we have done since 1987. He pleaded that we not make any more decent citizens kill another human being on behalf of the state. Our next task is to convince the committee to consider the measure and to pass it on for a floor vote. I think it remains a long shot as of now.

Several of the bills I sponsored or was the chief co-sponsor had a hearing since the last *MitchMessage*. I testified before the House Rules Committee on HJR 2, a constitutional amendment to be referred to the voters that would allow the legislature to propose a merger of counties, with the approval of the voters of the counties. As you may know counties are facing drastic fiscal conditions and this is a measure that might be needed in some circumstances. The House Education Committee heard HB 2337, my bill to provide matching funds for improvements in school security infrastructure. The House Transportation Committee heard HB 2277, a bill to create a permit for the use of studded tires. I am hopeful that some of these bills will move forward in some form or another.

There was an outbreak of Norovirus disease caused by a problem in the restaurant at the Zoo. It turns out that restaurant was exempted from inspection by the Multnomah County Health Department because it was run by a government agency (Metro). Sen. Shields and I proposed SB 621, removing that exemption for any restaurant run by a government agency, OHSU, or the Oregon State Bar. The bill was heard in the Senate General Government Committee on March 8. It was supported by Metro and by Multnomah County. It passed unanimously out of committee to the Senate floor.

The Health Care Committee is moving at a very fast pace, requiring a great deal of my attention as chair. We have well over 100 bills assigned to the committee and need to complete our work on House bills by April 18. Some days we can work very quickly. For example one day we passed eight bills out of committee, either directly to the floor or to the Joint Committee on Ways and Means. Other times — not so fast. Last week we spent the whole week hearing testimony on the four major bills needed to bring Oregon's health reform efforts into compliance with the federal regulations that are coming out of the Affordable Care Act. And we will not finish work on those bills before the end of next week. Bills passed by the Senate are beginning to come to the committee.

Despite the email jam caused by the gun folks, I remain delighted to hear from my constituents. And that flow of mail continues. We have lots of work remaining in the time between now and our scheduled ending date, June 28, so keep in touch.

The MitchMessage
March 24, 2013

The goal in the legislative game is 31, 16, and 1. That is, for a bill to become a law, it must get 31 votes in the House, 16 votes in the Senate, and the Governor's signature. (That is 36, 18, and 1 for a bill that raises revenue.) And the route to achieve that goal is generally very circuitous. I am moved to begin this message this way because of an email I received this week.

I have a bill (HB 2278) that would require an annual permit for the use of studded tires. Many people feel they need to use studded tires even though the tires are quite destructive to the highways. So HB 2278 would require ODOT to establish the price of the annual permit by a study to determine the cost of the destruction by studded tires. The price for a permit would be set to cover that cost. The first step in the legislative process is to get a committee to hear the bill. The second step is to get that committee to agree to hold a work session and vote the bill out of committee. We had a very useful hearing in the committee and I received several messages of support from advocates for restricting studded tires.

A question raised in the committee hearing was how recently had ODOT done a study upon which the fee would be based. It turned out ODOT reported that their most recent study was several years old. After the committee meeting the committee chair told me that my bill could pass if we restricted it to ordering ODOT to do an updated study. That would allow us, in a future session, to decide on the permit idea with a better estimate of the price of the permit. I agreed to get it amended and reported this was where the bill was headed in a press interview. I immediately received an email accusing me of having sold out to Les Schwab and abandoning the cause. When what I was really doing was finding a way to move the bill in a way that it can ultimately accomplish the objective, even though that will still be off in the future.

The whole thing reminded me that people outside the Capitol rarely get to see the negotiations and machinations that happen once a bill gets introduced. Legislators often play into that by promising all the things they will do when elected. Truth is, sometimes we can get things done, sometimes we have to compromise to get a part of what we want accomplished, and sometimes we fail altogether. It's a little bit like life.

Along that line we had a little victory this last week. For years insurance companies paid nurse practitioners and physician assistants the same rate as physicians for doing the same work. But a few years back some companies began to reduce the reimbursement to NPs and PAs. This had the potential to threaten the supply of primary care and mental-health services, especially in rural areas. This session we introduced HB 2902 to remedy the situation, after a similar measure had failed the 31, 16, and 1 test during past sessions. I heard the bill in my Health Care Committee and passed it out to the House floor with a "do pass" recommendation. Last week I carried the bill on the floor. Between when it passed the committee and when it got to the floor the Oregon Medical Association mounted an aggressive campaign against the bill. That led to a ferocious floor debate, characterized by what seemed to me to be mostly irrelevant arguments. The bill passed on a bipartisan 39–20 vote, with eight Republicans voting yes and three Democrats voting no. It is on its way to the Senate in search of 16.

Since the last message I testified on several of my bills. I argued the teacher competency bill (HB 2692) in the House Business and Labor Committee. That bill arose out of a massive layoff of teachers in the Beaverton School District. The school district argued that state statute only required them to consider seniority and teacher licensure when making transfers, competency to teach the class being an optional consideration. This bill would require considering competency to teach a class before placing a teacher into a class. Oddly a few Beaverton teachers testified against the bill. Since the hearing I have worked out an amendment with the Oregon Education Association that I believe does the job and which makes its passage out of the committee very likely. I will keep commenting on that bill as it moves along.

I sought the advice of a wise mentor (a senior Republican legislator) when I first entered the legislature. One thing he preached was that you could accomplish a great deal if you didn't care who got credit. That principle applied in a recent bill that passed the House. Many years ago a part of Bonny

Slope, known as area 93 was taken into the Urban Growth Boundary, over my strenuous objection. There did not seem any way for the land, in Western Multnomah County, to become urbanized. And much to the frustration of the land owners, it turned out that Multnomah County had no way to provide needed urban services. My constituents, living in that area, came to me and for several months I explored ways to deal with the situation. Finally, I realized that the area was on the border of urbanized, unincorporated Washington County and suggested the possibility of moving the area into Washington County. At first it did not seem possible, but eventually the idea gained the tentative approval of the critical leaders.

So I proposed a bill to do that, and said I would introduce the bill if the counties and Metro agreed to the move. All seemed to agree and I introduced HB 2347, even though the area was no longer in my district. Once the bill was introduced the Washington County and the Multnomah County folks wanted the bill to be changed to make the move conditional on several factors, and Senator Betsy Johnson entered the discussion on behalf of her new constituents. I backed out of the negotiations and a new bill was drafted. That bill was introduced and last week passed the House overwhelmingly. I was pleased to speak in support of the bill and wish it well on its way to the Senate.

We had a terrific hearing in the House Revenue Committee on HB 2275, my bill to increase the tax on cigarettes by $1 per pack. The importance of this approach is that it would significantly reduce the probability of teenagers getting addicted to nicotine, as kids are very price sensitive. If someone is not addicted to nicotine before the age of 21, their probability of becoming addicted is minimal. The bill was supported by medical and public health professionals as well as many anti-smoking advocates. In my testimony I pointed out that nicotine is more addictive than heroin and in some ways more dangerous. Because the bill would raise revenue it would require 36 votes in the House and 18 in the Senate. Consequently, despite the support of this tax in the public at large, it is unlikely to get out of the committee because it is unlikely any Republican will vote for it on the floor.

In another big event this last week HB 2787, the tuition equity bill, passed out of the Senate and is on the way to the Governor for his signature. The bill would allow for instate tuition at our state universities for children of undocumented parents, kids who were raised in Oregon and graduated from high school in Oregon. We have been working on that bill since my first session in 2003. It passed overwhelmingly in both the House and the Senate.

The mail continues to flow in, with much of it supporting better funding for schools. But my constituents feel free to chip in on many topics. I continue to get a great deal of mail on gun control but, since a Steve Duin column on my flood of hostile mail from the opponents of an assault weapon ban, the mail has overwhelmingly supported my position, and more specifically supported me for taking a stand. Keep the mail coming.

The MitchMessage
April 7, 2013

This is the weekend that gets me reflecting on the variable pace of the legislative session. The legislative leaders have set a very tight schedule, designed to get us out of Salem before the end of June. The Constitution would allow us to go a few days into July, but that is not the plan. Consequently, we face firm deadlines, including a very significant one this coming week. Most of the committees (excluding Revenue, Rules, and Ways and Means) must complete work on all of the bills originating in their chamber by April 18 and further, must announce by April 8 all of the bills to be considered at each meeting between the 8th and the 18th.

For some committees that is not too much of a problem. But the Health Care Committee is one of the busiest and most productive committees. At last count we have about 45 bills scheduled to have hearings and/or work sessions in the next five 105-minute committee meetings. That is going to require a great deal of discipline on the part of my committee colleagues and on my part as chair.

This has some significance for each member of the body, because if any of their bills is not listed on a committee agenda, and is not assigned to one of the three permanent committees, *that bill is dead.* All of that work and anguish invested and it is rest-in-peace for that bill. Consequently, much of last week was dedicated to scrambling to try to get committee chairs to schedule bills.

My staff and I did one of those scrambles to save an environmental bill that is important to me and to my constituents in northwest Portland. I had learned the bill, HB 2336, that Sen. Steiner Hayward and I introduced on behalf of the Neighbors for Clean Air, could not get out of committee in its original form. We worked with the committee chair and other members of the committee to produce an alternative measure which would attract the votes needed to move it out of committee. But because it could not be amended we had to get a new bill drafted at warp speed, gather some co-sponsors, and present it to the Chief Clerk of the House by 3pm Friday. It was given a bill number (HB 3492) in time to receive a first reading on the House floor on the 8th. The bill will, within two hours, be assigned to the Committee on

Environment. That gives the committee administrator sufficient time to post the bill before the 5pm deadline.

That bill switch also demonstrates the nature of compromise in the legislative process. The original bill was intended to force DEQ to change their permitting process for toxic air emissions. It required them to include, as a part of each permit, analysis of toxic air emission of the company to be permitted. The new bill does not relate to the permitting process, but does have the promise of reducing some of the toxic emissions in the district and moves the air toxic debate a bit further down the road. Mary Peveto, of the Neighbors for Clean Air, said, "this bill might not give us the apple pie we hoped for, but it does give us some apple seeds."

We received some other good news this week about HJR 1, the measure to refer the death penalty abolition constitutional amendment to the voters. The bill was about to die in the Judiciary Committee on the 8th. I was able to get the committee chair's agreement to move the measure to the Rules Committee. This required consultation with the Speaker's office and the chair of the Rules Committee and my agreement to amend the measure to alleviate the concerns of some that it was not written in a way to maximize its chance of passing the voters. It will be moved this week and we will begin working on amendments.

Others of our bills are alive and well, or at least alive. HB 2348, my bill to consider the regionalization of local public health activities, was amended to name a high-level task force to consider the future of public health services in Oregon. The bill, as amended, was supported by the Oregon Health Authority and by the counties. It is scheduled for a work session before the deadline and I am working on a final amendment to solve some of the concerns of local public health authorities.

HB 2337 moved out of the House Education Committee to the Joint Ways and Means Committee. It will create a matching fund to help school districts improve the safety infrastructure of Oregon schools. Under this bill $18.5 million would be available to match local funds for such improvements as card-key door locks, video systems to improve communications, and improved playground fencing. I think the most important thing about this bill, which came out of my observing what felt like a very unsafe school, is that it will stimulate school districts to assess the security of their buildings. I visited some schools in Forest Grove that have done a great job in increasing security in a very systematic way and the increased feeling of safety in those schools was palpable.

The Business and Labor Committee is poised to pass HB 2692, the bill that requires consideration of competence to teach the class when transferring teachers. I worked out a compromise with the Oregon Education

Association and the committee chair to include a modest amendment that makes the bill acceptable to all parties. That broke the logjam just in time. I expect that bill should pass out of the House and move to the Senate. I hope it will go to the Senate Education Committee where it should get a supportive reception.

Our attention will soon turn to bills coming out of the Senate and to working toward a balanced budget. A big part of this process is dealing with reducing the impact of PERS funding. The Ways and Means co-chairs began that process by developing SB 822, which saves the state more than $800 million overall, including $200 million as promised for the support of K–12 schools. That will bring the K–12 funding to $6.75 billion as requested by the school community to keep things no worse than they are now and it is considerably more than the $6.1 billion in the Governor's budget. I have said for some time I would support PERS reform if I considered it legal, fair, and that it would produce the needed funds to balance PERS and tax reform to get to a final budget. I believe this bill does that and creates a fair request for PERS retirees by modestly reducing expected COLA increases. The proposal does not reduce the COLA increases (2 percent per year) for retirees with a pension less than $20,000 and reduces the COLA increase on pensions of $60,000 by only $25 per month.

We expect to pass SB 822 in the next two weeks, at which time we will begin to work to reduce tax loopholes or search for other sources of loose change under the sofa cushions. That is to say, I do not expect any single major proposal for raising revenue.

I continue to receive tons of phone messages and email against gun control, partly fueled by the fact that all gun bills are not dead yet. In fact, we are considering two bills in the Higher Education and Work Force Development Committee, which are raising a great deal of heat, if little light. These bills take different approaches to weapons on college campuses. I expect the hearing to be the usual circus that attends any potential for improving our safety from gun violence. I wish people who accuse me of violating my oath to uphold the constitution would study the Supreme Court's decision that validated the right to carry weapons, but also made very clear that the second amendment does not provide totally unfettered access to each and every weapon. In the meantime, I really appreciate the supportive messages I have been receiving since the Steve Duin column on the topic I talked about in an earlier message.

And keep your messages coming.

The MitchMessage
May 5, 2013

The thrill of victory — the agony of defeat. The catch-phrase of the old TV sports show rang in my head as we headed back to Portland from Salem Thursday night. Thursday was a critical day on the legislative calendar, the day all bills originating in the House needed to be passed out of most House committees or they were dead for this year. The only exceptions are bills in the three standing committees, Rules, Revenue, and Ways and Means. One of my most important bills, HJR 1, the bill to refer repealing the death penalty to the voters, died a quiet death when the Judiciary Committee chair refused to open a work session to move the measure to the Rules Committee for consideration of amendments that were being crafted as the bill died. Losing that bill really made me feel terrible.

On the other hand, several of my critical bills escaped from committee during this hectic week. HB 3492, a bill designed to reduce hazardous air toxics, made it out of the Energy and Environment Committee about the same time HJR 1 was dying in Judiciary. This bill was the successor to HB 2336, which we designed working with the Neighbors for Clean Air. HB 3492 was crafted in a way to get the votes needed to move it. But it is a significant advance in its own right.

Other of my bills that made it out of committee this week include HB 2277, my studded tire bill (in an amended form); HB 2337, a bill that would create matching funds for school districts proposing to improve school security infrastructure; HB 3467, a bill to reduce the misuse of mug shots taken of people not convicted of a crime; HB 2279, a bill to improve the health insurance options available for local government; and HB 2348, a bill implementing a study aimed at improving the public health system in Oregon.

And I passed HB 2960 out of my Health Care Committee, but not without significant drama. This bill is designed to ensure that critical meetings within the CCO governing structure are open to the public. CCOs are the organizations we have chartered to transform care in the Oregon Health Plan. These 15 or so organizations are entrusted with more than $5 billion (that is a B as in billion) of public funds during the next biennium and operate with a limited antitrust exemption. Most, but not all, of them hold meetings in public. This bill would require all community advisory board meetings to be open and that a portion of each governing board meeting be open to the public. But a small group of these organizations are extraordinarily averse to having the light of public exposure shine on their activities. One even testified that the members of their community advisory board were kept confidential.

A group of these organizations (or at least their physician plans) contributed more than $250,000 during 2012 to a lobbyist, who spread that money liberally to the campaigns of several key legislators. And when that lobbyist opposes a bill, such as HB 2960, all hell breaks loose — as it did in my committee. The bill passed in my committee by a 5–4 vote on this last day we could work on the bill. By the end of the session the Republican member who had voted for the bill was ordered by his caucus to change his vote. That would have required a suspension of the rules, which is virtually never done if it changes the outcome of a previous action. Consequently, I refused to allow it, as it would have killed an important bill for me. Since we were done with our business, I adjourned the meeting. Not a happy day. I expect I will be reporting more about this bill in future messages.

When I adjourned that meeting of the Health Care Committee on Wednesday, after passing HB 3460, a bill to regulate marijuana dispensaries, we had dealt with more than 40 bills during the last four meetings of the committee. We are among the busiest committees in the House. We had 142 House bills assigned to us and passed 69. We heard and passed bills sponsored by members of both caucuses. We now move to considering bills that have passed the Senate. We have already had 25 Senate bills assigned to us, and will probably get that many more during the next week or two. The pace will be considerably more leisurely from now to the end of May when the deadline passes for working Senate bills.

In addition during this period, I was delighted to carry the teacher competence bill (HB 2692) on the floor of the House. The debate was pretty weird, not relating overly to the content of the bill. But that sometimes happens. The bill passed on a bipartisan vote of 38–21, with 5 Republicans joining with 33 Democrats. It really didn't seem to me that it was a partisan issue, but for some reason it turned a little in that direction.

During the next couple of weeks we turn to serious budget issues, as we consider the Senate bill on PERS (SB 822) and a first shot at a House bill that increases revenue. The budget requires significant decreases in PERS expense and a modest increase in revenue. Fortunately I have been getting great advice from my constituents on these issues. Here is a synopsis of my email on these matters.

- Change PERS, it's too rich — Don't change PERS, promises made
- Don't increase taxes — OK on corporations — job killer, OK on rich — job killer

- Need more money for schools, higher education, care of the elderly, state police — cut expenditures
- Change measure 11 — keep criminals in prison
- Driver license for everybody — no driver license for those …
- Don't destroy the second amendment — make schools safer
- Represent your constituents — represent the whole state
- Wolves, cougars, dogs, wolves, cougars, dogs

I really appreciate the help. So I am going to be on my own, but I am also getting lots of advice from my caucus that, as the majority caucus, has the responsibility for balancing the budget. And as you can imagine all 34 members of the majority caucus are getting the same kind of email advice I am, especially those new members from swing districts. And the minority caucus, without the responsibility of passing a budget, is free to simply focus on how to play things to improve their chances of becoming the majority caucus. Having spent two sessions in the minority, I clearly remember the feeling. Since balancing the budget will require raising some revenue, and raising revenue requires a supermajority of 36 votes in the House and 18 votes in the Senate, the fun begins when serious talks start with the minority members of both Houses. Finally, don't assume that the negotiations between the House and the Senate majority caucuses are easy. Tip O'Neill, the one-time Speaker of the U.S. House of Representatives, was quoted as saying "the Republicans are our opponents, the Senate is our enemy."

Finally, I keep hearing rumors that I am retiring. In an attempt to kill those rumors I am telling people I intend to be the first one to be a member of the House on his 100th birthday. Failing that, my current intention is that I will stay a member of the House as long as my health and Harriet's health allow it and as long as we continue to have as much fun (most days) as we both have. And in the short term, I will file for reelection on the first day it is allowed.

The MitchMessage
May 19, 2013

"The Legislative Assembly shall provide for raising revenue sufficiently to defray the expenses of the State for each fiscal year, and also a sufficient sum to pay the interest on the State debt, if there be any." — Oregon Constitution, Article IX, Section 2.

And therein creates the dilemma facing the legislature dealing with our most important legislative duty, creating a balanced budget. The problem is that Democrats and Republicans do not necessarily interpret that section of the Constitution to mean the same thing. Democrats generally believe the proper approach is to determine what is required programmatically to serve the critical functions of state government. That is to say, to determine what is required to provide appropriate K–12 education, higher education, state prisons, state police, social services, health care, roads and other services. It is then necessary to figure out how to raise the revenue to fund those services. On the other hand, Republicans generally believe the task is to determine how much revenue is available, without raising taxes, and then to allocate the available resources for each set of services in the most appropriate way.

The June revenue forecast exacerbated the debate to an exquisite point. Before the forecast, which predicted $272 million more in revenue for the 2013–2015 budget, the Governor was pushing for a deal that would cut several hundred million dollars more in PERS costs and add $250 million more in revenue. That revenue was needed to provide a minimum balanced budget. The revenue forecast produced enough to get that balanced budget. But if the Governor's proposed deal is approved the extra revenue could be used to buy back some of the $4 billion in service cuts we have made since the economic downturn. It could provide some extra funds for K–12, for higher education, for social services, and for public safety. So the negotiations continue. But the path to a balanced budget is much clearer now.

While all this budget intrigue is going on we are quietly working, passing a balanced set of bills out of both Houses and on to the Governor's desk. Most of the legislative package has passed out of its chamber of origin and is being considered by the second chamber or is in the Joint Committee on Ways and Means. During the past two weeks the House considered 56 Senate bills and only 13 House bills. Only ten of those 69 bills received less than 50 aye votes (out of 60 members). I raise the vote count to point out a fact that is rarely mentioned in the press. The bulk of work done in the legislature is completely bipartisan. Differences are worked out in committee or the bills have a relatively low probability of getting to the floor. Only five of those bills passed with less than 40 votes.

That is not to say there were no interesting debates. HB 2672B, which provides some worksite protections for domestic workers, touched off a contentious debate. Such questions as "If I take my nanny on vacation to Disneyland does she have to be provided time for eight hours of sleep?" were raised in debate. (The answer is that she is an employee and not a member of the family and needs to be treated as an employee.) That bill only passed on a 32–28 vote. Although a bill (HB 2669A) which provided certain workplace protections to interns working for educational purposes, passed on a 59–0 vote.

And we had our annual battle over a water rights bill. SB 199A seemed like a simple bill clarifying a water rights statute. It came out of the Senate on a 28–0 vote and out of the House committee with a single no vote. But a minority report was introduced and it turned into a battle with the bill finally passing on a 32–28 vote. Proving once more the old legislative saying "whiskey is for drinking — water is for fighting."

Some of the bills that were sent to Ways and Means are beginning to emerge, including some bills necessary to complete the technical work on the health insurance exchange and on the Oregon Health Plan transformation. There are still some fights there, including a Republican threat to hold up the bill for the hospital self-assessment, which brings in federal matching funds of more than $1 billion per biennium.

Several of my bills are moving along, with hearings in Senate committees and in Ways and Means. The Governor has signed one bill (HB 2918) and one (HB 2691) is on his desk awaiting his signature. HB 2918 improves the chances of a higher-speed rail corridor between Eugene and British Columbia. HB 2691 provides an easier mechanism for out-of-state health care professionals to provide volunteer services in Oregon if they are currently licensed in another state.

And some are in trouble. I introduced HB 2692 to require school districts to consider the competence of teachers as a factor in teacher transfers. I negotiated some amendments to the bill, which weakened it in some ways, but generally improved it. It passed out of the House and was assigned to the Senate Committee on Education.. I have heard that some of the very parents who urged me to introduce the bill are prepared to kill the bill if it cannot be changed. I will have to decide if I am willing to kill it. Or it might get to a conference committee for more deliberation.

A controversy between the House and the Senate led to the forming of a conference committee on HB 2897, a bill to restrict the use of sun tanning beds to people older than age seventeen. In order to get the bill out of the Senate committee it had been amended to allow 17-year-olds to use the beds. At the urging of OHSU cancer scientists the House refused to concur and the conference (which I chaired) recommended the original House version. The report was accepted in the Senate with exactly 16 votes and they passed the bill in the original House form. I am expecting a few other conference committees on Senate bills we are likely to amend in my Health Care Committee.

We have begun to move Senate bills out of the House Health Care Committee and only have about 15 more bills to act on before the May 31 deadline for policy committees to work bills. After the deadline we will continue to meet on an abbreviated schedule to begin to hold hearings on issues that we did not have time to consider during the regular session. It begins our interim work schedule.

Generally committee work slows down, except for Revenue, Rules, and Ways and Means as we begin the end game that guides the march toward adjourning *sine die*, perhaps by the end of June.

The MitchMessage
June 2, 2013

Another important deadline passed last week on our march to adjourning *sine die* by the end of the month. Friday was the last day that any policy committee could work bills. The only committees that can now consider bills are the committees on Rules, Revenue, and the Joint Committee on Ways and Means. My health-care committee finished our work two days early, although we had the heaviest load except for the House Committee on the Judiciary.

We had a total of 180 bills referred to us, including 143 House bills and 37 Senate bills. The Senate bills had already passed the Senate, but the House bills were being considered for the first time. We held public hearings on 130 bills, 95 House and 35 Senate bills. And we passed 104 bills, 71 from the House and 33 from the Senate.

Many of the House bills were referred to the Joint Committee on Ways and Means for further consideration, mostly for fiscal review before going to the floors of the House and the Senate. Because Ways and Means is a joint committee bills approved by them go directly to both floors rather than being sent to a policy committee in the second chamber. Since the Ways and Means Committee is also preparing the budget bills (more than 50 bills comprise the overall budget) it is sometimes difficult getting your bills considered.

Oregon's legislature is different from many other legislatures in that it has a strong committee process. The rules of both chambers prohibit amending bills on the floor of the chamber, putting a great deal of pressure on the committees to get it right the first time. Sometimes corrections can be made in Way and Means, but sometimes a bill sent to the floor needs to be moved back to a committee by means of a motion to refer made on the floor.

Last week I was working on a contentious amendment to be added to a bill being considered in the committee. It was a health bill and the amendment was a technical amendment. I was informed that both parties agreed to the wording of an amendment and we passed the bill with that amendment. The next morning I was informed that a couple of words in the amendment could lead to some unintended consequences. When the bill comes to the floor next week I will need to move to refer it to the Rules Committee to fix the slight problem and bring it back to the floor for action.

Because the committees were churning out bills against the deadline there was a great deal of action on the floor of the House. Many of the bills were technical bills that could be handled easily, but some created some floor action. For example, since the last *MitchMessage* I carried the four major bills finally conforming state statutes that reformed the Oregon Health Plan and established the health insurance exchange to federal regulations. We mostly avoided getting into another debate on "ObamaCare." They passed easily.

On a less grand scale, but vitally important to a few hundred people, we passed HB 2510A. There is a program that allows low-income senior citizens to defer property taxes until their house is sold. We passed a measure in 2011 that removes a property from this program that becomes subject to a reverse mortgage. HB 2510A allows people who were eligible for the program when the statute became effective to remain in the program even with a reverse mortgage. I received a great many protests on this topic from folks unexpectedly dropped out of the program.

We also passed SB 384A that allows the Oregon Health Authority to train people to use Naloxone to reverse opiate overdose. We are having an epidemic of opiate deaths. Naloxone instantly reverses the effect of an overdose with one application sprayed into the patient's nose and saves that patient's life. The bill passed through the House and the Senate with a single no vote.

Other bills were not so easy. For example, we considered HB 2387A, which directs the Oregon Historical Society to raise money and commission a statue of Mark Hatfield to be placed in Statuary Hall in the U.S. Capitol. The problem with the bill is that the Hatfield statue would replace a statue of Jason Lee in that hall. This caused uproar around the state in religious circles because Lee came to Oregon as a missionary with a mission to the Indians. An email barrage followed its introduction and a battle ensued on the floor. It passed 36–22 on a bipartisan vote. I was delighted to vote yes because I consider Hatfield one of the greatest Oregonians of the 20th century.

Another bill that passed with 36 votes, although more along party lines, was SB 281, which added post-traumatic stress disorder as an indication for the use of medical marijuana. The debate was mostly against the medical marijuana program, but the testimony we had received in committee carried the vote. We heard several PTSD patients talk about how traditional medication did not work for them and the only thing that let them get through the day was "illegal" marijuana. There were many people in tears during that testimony, including members of the committee.

We expect the busy pace of bills on the floor to continue for a couple more weeks as bills begin to emerge from Ways and Means, but the sense of tension relief was palpable around the offices at the end of the week. We are all going to be trying to get our own bills out of the Ways and Means

Committee. And waiting and watching as the Governor and the legislative leadership attempt to negotiate the end game, which could include a revenue/ PERS deal. It is beginning to look like that is possible. In which case we will be out of Salem by the end of June.

The MitchMessage
June 23, 2013

As we near the end of this 2013 legislative session and my committees have closed, I have more time to contemplate the nature of the world. The House debate on SB 132 this week set me to thinking about a strong anti-science belief system that seems to be emerging in America. Consistent with a growing distrust of government and general anti-establishment feelings emerging in our society there is a particular distrust of "official" science. It lives on both the left and the right of the political spectrum.

SB 132 was introduced in response to a growing disinclination of parents to vaccinate their children on entering school. State laws requiring children to be vaccinated are decades old and led to the virtual disappearance of dangerous childhood diseases such as whooping cough (pertussis), diphtheria, and polio. Under current law, when a child first enters school, a parent must either provide certification that the child has been vaccinated or is medically inappropriate for vaccination. Alternatively the parent may claim a religious or philosophical objection to vaccination. Over the past decade, partly facilitated by a court decision broadening the scope of possible philosophical objections, the unvaccinated rate in Oregon schools has tripled until it is the highest in the nation. There are classes in the state where the large majority of kids are unprotected. This bill requires a parent to certify that they had watched a video reviewing the evidence for vaccination before they claimed an exemption. The bill was modeled after a similar program in Washington that cut the refusal rate by half.

One reason for the growing exemption rate is hundreds of scientific articles and pseudo-scientific articles on the Internet pointing out ridiculous evidence on the danger of vaccination. In truth, because there are slight actual risks associated with vaccination, the best option for a parent would be not to vaccinate their child if they were absolutely certain every other child to whom their child was exposed was fully vaccinated. Their child would then be protected by "herd-immunity." But there is no way that can happen in an open society. In our kind of society everybody must take actions to maximize the common good or each of us is exposed to the possibility of suffering the consequence.

The protest against accepting social responsibility and the distrust of official science was also exhibited in the debate over the proposal to fluoridate Portland's water supply. Despite the scientific nonsense spouted by the opposition the enormous weight of scientific evidence is unequivocal in proving the efficacy and the safety of fluoridating the water at the levels currently recommended. But 60 percent of the voters said "no."

I am carrying on about this issue because these attitudes have consequences. Because of the destruction of herd-immunity, terrible diseases are reappearing. There were 800 cases of whooping cough in Oregon last year. Measles is returning. The measles death rate is one in every 500 cases. Because of the fluoride decision hundreds or thousands of kids will face serious dental problems, many of which will require hospitalization for treatment. Because many continue to disagree with national science academies the world over that human behavior is causing global warming, we refuse to take real action to save the earth, as we know it. And I feel helpless to stem the anti-scientific tide.

On a happier note, there has been significant movement, since the last *MitchMessage*, on my bills. I carried HB 2974, a major good government bill, on the House floor. It passed easily and should have no trouble in the Senate. This bill, and a companion to it I passed earlier, will streamline the way the Oregon Health Licensing Agency works. HB 2355, which was carried by Rep. Tomei (one of three chief sponsors), also passed easily off the House floor. This bill provides more resources from lottery profits to fund gambling addiction treatment.

SB 413, a very weak bill aimed at improving the health insurance rate review process, was assigned to my Health Committee after it passed the Senate. I worked with consumer advocates and crafted three amendments to strengthen the process, giving the insurance division more tools to keep health insurance costs under control. I carried the amended version on the floor of the House and it passed 36-23. However, when it went back to the Senate for concurrence the Senate refused to accept the amended version. A conference committee will be named to see if we can achieve a compromise. I hope we can do so, but the original bill was so weak I am willing to let it die if we cannot strengthen it.

And speaking of compromise I was really pleased with one recent occurrence. The Oregon Health Plan Transformation process uses Coordinated Care Organizations (CCO) as the main delivery model. These 15 organizations statewide are totally responsible for organizing and delivering care for Oregon Health Plan members. Each has a governing body and a community advisory council (CAC). It turns out that there is nothing in statute that requires them to hold their meetings in public. So, working with Sen. Chip

Shields, I crafted a Senate bill and a House bill to require more transparency in CCOs. We got a hearing in the Senate committee, but opposition emerged from a set of several CCOs, represented by a powerful lobbyist and the bill died in the Senate committee. I did not see much use in pushing the House bill at that time.

But, a series of meetings was set up bringing the opposition and me together, with the Governor's staff, to try to achieve a compromise. We did come to a compromise requiring open meetings in the CAC and establishing methods that the CCO governing bodies would use to make public what they were doing in the management of the organization. It turns out I had a Senate bill (SB 725) in my committee that had been introduced by that same group of CCOs. I amended compromise language that we all had agreed upon into that bill. I carried the amended bill in the House and it passed without opposition. The Senate voted to concur with the House amendments 20–9 and the bill is on its way to the Governor for his signature. It feels pretty good when you can reach compromise on a difficult issue.

It looks likely that we will finish this session's work in the next week or ten days. Two factors will determine when we get out. First we still have a couple dozen budget bills to finish. And there are several policy bills that have yet to emerge from the Ways and Means, Rules, and Revenue Committees, including a few of mine. What is left is just grinding it out and bringing everything through the process. We did a couple hundred of those bills during the past week or ten days.

But also we are in the middle of negotiations that could bring more revenue to increase the funds available for education and other elements of the budget and bring more changes to PERS. I am frankly concerned with both sides of a possible deal. The revenue deal could be troublesome if it comes at the price of reducing taxes on high-income taxpayers. The PERS side of a potential deal makes me anxious because we are considering things that are either illegal or unfair to PERS members, or both.

I am sure my next message will come after we adjourn *sine die*. Until then…

The MitchMessage

July 18, 2013 — Session in Review

A friend asked me how I rated this legislative session. After a brief consideration I answered that I would give it a solid B. The session produced some really important legislation.

For example, we made funding schools a top priority this session. The education community requested $6.75 billion to support the K–12 budget. I think it was agreed that was a rather aggressive ask. We did, however, produce that amount for schools, with $6.55 billion coming in a direct allocation and a $200 million reduction in the PERS contribution from public schools.

In passing SB 822 we achieved a reduction of nearly $900 million in PERS charges to all levels of government and reduced the overall PERS liability by more than $2 billion. I was pleased to vote for that bill because I believed it was fair to retirees, could most likely stand up to a legal challenge, provided immediate relief for hard-pressed budgets, and could muster the votes to pass both the House and the Senate. The bill did pass both the House and the Senate with most Republicans voting against the package and most Democrats voting for it. As you can read in *The Oregonian* most every day, the PERS discussion is not over. But I hope the next discussion includes the public employees unions at the table along with other concerned interests in the state.

This was a big year for post-secondary education. After ten years of struggle we passed a tuition equity bill allowing children of undocumented parents to receive in-state tuition at our state universities. These kids need to have lived in Oregon for years and have graduated from Oregon high schools.

After a struggle almost as long as tuition equity, we passed what appears to be a complete restructuring of higher education governance. Our actions basically eliminate the Oregon University System, bringing the Higher Education Coordinating Council more directly into the picture, creating local governing boards for Portland State University, University of Oregon, Oregon State University (likely) and the four regional universities (possibly). The future of the regionals is still a bit cloudy with a simplified OUS having some continuing function, especially in the area of shared services among the state universities.

In the post-secondary institutions we also held tuition increases down a bit and provided a great deal of support for construction projects, including funding the total amount of bonding requested for construction projects in the community college system to provide improved access for Oregon students in post-secondary education. As I listened to testimony in the House Higher Education and Workforce Development Committee I was amazed with the extraordinary progress that has been achieved by our community colleges, even during these recent difficult budget times.

As usual I spent a great deal of my time and energy on my duties as chair of the House Committee on Health Care. We passed more than 100 bills out of the committee, including a set of bills putting the final touches on the transformation of the Oregon Health Plan and on the implementation of the Oregon Health Insurance Exchange, now called Cover Oregon. The blockbuster work on these critical activities was done in the 2009, 2011 and 2012 sessions. But there remained much to do; including passing some very complex bills conforming Oregon statutes to federal law.

As 15 Coordinated Care Organizations (CCOs) began to operate across the state, many operational issues emerged, some of which required legislative action. For example, we received testimony that some CCOs meetings were not open to the public. I proposed a plan to make the CCOs subject to the public meeting laws — which met with furious opposition. After a couple of months of negotiations, I was able to reach a compromise and amend a bill before the committee to open the Community Advisory Committees to the public and to provide other channels of communication with the community.

We were able to extend the self-assessment (taxing) of hospitals and long-term care institutions, with the strong support of both of those communities. Medicaid matches the "tax" those institutions pay. The Medicaid funds are used to support the system and the tax is totally returned to the institutions in the form of higher reimbursement rates.

We also implemented the expansion of the Oregon Health Plan by adding 220,000 new participants. The federal expansion increased the financial limit to 138 percent of the Federal Poverty Level and took away categorical requirements. All adults under that income limit now come into the Health Plan financed totally by federal funds for the first three years. Federal support gradually, over the next several years, reduces the federal contribution to 90 percent. These additional dollars will not only provide access to care for many whose access is currently limited, but will also pump billions of dollars into the local economy over the next several years. Since this money pays doctors, nurses, and other health-care workers, it is one of the major jobs programs we put in place this session.

We added autism behavioral treatment insurance payments to other health insurance mandates. The autism community has been working on that problem for years. In another bill that has taken years to develop, and thanks to the work of Rep. Keny-Guyer, we will now require direct-entry midwives to be licensed. It was a struggle, but it has significant promise to improve the safety of home-births in Oregon.

In another very significant action we licensed and regulated medical marijuana dispensaries. In recent years some 200 dispensaries have opened that are completely unregulated. We crafted a bill to regulate these dispensaries to create a safe channel of high quality and safe marijuana to people who have a legitimate and a legal right to use it. The Oregon League of Cities, Oregon's Attorney General, and Congressman Earl Blumenauer supported the final version. With some late session amendments, even the association representing the state's district attorneys did not oppose the bill.

I began the legislative session with a long list of bold bills and had some major disappointments among the successes. One bill I introduced at the request of some constituents living in the Beaverton School District would have changed the statute on teacher transfers to make competence to teach a mandatory factor to consider. I negotiated some language changes with the teachers union and passed the bill out of the House. The bill got to the Senate Education Committee, chaired by Senator Mark Hass. Stand for Children objected to some of the language in the bill as it came from the House. I began to draft amendments to meet their objections, at which time the representatives of Stand informed Sen. Hass they preferred the bill to die. And it indeed died; illustrating that compromise does not always get the job done.

But there were some significant bills of which I was the chief sponsor or a chief co-sponsor that passed to the Governor's desk. One of those bills brings restaurants managed by governments under the protection of health inspection. This bill was triggered when a Norovirus event occurred at the Zoo restaurant (run by Metro). It turned out that such restaurants were not required to have mandatory inspections. Metro supported changing the law.

We increased lottery funds used to fight problem gambling. A bill passed to help pay for alcohol treatment aimed at making it easier for first time DUII offenders to get services. We even made it more difficult to exploit people who were arrested but not convicted. Businesses were posting their mug shot on the web and then charging exorbitant rates to remove the photo. We put some barriers in place to make that more difficult.

We passed my bill to create a task force to assess the future of public health in Oregon and to make recommendations about such issues as the regionalization of the local public health system. With counties facing increasing financial pressures it appears unlikely that the current public health system model can survive, especially with the potential threat of pandemic influenza or other contagious diseases. State and local public health authorities enthusiastically supported the bill, after it was amended to deal with some of their concerns.

Continuing my interest as past chair of the legislative choo-choo caucus, I worked with Rep. Nancy Nathanson to pass HB 2918. Federal authorities have named Eugene to Vancouver B.C. as the Northwest High-Speed Rail Corridor. This bill facilitates ODOT working with Washington and British Columbia rail authorities to plan for the future of this rail corridor, and requires ODOT to maintain at least two train round trips a day between Eugene and Portland.

As I look toward the short session of 2014 and the 2015 long session I realize I still have a great deal of work to do. I remain concerned about cigarette smoking in Oregon and neither of my anti-smoking bills moved, including my plan for a major increase in tobacco taxes. I remain concerned about the joint future of OHSU and PSU, as SB 270 has made it more difficult to imagine the move to joint governance. And I continue to worry about the future of Forest Park. I did not push my Forest Park agenda this session, as the city park leadership changed with the new mayor in Portland. I recently reviewed my first *MitchMessage*, before the 2003 session and named these as three of my five key agenda items going into the session, the other two being improving passenger rail in the Cascade Corridor and creating an independent health agency in the state. I guess two out of five for a decade isn't that bad. It simply means I need to look forward to another decade in the legislature to finish what we have begun. □

WHAT IS ONE TO MAKE OF THIS WHOLE THING?

OREGON HOUSE OF REPRESENTATIVES, 2003–2013

Serving in the legislature is a personal experience. This retrospective chapter gives me the opportunity to reflect on the material presented in the seventy-five or so *MitchMessages* that comprise the body of this book.

The first thought that comes to mind is how personal the experience of being a legislator is. I point out in the introductory chapter that these messages are different than the communications sent out by other legislators, in that mine are less formal and are designed to reflect my experience in the legislature. Most other legislative newsletters are written by staff and are designed to shed glory on the achievements of their bosses. They are a part of the legislators' reelection campaign.

But it became clear to me as I prepared the *MitchMessages* for publication in this book that the experience of being a legislator is, in its own right, intensely personal. While we share some elements of a universal experience during service in the legislature our reaction to that experience is unique. Our perception of that experience is filtered through our life history, our attitudes, our present home and work situation, and many other intangibles. As I pondered my experience over my first six terms in Salem I reflected on how the legislator in the next office is experiencing the situation. She is a young lawyer in her first term. She had her first child during the last month of her election campaign. She brings the child to work with her each day and takes him to a daycare center near the Capitol. Down the hall are others with similarly disparate situations from my own.

I do not point this out because I believe that reading my personal reaction to the legislative process is useless to the extent to which it is unique — on the contrary, I think my personal background as a trained researcher brings a particularly valuable perspective to my observations about the process. But as with any case study it is useful to fit the limited data set into a conceptual framework. Any framework matures as qualitative data is fit into it. Even though the material in this book remains the reflections of a single participant in the process, it may prove helpful in crafting a wider view of the legislative process.

WHAT IS NOT IN THE BOOK?

As I was discussing the development of this book with a professor of political science, he reminded me that while the immediacy of the book was one of its advantages the material has been written and circulated by a very active participant in the political process. He pointed out how that situation certainly imposed implicit and explicit constraints on what I was willing and/or able to share with constituents and with the general public. To a certain extent that is true and there were some things I generally chose not to explore, or not to explore in great depth. There were other things upon which I simply chose not to focus because I did not think the *MitchMessage* was the proper medium for those explorations.

Among the former issues to which I did not devote much space or attention was the role of the caucus in the life of a legislator. That is to say, I chose not to report on the internal workings of the caucus to some extent, because I was constrained by confidentiality agreements of the caucus. But I think the more important reason is that the extent to which the actions of the caucus were relevant to my messages it was the public behavior of the caucus that counted. And I did report on those actions.

An exploration of the factors influencing legislative decision making is another example of a topic that was not covered extensively in the messages because the messages were not the right medium for that discussion. It is my impression that there remains a great deal to learn about how individual legislators, both at the state level and at the federal level, come to decide how to vote on individual pieces of legislation.

The legislator brings a built-in set of attitudes and opinions to the table. These positions are hardened through scores of times when questions were asked in debates, public appearances, and conversations with constituents: "What is your position on … abortion? taxes? global warming? land use? etc." That brings the legislator to the starting line on most topics. Then many other factors come into play. The lobbying begins, bringing to bear the influence of powerful interest groups, including those that have supported the legislator's electoral campaign. Each of us wants to make and keep friends, especially those friends who are or have been particularly helpful.

At critical times in the debate on any issue we hear from our constituents, usually on both sides of an issue. We commonly get "you must remember you represent us." This raises an interesting question for a legislator, which is the extent to which a legislator represents his or her constituency or the whole state. This plays out in the real world situation when the legislator believes a certain vote is required for the good of the state, but is quite certain it would not be the vote chosen by the majority of the district's constituents. In many districts this causes a great deal of anguish for a legislator considering a vote to raise taxes, or even to refer a tax increase to the voters. Tea Party activists mounted a primary challenge to two rural Republicans after each joined the Democrats in a vote to refer a temporary personal and corporate tax increase to the voters during the 2011 session. Both withstood the challenge with the support of many groups that usually support Democratic candidates.

And other factors emerge. We often get pressure from those of our colleagues who are the main supporters of a bill. Whenever possible we like to support our colleagues, particularly when we know their support is likely to be vital to pass one of our own main bills. And then occasionally, one gets some pressure from one's own caucus whips, to support a position important to the caucus.

These things don't necessarily play out when the legislator has a firm ideological or policy position on a topic. Nobody is going to try to get me to take a position against a woman's right to choose — and they wouldn't even bother to try.

But as I have described, many bills are important to one faction or another that are not necessarily important to other legislators. That is when the pressure comes out. This is clearly a topic rich with analytical possibilities.

SOME TAKE-HOME MESSAGES

Working in the legislature is an exhilarating experience.

I hope what comes through in reading the messages is that being a legislator is an honor, a responsibility, and a joy. People frequently say to me that working in the legislature must be a burdensome experience. And I reply that the dirty little secret is that being a member of the Oregon House of Representatives is both great fun and very rewarding. Why else would an intelligent person struggle to raise $500,000, knock on thousands of doors, and totally disrupt his or her life to win a seat in the House? It is especially rewarding for those of us who are fascinated by strategy and tactics, because during session many of us wake up each morning planning strategy and tactics.

Work in the legislature is a continuous, rather than an annual process. There is no way for one legislative session to bind another session. But as my messages point out there is a great deal of work that is begun in one session and continues into one or more future sessions. While there is considerable turnover among members of the legislature there is also significant continuity of membership, especially in states like Oregon, without term-limits.

A prime example of the continuous nature of legislative work in these messages is the work on health-care reform. There is some mention of Medicaid reform toward the end of the 2003 session, a session in which I was only marginally involved in the Health Care Committee. Some mention of health-care reform can be found in the 2005 session, but it wasn't central to the work of the legislature until I became chair of the Health Care Committee in 2007. From that point on, because of factors in Oregon and nationally, health-care reform rolled on a fast track through each session from 2007 through 2013, with both Democrats and Republicans taking an active part in the deliberations. Each session began with a clear mission, if not with a clear legislative mandate.

Much of what the legislature does is of a routine nature. It should be evident from the mass of the messages that much of the work of the legislature is routine work that is needed to keep the government running smoothly. We pass about 1000 bills a session, the majority of which are passed with between fifty and sixty yes votes in the House. These bills were worked out in committee and address issues raised by agencies or interest groups that are either technical fixes to problems that have arisen or are policy changes that are supported by all who are affected by the change. The typical path for a bill of this kind, especially if it does not have a significant price tag, is one hearing in the committee, onto a vote in committee, where it passes with little or no dissent; then to the floor of the House, where it passes without debate. This does not mean the action was trivial, but it does mean it does not cause much controversy.

BRINGING TOUGH ISSUES TO THE LEGISLATURE

On the other hand, I believe it is part of a legislator's central job to bring tough issues to the body, issues that might take several sessions to pass, or might never pass. For years during the Republican leadership we debated the futile question of self-service for gasoline. (Self-service of gasoline is outlawed in Oregon and in only one other state.) While I have not seen a proposal on the topic during the last few sessions, I am sure it will return sometime in the future.

Getting access to health care for more Oregonians is an issue some of us keep raising and we have moved during my career in the House to add several hundred thousand to the group of Oregonians who have access to health insurance. On other issues, I continue to try to figure out how to ensure proper planning for the future of Forest Park, to move PSU and OHSU closer to a merger, and to advance the cause of passenger rail in the Northwest.

A SPECIAL NOTE ON THE POWER OF THE SPEAKER AND OF COMMITTEE CHAIRS

I believe the Speaker of the House has a great deal of power in most state legislatures, but the Speaker has extraordinary power in Oregon. The Speaker names all of the committee chairs, as well as the House co-chairs of the joint House/Senate committees such as Ways and Means. In addition, the Speaker names all of the majority and minority members of each committee. If the Speaker is smart those appointments will be made after consultation with each member of the House and with the minority leader. The Speaker may choose to chair or sit on any committee and generally chooses to co-chair the Emergency Board, which is in charge during the Interim.

The Speaker controls the flow of bills through the House, beginning with the assignment of all bills to a specific committee; after a bill passes out of committee, the Speaker controls when it gets on the agenda of the House. In addition to all of this formal power, the Speaker has enormous informal power, being able to influence individual members on individual issues because of the ability to shower goodies, such as plum appointments, on a member.

Given this strong role of the Speaker, it is interesting to note that the various committee chairs also have a great deal of mostly unfettered power. The committee chair has absolute power to create the agenda of the committee deciding which bills will be heard and which won't. The chair decides which bills will be brought to a vote after they are heard, or which will die in committee. When a bill goes to the other chamber and is amended it is up to the chair to decide whether to recommend to the body whether the amendments shall be accepted or rejected. If the amended version of the bill is rejected the chair generally sits on the conference committee or recommends who does.

It is true that all of this is done in consultation with the Speaker's staff, but it is pretty rare that the decision of the chair is overridden by the Speaker's office. On the other hand, the more astute chair knows when to fight and when to back off and go along with the Speaker. The chairs generally remember that the Speaker always has the power to remove a chair, although that is a very rare event. I don't remember it happening in the House since 2003. Although I did hear a story about the Arizona House where the Speaker got mad at the Health Care chair and did not assign a single bill to that committee for a whole session. I am certain other chairs noticed that punishment and became a few degrees more compliant.

A FINAL NOTE

At the time I was finishing this book the U.S. Congress was engaged in an extraordinary self-destructive exercise of organized legislative malfeasance. With a Democratic president and a Democratically-controlled Senate, the Republican-controlled House of Representatives and the Republican minority in the Senate decided that their most important function was to make life impossible for the President, even if it meant bringing the government to a standstill through the use of such tactics as sequesters, shutting down the government by passing neither a budget nor a continuing resolution, and threatening to refuse to raise the debt limit. This triumph of organized idiocy caused the citizens' favorable assessment of the Congress to fall to less than 10 percent.

That leads me to speculate on why the picture I have presented of a decade of life in the Oregon House of Representatives is so different a picture than that presented in the Capitol in Washington. As I consider several factors that might provide an answer the first thing that comes to mind is the factor of size. We are a small state with a relatively small legislature. There are only sixty members of the House, not 435 and only thirty senators, not 100. We know each other and individually have much closer relationships than are possible in a body the size of the U.S. House of Representatives.

There have been times in Oregon when the legislature and the Governor were at loggerheads. During all of Governor Kitzhaber's first two terms he faced a Republican-controlled legislature. He became known as Dr. No because of the large number of bills he vetoed during those eight years. He complained upon leaving office that the state was ungovernable. But during that whole period we kept the state running, with a balanced budget, and with the business of the state carrying on apace. There were no threats of shutting down government in Oregon and certainly no threats of defaulting on Oregon's debts.

Certainly another factor that colors the behavior of the legislature is that we have a citizen legislature. Our senators and representatives have a life outside the building. Since we are only paid as part-timers, we go back to the real world after sessions and need to face the reality of real work and a real life. It is clear that the members of the U.S. Congress live a sheltered and pampered life.

In Oregon that member would be going back to a law practice or a college classroom, where people would ask about the crazy behavior they were displaying in Salem. Because we have this part-time legislature we have some excellent people willing to run for the legislature, people who would have to take a significant pay cut to take a full-time legislative position. At one time I counted that 80 percent of the members of our caucus had an advanced degree. That does not inoculate against craziness, but it does, at least, ensure a certain level of intelligence.

Finally, after fifty years of living in Oregon I believe the culture of the state moderates such behavior. Our pioneering spirit provides a can-do approach to solving problems that would simply embarrass us to behave in such an absurd way.

If there is a most important take-away message from reading this book it is that the Oregon Legislature comes to work and generally gets the job done, however difficult that job may be. □

| CAPITOL LETTERS | # ACKNOWLEDGMENTS |

First I want to acknowledge my wife and key staffer Harriet Greenlick. Harriet has been my inspiration and my helpmate during my whole legislative career, directing my office and managing my daily legislative life. She was a member of the editorial team for the *MitchMessages*, editing and proofreading every single one of my drafts over the decade reported in this book. The other member of the editorial team was Geoff Sugerman, who has been my media consultant from my first campaign for the Legislature in 2000. Geoff did the final editing on each message and was responsible for its electronic distribution. He is a great friend and an amazing consultant.

I had great support turning the individual *MitchMessages* into a coherent document. Angela Rico, who was a PSU intern in my office, did a remarkable job reading the messages session by session, highlighting the themes of each session. This helped me develop the introductory material for each chapter. Her PSU advisor, political science Prof. Richard Clucas, has provided very helpful and sage advice to me at various stages of getting the manuscript ready for publication.

I crafted the final manuscript for *Capitol Letters* while I was a fellow at the Center for Advanced Study in the Behavioral Sciences at Stanford University (CASBS) during the 2013 fall semester. My fellowship provided a wonderful experience for Harriet and me. I am indebted to the Center, its management and the other fellows at CASBS that year from whom I learned so very much. I especially want to thank the director, Iris Litt, for her support and fellow Donald Lamm, who was particularly generous sharing wisdom gained during his extraordinary publishing career.

The search for the right publisher took me to Ross Hawkins at ACS Publishing and the Arnica Foundation, who was extremely supportive and worked with me to create a path to this publication. Editor-in-chief Gloria Martinez was fantastic to work with as we edited the manuscript chapter by

ACKNOWLEDGMENTS

chapter. And the very talented Aimee Genter-Gilmore did a wonderful job designing the book and cover.

My daughter Vicki Ambinder, who supported the whole project, joined in on the final proofreading. Her husband Harris Ambinder, an English teacher, gets credit for suggesting the title, *Capitol Letters,* which truly characterizes the book.

My longtime friend, Bruce Bishop, served as a supportive critic from the first *MitchMessage.* After reading that first *Message,* Bruce was quick to teach me how to spell the name of the building with the gold man on the top. He served penance for all of his harassment with the great job he did proofreading the penultimate version of this manuscript.

Kerry Tymchuk, executive director of the Oregon Historical Society, facilitated the donation of my proceeds from the publication of this book to OHS and was helpful throughout.

And finally, I owe a huge debt of gratitude to my dear friend, the political cartoonist extraordinaire and genius social critic, Jack Ohman of the *Sacramento Bee.* Jack generously provided a set of his cartoons done contemporaneously with the *MitchMessage* sessions. These cartoons, taken as a body of work, provide their own unique lens with which to view Oregon politics. □

HOUSE JOINT RESOLUTION 100 FLOOR SPEECH

DELIVERED FEBRUARY 13, 2008

Opening statement:
Thank you, Mr. Speaker.
To the resolution.

WHAT IS HJR 100?

HJR 100 refers a critical question to the citizens of our state. It asks them if they believe the following statement should become a part of the Oregon Constitution: The people of Oregon find that health care is an essential safeguard to human life and dignity and that access to health care is a fundamental right. In order to implement that right, the Legislative Assembly shall establish by law a plan for a system designed to provide to every legal resident of the state access to effective and affordable health care on a regular basis.

WHAT ARE RIGHTS AND FROM WHERE DO THEY DERIVE?

The Declaration of Independence declared that we are endowed with a set of inalienable rights including the right to life, liberty and the pursuit of happiness. Those rights seemed particularly important to a group of men who were about to commit treason in aid of a revolution against the mightiest power on the earth. Their life, liberty, and their pursuit of happiness were clearly at risk, as they pressed ahead against England.

When independence was won, the former colonies were faced with approving a constitution that focused on defining the relationship between a newly created national power and the original colonies, redefined as states. As a price of ratifying the new constitution the citizens of the states insisted on a set of amendments to the proposed constitution, the Bill of Rights that limited the power of the national government vis-à-vis individual citizens. That leads us to ask why this statement of rights was so important to the citizens of the new nation. And the answer is clear. It was important because they were recent victims of what they viewed as wrongs on the part of their former ruler.

RIGHTS ARE A PRODUCT OF WRONGS — THEY COME FROM HUMAN EXPERIENCE, PARTICULARLY EXPERIENCE WITH INJUSTICE.

Because of the experience of the founders with what they viewed as unjust behavior on the part of an unfettered crown, their concern was with specifying rights which would protect citizens against the power of the government.

Now move with me from the 18th century to the 20th century. American experience in the mid-20th century was extraordinarily traumatic, with a depression that fractured the social fabric of our society and a World War that threatened our national autonomy. In the 1941 State of the Union Address, President Franklin Roosevelt proposed four freedoms to a nation reeling from the Great Depression and facing the inevitable entry of our country into a cataclysmic war — freedom of speech, freedom of religion, freedom from want, and freedom from fear.

Four years later, now armed with both the Depression experience and the experience of mobilizing a country to fight a great war, President Roosevelt began to lead the country into a new era. The United States had become the most powerful country in the world. Roosevelt was determined to guide the country into a peacetime prosperity fueled by a free enterprise, free market economy. He believed that in order for that to happen we needed a Second Bill of Rights, which he proclaimed in his January 11, 1944 State of the Union Address. That Second Bill of Rights proclaimed that every American is entitled to:

- *The right to a useful and remunerative job in the industries or shops or farms or mines of the nation;*
- *The right to earn enough to provide adequate food and clothing and recreation;*
- *The right of every farmer to raise and sell his products at a return, which will give him and his family a decent living;*
- *The right of every businessman, large and small, to trade in an atmosphere of freedom from unfair competition and domination by monopolies at home or abroad;*
- *The right of every family to a decent home;*
- *The right to adequate medical care and the opportunity to achieve and enjoy good health;*
- *The right to adequate protection from the economic fears of old age, sickness, accident, and unemployment; and*
- *The right to a good education.*

President Roosevelt died the next year, but the rights he proclaimed lived on and became the conceptual basis for the Universal Declaration of Human Rights, which was signed by all of the countries, including the United States, joining the United Nations after the end of World War II. The Declaration includes Article 25, which is most relevant to the motion before us today. That article reads, in part:

Everyone has the right to a standard of living adequate for the health and well-being of himself and of his family, including food, clothing, housing and medical care and necessary social services, and the right to security in the event of unemployment, sickness, disability, widowhood, old age or other lack of livelihood in circumstances beyond his control.

The Congress acted on the components of the Second Bill of Rights as a part of the plan to rebuild America after World War II. For example, the right of every family to have a decent home was central to the plan for post-war America. The GI Bill of Rights provided, among other benefits, low-cost houses to hundreds of thousands of returning veterans and their families. The Federal Housing Administration also facilitated the purchase of homes by millions of other Americans. And a most important piece of ensuring the right to a decent home has been embedded in our income tax policy, which allows taxpayers to deduct the cost of interest on home mortgages from state and federal income taxes.

Other of the rights proposed in the Second Bill of Rights have also been addressed in federal and state policy as well, including, I would argue, the right to food and to a decent education. But the right of access to effective and affordable health care has not fared so well. There were serious attempts to implement that right by federal action by presidents Truman, Nixon, Kennedy, Johnson, and Clinton. And we did succeed in creating the right to health care for segments of our population, including senior citizens, veterans with service-incurred injuries, members of the military, and the very poor — but not *all* Americans.

WHY DO WE NEED THE PROPOSED REFERENDUM AND WHY DO WE NEED IT NOW?

It is clear to most observers that the fact that more than 50 million Americans are without access to health care makes this a national problem, crying out for a national solution. But it is equally clear that there is not the national will to address it in a comprehensive way. Consequently, the majority of states in the nation are currently addressing what they view as a health-care crisis. In Oregon 500,000 citizens are without health insurance, a critical element in their ability to access appropriate health care. The cost shift from the uninsured to the insured is driving up the cost of health insurance to the point where employers cannot continue to provide coverage for their employees and their employees' families without jeopardizing their competitive position.

We received compelling testimony on the deprivations our citizens faced without regular access to health care. The plight of our uninsured Oregonians and other problems in the health-care system led, during the recent regular session, to SB 329. This bill created a process for developing a plan to reorganize Oregon's health-care system, including a promise of universal access to health care for Oregonians. That measure passed this House with more than fifty affirmative votes. The Oregon Health Fund Board, created by SB 329, is hard at work crafting a plan to be put before the legislature in the 2009 session.

The debate on that plan is going to be a difficult one. But that difficult debate can be facilitated by passing House Joint Resolution 100 and sending the HOPE amendment to the ballot in the November 2008 election. I believe that Oregon's citizens will support the idea that access to effective and affordable health care is a fundamental right and that they will instruct us to implement a plan by which that right can be ensured. But even in the event that I am wrong and the voters reject that proposition, that information will be invaluable as we struggle with the difficult task of improving our crippled health-care system.

I urge you to join me in providing our citizens a chance to weigh in on this important issue, by voting to accept HJR 100.

Statement closing the debate:

WHAT IS HJR 100 NOT?

In my opening statement I focused on what HJR 100 *is*. After this most interesting debate I want to focus now on what HJR 100 is *not*. HJR 100 is not a bill to create a system of socialized medicine. The extent to which there is a significant change in the government's role in financing or delivering health care, it is going to require action on the part of the legislature and the Governor — and ultimately an affirming action of the voters. Voter approval of the measure that follows from HJR 100 does not put a right to health care above any other constitutional right — it simply gives that right constitutional standing. And it does not produce any specific or immediate changes in the way health care is delivered to, or financed for, those of us who are currently happy with our health-care arrangements. It does none of those things. So why do we need it?

Rights come from wrongs — personal story

I argued in my opening statement that rights come from wrongs and the most powerful way to understand what that means is to consider personal stories. I am willing to wager that each of you has heard a personal story depicting the wrongs that come from people not having access to effective and affordable health care. I want to share my story and how my story leads me to the passionate belief that access to health care is a fundamental right of our citizens.

Three years ago this month I went to a routine dental examination. That visit, and the subsequent visits I will share with you, were all paid for by the health insurance we receive as members of the Oregon Legislature. During that dental exam the dentist spotted something suspicious and suggested I visit a dental surgeon. I visited the dental surgeon, who found the spot for which I had been referred was benign, but noticed a lump on the roof of my mouth. He suggested I visit an otolaryngologist, which I did. The otolaryngologist did a biopsy on the lump, and the biopsy suggested the possibility of mantle-cell lymphoma. An MRI and a PET scan, a further biopsy, consultation with a geneticist and a pathologist, confirmed that diagnosis.

That led me to an oncologist and an oncology consultant at OHSU, providing further confirmation of the diagnosis and the development of a treatment plan. It was clear to me that my physicians were not very sanguine about my prognosis, but were ready to proceed with a vigorous, and somewhat experimental treatment plan. I consequently entered into a round of chemotherapy and behavioral therapy for a period of more than six months. By the end of three months I went into remission and remain in total remission to this day.

Why am I sharing this story with you today? The point of this story is that I believe that if I did not have access to effective and affordable medical care, I would not be standing here today — *I would be dead.* The difference between life and death in this situation was the extent to which I occupied a privileged place in our society. If I were a fifty-year-old worker in a minimum-wage job without health insurance with the same medical condition it would not have been discovered or treated before it was too late. I would not have been at a dentist for routine care. I would not have accepted a referral to a dental surgeon. I would not have gotten the remainder of medical care necessary for my survival. We heard story after story that people without access to health care waited until their medical condition was far advanced before they showed up at an emergency room. In far too many circumstances that was too late.

Note: HJR 100 passed the House 31–29. □